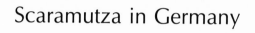

Scaramutza in Germany

Scaramutza in Germany

The Dramatic Works of Caspar Stieler

Judith P. Aikin

The Pennsylvania State University Press
University Park and London

Library of Congress Cataloging-in-Publication Data

Aikin, Judith Popovich, 1946-
  Scaramutza in Germany : the dramatic works of Caspar Stieler /
Judith P. Aikin.
        p.   cm.
  Bibliography: p.
  Includes index.
  ISBN 0-271-00656-0
      1. Stieler, Kaspar, 1632-1707—Criticism and interpretation.
I. Title.
PT1793.S7Z53 1989
832'.5—dc19   88-25238
                                                              CIP

To my husband, Roger,
who has put up with that other man in my life,
Caspar Stieler, quite long enough.

Contents

Acknowledgments

I would like to acknowledge the help of Mr. Tim Parrott, M.A., whose research efforts into Stieler's idioms and slang expressions on my behalf are particularly apparent in the sections on language, classical allusions, and humor.

Libraries and librarians particularly helpful in my research for this book warrant my heartfelt thanks here: Dr. Julie Meyer at the Herzog August Bibliothek, Wolfenbüttel; Oberbibliothekar Heinz Kürsten at the Kreis-Bibliothek in Rudolstadt; Stellvertretender Direktor Starke at the Universitätsbibliothek, Halle; and dozens of others who have provided microfilms and photocopies of needed texts or some necessary bit of information not otherwise available to me. I also owe a great debt of gratitude to the University of Iowa library, and to my colleague Professor John ter Haar, who is largely responsible for the excellence of its collection in seventeenth-century German literature.

Many individuals have, over the eight years encompassed by the writing of this study, contributed to my understanding of Stieler's place in seventeenth-century German literature, and I cannot begin to mention them all; most are named in the Notes. But a few who particularly merit mention here are Martin Bircher (whose comments on a draft of part of the manuscript were very helpful), Blake Lee Spahr (who "set me right" on Anton Ulrich and promoted publication of this volume), Mara Wade (whose work on Baroque *Singspiele* has been especially useful, and who is always ready to help with information and ideas), and my colleague in the Music School at the University of Iowa, D. Martin Jenni (who first brought *Seelewig* and some of Stieler's songs in the *Geharnschte Venus* to audible life for me).

Above all, I would like to express my appreciation to the University of Iowa for generously making time, research funds, and computer facilities available to me for this project. The Office of the Vice President for Educational Development and Research of the University of Iowa also provided a publication subvention in support of this volume. Some of the preliminary research for this study was carried out with financial assistance from the American Philosophical Society, whom it is my pleasure to thank once again.

Abbreviations

Because of their bulky form, the following works by Stieler will be cited as two-letter abbreviations:

VP = *Der Vermeinte Printz*
EU = *Die erfreuete Unschuld*
BB = *Der betrogene Betrug*
GA = *Der göldene Apfel*
GV = *Die Geharnschte Venus*

All the plays will be cited in the text without reference notes; complete bibliographical references are given in the Bibliography of Stieler's Plays Cited in the Text at the end of this study. Since pagination in EU recommences after the first act, Roman numerals will indicate first or second pagination (e.g., I, p. 38 = p. 38 in the first pagination).

Other frequently cited texts or series:

RF = Conrad Höfer, *Die Rudolstädter Festspiele und ihr Dichter*
DLE = Deutsche Literatur in Entwicklungsreihen, Reihe Barock, *Barockdrama*, ed. Willi Flemming
WBG = Wissenschaftliche Buchgesellschaft

I

PROLOGUE

Scaramutza in Germany

1

The Comic Spirit and Comedy
in Baroque Germany

Scaramutza, inspired by the famous comic figure of the Italian commedia dell'arte in Paris (Scaramuccia or Scaramouche), is a German fool who appears in a number of German dramas beginning in 1665; most of these plays have been shown to have been written by Caspar Stieler (1632-1707), a Thuringian dramatist who created theatrical events for several Thuringian and Saxon courts. In these plays Scaramutza serves as the author's mouthpiece, guiding audience reaction, offering biting satirical barbs, and personifying the very spirit of comedy on the Baroque stage. The function of this comic figure was not limited to arousing laughter, although the slapstick, verbal humor, and ridicule connected with Scaramutza were designed to do so. Stieler's German fool is, in addition, the purveyor of a cheerful tone and the guide through the maze of appearance and reality to the inevitable happy ending, complete with multiple marriages. He is, in short, the very embodiment of a particular kind of comedy that made its appearance in seventeenth-century Germany, as well as in late sixteenth- and early seventeenth-century Italy, Spain, France, and England: the romantic or heroic comedy of which Shakespeare's *As You Like It* is probably the definitive example.

This sort of comedy[1] has usually been ignored or even tacitly maligned by Germanists: one gets the distinct impression that it is beneath the notice of this dignified profession to deal with works in which the protagonists get married at play's end with every expectation of living happily ever after. In contrast, a number of scholars have concerned themselves with satirical comedy, since it purportedly has a serious social function which sets it above its supposedly more frivolous cousins. Explicit or implicit in the excuses given for the exclusion of romantic comedy from serious studies of the genre or the period are two questionable assumptions: (1) romantic comedies—indeed, any literary works with happy endings—are trivial literature, and (2) German romantic comedies of the Baroque are derivative, merely slavish imitations of a foreign fashion.[2] Such statements only betray the regrettable elitist and xenophobic tendencies with which *Germanistik* has been burdened since before World War I—prejudices which, fortunately, show every sign of abating, leading to the creation of a fresh scholarly climate in which German literature can be allowed to take its place as a European literature participating in pan-European movements and traditions. However, it is still necessary today to turn to certain scholars of English, French, Italian, and Spanish literature in order to find serious treatments of romantic comedy as a genre, and particularly of the theoretical raison d'être of the requisite happy ending.

In the especially fruitful realm of English language theory of comedy one finds a tendency to elevate comedy, particularly Shakespearean or romantic comedy, to a level of cosmic significance not exceeded by that of tragedy. Joseph Campbell[3] and Northrop Frye,[4] for instance, have tied comedy to archetypal myths and rituals of regeneration and resurrection, while Susanne Langer sees in comedy the celebration of the life force.[5] In fact, these theorists[6] tend to ignore laughter and to focus on light-heartedness and gaiety as the true mood of the genre. Most German treatments of comedy, instead, focus on "Humor" and "Komik," or on psychological or physiological theories of laughter, and pointedly ignore romantic comedy and its happy ending.

In recent scholarship devoted to the German Baroque novel, it is interesting to note that two generic types have been identified which parallel my own division of Baroque comedy into romantic (heroic) and satirical. Using Christian Thomasius's musings on the novel of 1689, Kafitz identifies the heroic and satiric types (Thomasius also posits a third, the pastoral novel).[7] It has been pointed out that eighteenth-century theorist Gottlieb Stolle likewise identified the two main kinds of novels in precisely these terms.[8] The standard definition of the heroic-gallant plot, in fact, seems to apply, except in terms of breadth and multiplication of characters and plot-strands, to the romantic comedies of Shakespeare and of the German Baroque: "the hero falls in love with the heroine—but their ultimate union is delayed by all sorts of obstacles. . . . She is threatened by her abductor, or by the usurper of the throne, with marriage—if necessary by force—or more simply her chastity may be endangered. . . until at the conclusion, in spite of all difficulties thus far encountered, the couple is finally united in wedlock. . . . [The work ends] in a celebration, with marriage and the security of a throne. A seemingly eternal order has prevailed."[9] Yet instead of seeing a parallelism between

these two types of novels, heroic and satirical, and the two possibilities for comedy, these scholars and theorists incline to see an
analogy between the "high" or heroic-gallant novel and the "high"
drama or tragedy on the one hand, and the "low," "picaresque," or
"satirical" novel and the "low" drama or (satirical) comedy on the
other—a patent neglect of the importance of the happy ending to
the "high" novel, in my opinion, as well as of the forgotton half of
the comic genre.[10] But apart from this inaccurate analogy, several
scholars of the Baroque novel have indeed come to terms with the
happy ending that is as necessary to the "high" novel as to the
"high" comedy, and their findings can indeed be applied to that
truly analogous dramatic type, the romantic or heroic comedy,
which we might quite accurately term "heroic-gallant comedy."
Spellerberg, for instance, speaks of the immediacy of Divine
Providence and its rewards for the virtuous in the heroic-gallant
novel, as opposed to the less explicit sense in the Baroque tragedy
that virtue will eventually triumph over evil. He speaks of a
"dichterische Theodicee der Geschichte" in the novel[11] which
certainly should be equally applicable to the joyful resolution at
the end of each romantic comedy. This study on the comedies of
Caspar Stieler will provide a first step following in the traces of
scholarship on the Baroque novel, which once elevated the satirical
exemplars by Grimmelshausen, Beer, and Reuter to the sole position of honor, while it neglected the sort which ends happily in
the multiple marriage of lovers from the courtly sphere.

The German seventeenth century actually had a theory to
account for the properties of the heroic or romantic comedy
described in English scholarship and for the happy ending, and
while it is not as metaphysical and universal as those theories of
Frye, Campbell, or Langer, this theory takes itself and its object
very seriously indeed. According to both Jakob Masen, the Jesuit
theorist and dramatist, in his *Palaestra eloquentiae ligatae* of 1657,
and Sigmund von Birken, the Nürnberg poet and dramatist, in his
Teutsche Rede-Bind- und Dicht-Kunst, published in 1679,[12] the
function of comedy is to arouse in the audience two emotions
which are the opposites of the Aristotelian requirements for tragedy. Instead of fear and horror, a comedy is to evoke feelings of
hope for a similar happy outcome in the spectator's life (*spes*;
Hoffnung), and instead of pity, a sense of vicarious joy that the
problems were satisfactorily solved (*gaudium*; *Freude*). Masen

defines these concepts in Christian terms as hope for one's own salvation and joy at the manifestation of God's grace in the play; Birken's examples, all religious allegories, seem to show that he agrees. Thus both ally (romantic) comedy with that older concept of Christian *comoedia* evident in Dante's *Divine Comedy:* comedy involves the revelation of the ultimate truths about divine grace in an optimistic account of man and his world.

The key to this Christianized comedy lies, at least in part, in a popular exegetical tradition and the imagery associated with it. The allegorization of the Old Testament Song of Songs (*Das Hohelied*) by St. Bernard of Clairvaux as the spiritual marriage of the soul and Christ[13] gave the institution of human marriage the aura of sacred cipher. It is a tradition called upon by Abelard as he exhorts Heloise to renounce her earthly love and by Friedrich von Spee when he has his persona woo Christ in a series of love poems. The *unio mystica*, the ultimate state in the human condition according to mystical Christian views, is thus symbolically present in the marriages which provide the standard closure for the typical romantic comedy from the Age of Faith.

Naturally, other, more secular perspectives also place on marriage a value that raises it above the trivial. Just as physical survival of the social group depends on procreation of children within a defined family unit, so the survival of the feudal polity depends on the stability and continuity provided by the heirs of a dynastic marriage; indeed, in many cases the peaceful solution to conflicts or the peaceful transfer of the reins of government is accomplished by such a marriage. And while these marriages, normally arranged in the best interests of the state, have little to do with love and romance, it is notable that the imagery traditionally associated both with "love in the western world"[14] and with the spiritual union perceived in the Song of Songs is ubiquitously associated with the public displays of the occasion. Other events of dynastic importance, such as the birth of an heir and the birthdays of the prince or his close relatives, co-opt this imagery as well, thus firmly connecting dynastic interests with the symbolic significance of marriage. One of the forms these displays are likely to take is the performance of an appropriate play, usually a "heroic-gallant" comedy, during the courtly festivities. Most of the plays written by Caspar Stieler participate in precisely this sort of dynastic celebration.

2

Caspar Stieler: State of the Scholarship

Between 1665 and 1667 six assorted comedies appeared in print
anonymously in Rudolstadt and Jena: *Der Vermeinte Printz* and
Ernelinde, oder die Viermahl Braut in 1665, *Die Wittekinden* and
Die erfreuete Unschuld in 1666, and *Basilene* and *Der betrogene
Betrug* in 1667. The title pages note that each play was performed
for a particular festive occasion at the court of the count of
Schwarzburg-Rudolstadt. Similarities in tone, use of Romance-
language sources, and appearance of the comic figure Scaramutza
in all but one of the plays have led bibliographers and historians
to group the plays together under the assumption that they are the
product of a single author.

The collective title page often attached to volumes containing
more than one of the six comedies, *Filidors Trauer- Lust- und
Misch-Spiele*, gives little more information about the identity of
the author than the title pages of the anonymous single plays, for
Filidor was a popular pen name in the seventeenth century. No
author of the period ever claimed these plays, or indeed the song
cycle of 1660, *Die Geharnschte Venus*, which exhibits similarities
in language and whose author likewise titled himself Filidor. A
series of guesses by historians of later centuries includes such figures as Johann Rist, Johann Georg Schoch, Lorentz Wolfgang
Woitt, Jakob Schwieger, Georg Bleyer, and Caspar Stieler. Joachim
Friedrich Feller, editor of the 1726 edition of Stieler's *Sekretariat-
Kunst*, attributes the song cycle to Stieler but does not mention
any plays in his list of Stieler's works.[15] Two of the earliest
attributions, those by Falkenstein and Motschmann in the first
half of the eighteenth century,[16] are to Stieler, but both authors
also include works now known not to be by Stieler, thus calling
their credibility into question. And in any case, later scholars
knew nothing about these attributions. Gottsched, who includes
four of the Rudolstadt plays in his *Nöthiger Vorrat* of 1757-65,
attributes three of them to a single but unknown author.[17] The
attribution of the plays and the song cycle to Jakob Schwieger,
whose pen name in the *Schwanenorden* was indeed Filidor, first
appeared in print in the *Cimbria literata* of Johannes Moller in
1744,[18] followed by such works as Jöcher's *Gelehrten-Lexicon* of
1751,[19] Vilmar in the early nineteenth century,[20] Goedecke in

1884, and Theodore Raehse in his edition of the *Geharnschte Venus* of 1888.[21] Many catalogs and bibliographies actually retain this erroneous attribution.

In 1897 Albert Köster revolutionized scholarship on the *Geharnschte Venus* and on Caspar Stieler in his book *Der Dichter der Geharnschten Venus*,[22] in which he demonstrates conclusively through vocabulary, dialect characteristics, and anagrams that Caspar Stieler, not Jakob Schwieger, was the author of the song cycle. In passing, Köster mentions his belief that the Rudolstadt plays were likewise Stieler's. His student, Conrad Höfer, took up the challenge and in 1904 published the results of his dissertation on the authorship of the comedies, *Die Rudolstädter Festspiele aus den Jahren 1665-1667 und Ihr Dichter*.[23] While his proofs could not be as conclusive as Köster's, since there were no convenient anagrams to decipher, he certainly established Stieler's authorship beyond any reasonable doubt.

Still, doubters emerged. Willi Flemming proposes a new possibility in 1933 in his collection of *Festspiele* which included *Die Wittekinden*: the musical secretary at Rudolstadt, Georg Bleyer.[24] But as Höfer demonstrates in a rebuttal of 1941,[25] Bleyer came to Rudolstadt too late for consideration (late 1666) and was too young in 1657 (ten years old) to have written the song cycle. This article by Höfer also brings more documentary evidence about Stieler's sojourn in Rudolstadt to light and thus constitutes a strengthening of Höfer's original attribution. Walter Hinck was still not convinced in 1965,[26] and doubted all previous attributions, primarily because present knowledge about Stieler did not account for the experience with Romance literatures, especially Italian, which is evident in the Rudolstadt plays. But Herbert Zeman's dissertation of 1965, *Kaspar Stieler: Versuch einer Monographie*,[27] which reveals in detail Stieler's travels and activities in his early years on the basis of newly discovered documentation and the personal comments in Stieler's non-literary oeuvre, should be enough to convince the last doubter that this attribution is justified.

While the *Geharnschte Venus* song cycle has found appreciation in every century, the Rudolstadt plays have long been maligned or ignored. Even Conrad Höfer regrets their mixture of various types of language: "Zu einem günstigen Urteil über Stielers Sprache wird man nach der vorstehenden Auseinandersetzung kaum kommen" (RF, p. 130). Hankammer feels that the effort spent to detect the author was not worth it; Newald indicates that the plays are of lower quality than the song cycle.[28] Most point to Stieler's own excuse that he was in too much of a hurry to write them properly.[29]

All histories of German comedy, with the exception of Hinck's work and an unpublished dissertation by Horst Hartmann,[30] ignore the six comedies and their author, but it is not clear whether this omission stems from intention or ignorance. Certainly Roy Pascal betrays ignorance when he terms the comedies "allegorical masques."[31] Hinck sees their importance primarily in the scenes dominated by the comic character Scaramutza. Flemming finds *Die Wittekinden* important in its portrayal of German history. Sowinski treats Stieler as a regional writer: "Der bedeutendste thüringische Dramatiker des 17. Jahrhunderts bleibt jedoch Caspar Stieler aus Erfurt."[32] Zeman stresses the quality of two of the plays at the expense of the others: *Der Vermeinte Printz* and *Der betrogene Betrug*. Yet both Höfer and Zeman have claimed that all of Stieler's Rudolstadt plays, as nearly the sole representations of a particular kind of comedy in the German Baroque, should be taken into account in any discussion of the comedy of the period.

The dramatic works of Caspar Stieler dating after 1667 have received far less attention in German scholarship, and are almost never even mentioned in literary histories, due in part, no doubt, to the relative rarity of copies of the texts. Rudolf Schoenwerth included a description of *Bellemperie* (1680) in his book *Die niederländischen und deutschen Bearbeitungen von Thomas Kyds 'Spanish Tragedy'* of 1903,[33] and pointed out many of the changes from Stieler's source, without, however, discussing the results or the possible reasons for the alterations. It was left to Conrad Höfer to treat the late dramas of Caspar Stieler from the perspective of the complete oeuvre: in Höfer's *Rudolstädter Festspiele* of 1904 he included brief treatments of *Bellemperie* and *Willmut*, although primarily in order to demonstrate that their authorship was the same as that of the Rudolstadt plays (pp. 22-37 and note 3, p. 186). Höfer likewise includes in this work a short section on the Stieler translation of *Il Pomo d'oro* (pp. 149-50). Höfer is also responsible for the first treatment of the theatrical activities of 1684 in Weimar in his "Weimarische Theaterveranstaltungen zur

Zeit des Herzogs Wilhelm Ernst."[34] Zeman includes discussions of all these works in his *Monographie* of 1965, without, however, adding new substance or perspectives to the discussion. My own survey of German Baroque drama contains analysis and interpretation of *Bellemperie* and *Willmut*,[35] and my article on plays and audiences within Baroque plays includes a discussion of *Bellemperie* from this perspective.[36] The pastoral play of 1668, *Melissa*, will be discussed for the first time in this study; the opera libretto *Floretto* has only been discussed in a study on the Hamburg opera,[37] and then without reference to Stieler. All of the plays will receive introductory treatments in the forthcoming edition.

Any further discussion of the dramatic works of Caspar Stieler must appreciate the plays on the basis of a complete understanding of them in their context; this study should help to provide that basis. Involved are analyses of the plays in terms of genre or type of comedy to which each belongs, revelation of the function of the comic scenes within the whole, examination of the relationship of the plays to their sources, determination of the functions of the performances of the plays at court, and deductions about Stieler's view of his society and his world.

3

Filidor and "der Spahte": A Short Biography

Caspar Stieler was born March 25, 1632, in Erfurt. At the tender
age of four years he lost his father, Ernst Stieler, and his grandfather, Caspar Stieler, both pharmacists and prominent citizens.
His mother, the former Regina Quernt, then married Johann Mar-
tini, likewise a pharmacist, who is remembered in later years by
Caspar Stieler as a kind and loving step-father.[38] Caspar Stieler
attended a succession of Universities—Leipzig, Erfurt, and Giessen—in his first few years of higher studies, 1648-50, and in 1650
was expelled from the University at Giessen for picking a fight,
dueling, resisting arrest, and escaping.[39] Perhaps sobered by this
serious reprimand, or possibly under the influence of a new
friend, Martin Posner, with whom he roomed in his new place of
residence and study, Königsberg, Stieler seems to have become
more interested in literary and language studies. But the colorful
life of this adventuresome young man continued to collect new
experiences. In 1654, possibly due to shortage of funds, Stieler
joined the Prussian army as an official of the military court and
accompanied his regiment on a campaign in Poland. In the fall of
1656, still apparently in this position, Stieler became severely ill,
possibly with the plague which reached epidemic proportions in
Prussia that year. Nursed by friends in Königsberg, he finally
regained his health, but determined to leave the insalubrious
northern climate. Upon departure from Königsberg in 1657, he
carried with him his first literary work, *Die Geharnschte Venus*, a
cycle of love poems written during his years as a soldier, which
was to appear under a pseudonym three years later in Hamburg.

After a visit to his home in Erfurt and a stay in Hamburg,
Stieler began a *Bildungsreise* around Europe in 1658. He traveled
in Holland, stayed for a time in Paris perfecting his French language ability, then (probably again in need of money) joined the
French army. He participated in the siege of the Catalonian
fortress Rosa and was apparently a prisoner of war there for a
time. In 1659 he again pursued his travels through southern
France, in 1660 is found in the employ of the nobleman who was
regent in Orange, and in 1661 continued his journey in the company of another nobleman. He visited Rome and Florence and

other Italian cities, where he learned Italian, then returned to Erfurt in 1661 via Switzerland.

While visiting in Erfurt, he met his wife-to-be, Regina Sophia Breitenbach, and suddenly the brawling, adventurous picaro of the previous thirteen years disappeared. Stieler now enrolled at the University of Erfurt to complete his legal studies and actively sought a remunerative post. Opportunity presented itself in 1662: the count of Rudolstadt, Albert Anthon, had attained his majority and was seeking talented men to participate in the new government. Stieler did some research and penned a laudatory poem which presented the deeds of the count's illustrious ancestors, ending with a request for employment. Albert Anthon offered Stieler the position of secretary with a salary large enough to get married. Stieler married Regina Sophia in 1663, and the first of seven children arrived in 1664.

While in Rudolstadt, Stieler had a multiplicity of responsibilities as secretary: he must take care of the usual secretarial duties (letter-writing, record-keeping, making of various kinds of documents, contracts, etc.), he must read the news aloud at table to the count's family, he must see to the education of various pages and courtiers in style and languages, he must help provide musical entertainment, and he is to write, direct, produce, and perform in plays for festive occasions. He produced six plays from 1665 to 1667, one a translation (*Ernelinde*), but the other five original comedies based on novellas, chronicles, or (in one instance—*Basilene*) existing plays in other languages. Each served to celebrate a festive occasion: marriages, birthdays, birth of an heir. Stieler liked his employer, as later comments show, but the income was too small to support his growing family, and the work-load was too great, so when another opportunity presented itself in 1666, Stieler was quick to grasp it.

Stieler then served as secretary in Eisenach to the Dukes of Saxony-Weimar from the middle of 1666 to the end of 1676 at a salary some three times that of his previous position. Still, money problems forced him to spend his few leisure hours as a free-lance writer, providing handbooks on a variety of subjects. As a member of the *Fruchtbringende Gesellschaft* after 1668, under the pseudonym "der Spate," Stieler found a new literary métier: he wrote books about style and language and guides for the professions whose tools these are. He was productive and happy in these years in Eisenach. The death of his wife in 1676 as a result of childbirth was such a shock to Stieler, however, that he was rendered unable to fulfill either his secretarial duties or his publishing agreements for the greater part of a year. He resigned the secretarial post by the end of 1676 and until 1678 he does not appear to have had another post.

In 1678 he accepted the position of secretary to the University of Jena, and his activities there included teaching German grammar and style. In 1680 he resigned this position to return to employment in Saxony, this time in Weimar, where he stayed for some five years in a position which gave him ample time for his own publishing ventures. This position also encouraged him to turn his talents once again to the writing and production of drama. In the second half of this decade he obtained a position with the Duke of Holstein-Wiesenburg which brought him to Copenhagen for a time.

By 1690 Stieler seems to have retired to Erfurt, where he continued his writing and publishing activities until his death in 1707. In 1691 he published his *Teutscher Sprachschatz und Stammbaum*, a dictionary which formed the basis for later lexical work in Germany. He died in comfortable circumstances, honored and respected by his hometown and by *literati* and bureaucrats all over Germany. Only his poetic and dramatic talents were forgotten, presumably because Stieler himself preferred to forget them.[40]

II

THE PLAYS

". . . The play's the thing
wherein to catch the conscience of the king."

4

The Rudolstadt Plays (1665–1667): A New Look

One of Stieler's duties as secretary at Rudolstadt, as at Weimar later in his career, was the writing, production, direction, and performance of plays for the entertainment of the courtly audience on festive occasions celebrating dynastic continuity—state marriages, births, birthdays. While the more usual context of playwriting in seventeenth-century Germany, the schools for the upper middle classes, has tended to attract more notice in the scholarship, the relationship of all dramatists of the period to the greater and lesser royal courts should not be forgotten: Gryphius wrote several non-tragic plays for festive occasions at the local Piast court; Lohenstein dedicated his plays to various courtiers and even apparently sent two of his *Trauerspiele* to Vienna as festive plays honoring two of the emperor's marriages; Hallmann likewise designed his dramas for performance at the imperial court; and even Christian Weise's and Sebastian Mitternacht's plays were often dedicated to members of the local nobility in the audience.

Der Vermeinte Printz, the first of the Rudolstadt comedies to be written and performed, was intended to honor the marriage of Albert Anthon, Count of Schwarzburg-Rudolstadt, to Aemilia Juliana, Countess of Barby, in 1665, as the elaborate title page indicates. Stieler himself reveals in his short preface that the source of the plot is an Italian novella by Ferrante Pallavicino called *Il Principe Hermafrodito*.[1] Stieler's plot follows that of the source in great detail, although some differences can be noted: Stieler adds the bawdy puns (the novella contains very few), but reduces the titillation of the hermaphroditic theme to a minimum in his version. Many speeches, contained in the novella as direct discourse, are translated verbatim, but in the shift to the dramatic genre, Stieler has dramatized the situations, replacing long monologues with rapid conversational exchanges. The most obvious change is the addition of the subplot of the servants, Scaramutza and Camilla (borrowed from the commedia dell'arte but altered to his own tastes), which does not appear in the novella at all. Stieler's process of dramatization of a narrative source is comparable to that of Shakespeare in many particulars.

The "unerhörte Begebenheit" which provides the focus for the novella is also central in Stieler's dramatization: the king of Sicily, whose wife loses the ability to produce further children as a result of the complications of childbirth, raises their infant daughter, Zelide, as a son, Floridor, in order to allow the child to inherit the throne. After veiled hints as to the female gender of the assumed prince in the title and mythological prologue, the first scene portrays the discovery of the eighteen-year-old "prince" that she is in fact a princess. At first she agrees to continue the masquerade and thus do her father's bidding, but the arrival of a handsome stranger at court (actually the exiled prince of Castille, Alphonsus, who has come disguised as a minor nobleman) brings about a crisis, for the princess falls in love. She initiates two bold intrigues designed to allow her to win her prince and assume her true identity without endangering the stability of the kingdom or losing her inheritance. As Floridor, she confides to Alphonsus about the existence of a twin sister, Zelide, and arranges a meeting between the two. Her matchmaking works, for Alphonsus falls in love with Zelide. And she urges a local countess who wishes to marry Floridor to have Parliament abolish the current laws of succession, supposedly in order to allow a marriage to a woman of lower social class, but actually in order to negate the clause concerning male-only succession. Meanwhile, the princess of Naples has arrived in male disguise in order to woo the supposed prince. When Zelide has Alphonsus dress in women's clothing in a further intrigue, the chaos of disguise and false gender is total. But with Alphonsus in love with Zelide and the laws of succession overturned, the successful princess makes public her feminine identity, turns away her female suitors, marries her prince, succeeds to her kingdom, and lives happily ever after.

The verse choruses (prologue, *Zwischenspiele*, epilogue), probably set to music and possibly choreographed, depict the divine truths underlying the plot. In these scenes the ancient gods, as personifications of the qualities they traditionally represent, guide the events on the human plane. Jupiter, as personification of political wisdom, sets the god of shape-shifting, Vertumnus, to work to solve the political problems caused by the birth of an heir of the wrong sex. But Amor, god of love, ousts Vertumnus and solves the problems in his own way.

Mistaken identity, disguises, and deceptions in this play form a network of intrigue and complication based on the disparity between appearance and reality, between the artificial and the

natural. Close calls with "crimes against nature" such as trans-
vestitism, transsexualism, and homosexuality are the result of
insistence on an "unnatural" law (the Salic Law of male-only succession) and upon deception as the solution to the problems it
causes. The legalized discrimination against women practiced in
Zelide's society is exposed as an unnatural rule, to which it is
impossible for loving parents to adhere. But the princess's "natural"
feelings—love for her prince—intervene in the network of artificiality and sham.

Not only does the nexus of complications and intrigues
involve confusion about gender, but humor in this comedy likewise depends to a large extent upon hidden sexual identities. The
play opens with a delightfully silly scene in which the kingdom's
heir, now eighteen, is vigorously disputing the statement by one of
the king's advisers that the nude figure in a painting is female.
The "prince" naturally assumes that the body which resembles
his/hers is male, since he/she thinks himself/herself male. The
advisers, not in on the deception, are puzzled, and the audience,
which has already been enlightened as to the true state of affairs,
must suspend its disbelief that the child could have been kept
ignorant of its true gender so long.

The assumed prince soon learns her true identity, but humor
continues to be based primarily on the confusion of sexual
identities. Another woman dressed as a man falls in love with
"Floridor"; the beleaguered king is horrified to find his "son" in a
compromising situation with a "woman"; a virile man, accused of
being a woman mascarading as a man, is forced to don woman's
clothes and move into the women's suite of rooms. Even the
reality of the stage performance may have contributed to this
humor, as in Shakespeare's original performances, for female roles
were likely played by men.

In the end, the potentially tragic disparity between appearance
and reality is turned into a weapon for the cause of Nature and
inclination—in the form of the princess's intrigues—and then
finally vanquished altogether by the unifying magic of love. Amor
replaces Vertumnus, and Jupiter—political wisdom—expresses
divine approval of the result, for the princess's marriage links two
kingdoms and provides stability and dynastic continuity for both.
These themes are appropriate for a comedy, the function of which
at its first performance was to honor a royal marriage. The mar-

riage of Albert Anthon and Aemilia Juliana would, it was hoped, likewise unite two principalities and two dynasties, and provide a single heir to rule both. But this play had an additional function not seen in the usual marriage play, for Aemilia Juliana had lost her claim to her patrimony due to the same Salic Law which causes the complications in the play. The play, then, in spite of its obvious entertainment value, can be seen as a polemical piece designed to lay claim to a particular territory for the patron. It may even go farther, urging continuing resistance by the small central German principalities to their expanding neighbor, Brandenburg-Prussia under Friedrich Wilhelm I, the Great Elector.[2]

The clue to this political stance in the play is Stieler's insistence that the Salic Law ("das Salische Gesetz") is to blame for the unjust disinheritance of the female and thus for the dilemma in which Zelide finds herself. Stieler mentions this "law" already in the plot summary, and makes his happy ending contingent upon its removal (pp. A2v-A3r). The father of the assumed prince tells her why he had hidden her true sex from the world, and even from her: "Das Salische Gesetz/ so denen Weibspersonen die Nachfolge im Reiche untersaget/ beraubet euch des Sizilianischen Stuels" (p. 5). In Stieler's play and in its source, the Salic Law also involves prohibitions against royalty marrying below their own class—important for the plot but having no historical or even traditional basis, as far as I can determine.

However, the "Salic Law" is very much connected, historically and traditionally, with the rights of female succession. The actual Salic Law is an entire legal code of pre-Carolingian origins, containing one article which states that Salic Franks may not pass their lands on to female relatives: "De terra vero Salica nulla in muliere hereditatis transeat porcio, sed ad virili sexus tota terra proprietatis sue possedeant."[3] The concept of the Salic Law contained in Stieler's play is not based on the actual code, but on a polemical tradition begun in the fourteenth century by the French at the onset of a long dispute over the French throne. King Edward III of England, whose mother was the only direct heir of France's King Louis X, laid claim to the French throne in 1337. His claim by direct descent to the throne currently in the possession of a mere paternal cousin, Philipp of Valois, was acceptable under English law and custom, but was forbidden by a French decree of 1316 which disinherited Edward's mother and her descendants. Edward attacked this decree and declared war against France—the start of the Hundred Years War—in order to press his claim. He also placed the French fleur-de-lis on the English royal coat-of-arms, where it was to remain as visible sign of English claims until 1670. Lawyers for the Valois government responded with a precedent for the decree forbidding female inheritance: the old Salic Law. These findings were given the trappings of erudition in 1402 in a treatise by Jean de Montreuil, which created a pseudo-history of the codex, attributing the Salic Law to King Pharamond and connecting it to the origins of French law. Claims and counterclaims continued to be forwarded by the descendants of Edward and Philipp; perhaps the most famous representing the English side was immortalized by Shakespeare at the beginning of his *Henry V* (in the speech of the Archbishop of Canterbury).[4] In this polemical tradition, the name of the entire codex came to stand in popular parlance for the one small article forbidding female inheritance. Stieler notes these dubious origins of the Salic Law in the words of one of the king's advisers:

> Ohne/ daß dieses Recht keinen gewissen Ursprung hat/ als/ daß man darfür hält/ es sey an dem Ufer eines Flüsses von Barbarischen Völckern/ so etliche vor Franzosen halten/ gestifftet worden: So ist es in diesem Stücke höchst unbillig/ daß es ehrlichgebohrne Kinder ihrer Eltern Erbe entsetzet.
>
> (p. 96)

He goes on to make a reasoned plea that such a foreign fabrication should not be allowed to rule present events.

While in France in the later centuries inheritance continued to follow the formula provided by the Salic Law, in England and on the rest of the European continent, for the most part, kingdoms and principalities continued to be inherited by or through females in the absence of male heirs, as had been traditional throughout the age of feudalism. And yet, in the seventeenth century, the French royal claims for the validity of the Salic Law did indeed seem at times to have affected questions of succession elsewhere. And a case in point is the very situation with which Stieler's *Der Vermeinte Printz* is concerned.

Stieler's comedy was written to be performed as part of the celebration in Rudolstadt honoring the marriage of the Schwarzburg count Albert Anthon to Aemilia Juliana, a daughter of the

Count of Barby. Like the Schwarzburg counts, those of Barby had long controlled a small principality in central Germany which had its origins in the early medieval period. The territory, which included the economically valuable juncture of the Elbe and Saale rivers, lay hemmed in by Magdeburg and Brandenburg to the north, Saxony and Anhalt to the South and East, and Halberstadt to the West. It had been declared "Reichsgrafschaft" in 1497, and had remained a constant entity since that time. Aemilia Juliana's father, Albrecht Friedrich von Barby, had died in 1641, leaving her and her siblings orphans (the mother had died previously). Little Aemilia Juliana, aged four, was brought to Rudolstadt to be raised by the Schwarzburg family, while the other children—including the infant Count August Ludwig von Barby and three sisters—were brought up in the household of the ducal family of Braunschweig-Wolfenbüttel. Count August Ludwig von Barby died in 1659 at the age of twenty without leaving an heir, however, and Barby, instead of passing to one or more of his sisters, was split up among Anhalt-Zerbst, Sachsen-Weißenfels, and Magdeburg—all of which had some claims to the territory as nominal feudal overlords.[5] The daughters had lost their patrimony.

In the play celebrating the marriage of one of these daughters six years later, a parallel problem of inheritance and succession is dramatized: a princess of Sicily, who would be denied her patrimony, the royal succession, under the terms of the prevailing Salic Law, is raised by her father as a boy. Zelide/Floridor laments the situation in terms which reflect Aemilia Juliana's fate: "So lange dieses verfluchte Gesetz seinen Ansehen erhalten wird/ kan Zelide nicht herrschen/ nicht erben/ und wird diese Krohne den Fremden außgebothen" (pp. 89-90). The attack in Parliament declares that a law which cheats women of their patrimony is unnatural and ungodly: "Das Gesetz ist billich verwerfflich/ so wider die Natur gebeut" (p. 91); "was hat vor alten Zeiten die Schatzkammer des Reichs mehr erschöpffet/ und die innerliche Ruhe zerstöret/ als die Gottlosigkeit dieses Gesetzes?" (p. 97). This play, performed in the context of the marriage of Aemilia Juliana of Barby, then, in attacking the Salic Law of male succession, seems to be supporting the idea that one or more of the surviving children of the previous Count of Barby, although all daughters, should inherit his lands and titles, and be able, as Princess Zelide does, to confer them on their husbands and children. The comedy thus makes a claim for the lost patrimony, not only for the bride in behalf of her bridegroom, but also for at least one other member of the audience: the future Duke of Braunschweig, Rudolf August, who was married to Aemilia Juliana's eldest sister, Christiana Elizabetha.[6] The other sisters, both married to North Central German princes, may also have been in the audience. The appeal made through this play to Rudolf August and those other husbands would have been for a partnership in the venture to reclaim Barby. That the plea was not successful is indicated by the fact that no traces of any formal claim by these potential claimants to Barby can be found; indeed, on his wife's tombstone decades later a disappointed Albert Anthon was to eulogize her as "letze Gräfin von Barby."[7] Other political interests seem to have won the day,[8] but the play which took a stand on events of 1665-66 has lasted longer than the territorial entities with which it was concerned, and can now be read as a plea for property rights for women.

The companion piece, *Ernelinde oder die Viermahl Braut*, also performed in 1665 for the marriage, is a capable literary translation[9] of Giacinto Andreas Cicognini's *La Moglie di quattro Mariti*, an Italian comedy first published in 1659. Stieler terms it a *Misch-Spiel* (tragicomedy). As Höfer notes (RF, pp. 144-48), the differences between the original and the translation have two bases: substitution of German slang and maxims for the Italian, and addition of polite formulas of address from Stieler's perspective in the chancellery of a small court (*Kanzleisprache*). He changed two comic character names (Cassiopeia to Empelonie and Ghiribizzo to Gernwitz) and added a prologue and three *Zwischenspiele*, to be discussed below. But even without these additions Stieler's *Ernelinde* is no literal translation of Cicognini's play, but rather a creative transformation of the colorful colloquialisms of a foreign language into those of his own. As a result, the various editors of Jakob and Wilhelm Grimm's great dictionary found this work such a treasure trove of idioms that they chose to use it as a source for volumes 1 and 5, at least, of the *Deutsches Wörterbuch*. Many of the examples Höfer proffers in his discussion of Stieler's translation are thus to be found in Grimm with *Ernelinde* listed as the source.[10]

Ernelinde, Princess of Norfolk, who is an orphan, lives at the royal court of England under the protection of the young king,

Heinrich. Due to misinformation about her parentage and that of her suitors, she is affianced first to the king (who is actually her father), then to Ferramond (who is then falsely discovered to be her twin brother), then to Filander (who is actually her twin brother), and finally to Ferramond again.

Hidden or uncertain parentage provides the focus for tragic, near-tragic, and even comic elements in the plot. Near-tragedy in the form of incest is avoided in Ernelinde's case by revelation of the truth, but the necessity for revealing the truth is also the source of tragedy in the play, for the unknown mother of Ernelinde and Filander—the king's step-mother, Isabelle—commits suicide after revealing her shameful secret: many years before, she had crept into Heinrich's bed, disguised as a servant girl, and had conceived the twins, whom she had given to two noblemen to raise. The queen stabs herself with a dagger and writes the letter revealing the hidden consanguinity with her flowing blood. Nemesis, as the chorus to Act III announces, has carried out divine retribution for Isabelle's sin.

But comedy is likewise dependent on uncertain parentage. Ferramond has come to court for love of Ernelinde, but has disguised himself as a poor nobleman, and as such is made her secretary and advisor. By hiding his princely heritage which would have made him Ernelinde's equal, he nearly loses the opportunity to marry her, in spite of the fact that she loves him as much as he loves her. His quandry yields much of the humor of their scenes alone together. Even the comic characters—the servants—seem always to be bantering about parentage, and their bickerings seem to parallel the serious situation in the main plot: Empelonie rambles on about her grandmother and grandfather (p. 10). Her son Gernwitz conjures up a bombastic pseudo-ancestry in his "Bittschrift" (p. 12) which his mother refutes ("Er kann uns nicht verleugnen/ und wenn Er biß ans Ende der Welt zöge," p. 13). Gernwitz later cites his parentage to refute the accusation that he was "ungeschaffen" ("idle" or "awkward," but taken literally in the sense of "not created," not born of parents, p. 106).

The centrality of questions of parentage in his source may have attracted Stieler to Cicognini's play, for the circumstances of the marriage could be construed to be similar. The bride, Aemilia Juliana of Barby, was, like Ernelinde, an orphan heiress brought up at a neighboring court under the protection of its rulers and as a foster sister of the count she has just wedded, Albert Anthon. While no doubt of the bride's parentage existed, it seems likely that this marriage, too, was a love match; but in reality, as in the final outcome of the play, natural affinity coincides with what God has destined for the good of the state. The two temporary siblings fall in love and marry.

While the question of parentage provides a structural framework for the play, the core of the plot is a series of scenes between Ferramond and Ernelinde in which each alternately reveals and conceals true feelings. Ernelinde makes ambiguous statements, allows love letters to fall into his hands, and otherwise teases him with hints of her affections towards him, but whenever he presumes to pursue the matter, she puts him in his place with a harsh-sounding command: "dienet und schweiget!" On the one hand, this abasement seems to reflect their respective (apparent) status in the feudal hierarchy, but on the other it reminds one of the vocabulary of courtly love, in which the man "serves" his lady in order to win her favors. In a clever variant of the echo poem found in most pastoral dramas,[11] Ernelinde feigns sleep and her mumbled "echoes" of Ferramond's love-sick monologue reveal— and conceal—reciprocation. At the end of the play, when Ernelinde and Ferramond are finally affianced, she teasingly claims precedence one last time, but yields to his claims of equality and in fact offers to be his humble servant in the future. He promptly turns the tables on her and now repeats the command to her: "Hola! dienet und schweiget!" (p. 127).

This bold and naughty heroine, so similar to Stieler's others, must have provided a part of the appeal Cicognini's play had for Stieler. Yet unlike Zelide or other Stieler female protagonists, Ernelinde also demonstrates a disturbing passivity in her acquiescence to the various marriage arrangements made by the king. In spite of her love for Ferramond, she does not initiate intrigue in order to marry him, but merely follows where she is led. One of her actions serves to illuminate this aspect of her character in terms of significant imagery. When the king asks her what she holds in her hands, she tells him that it is the picture of her beloved; but in actuality it is a mirror in which the king—or any other suitor—will be able to see himself. Like the mirror, she will accept whatever lover is impressed upon her by outside forces. Luckily for her, divine destiny itself arranges the happy outcome.

Passivity in women is rewarded, but so is passivity in men, for Ferramond too has patiently waited for a happy outcome, rather than indulging in plots and counterplots.

To Cicognini's plot and characterization Stieler added little, but he did provide the verse prologue and three choruses. Two— the prologue and the chorus following the final act—are congratulatory. They offer Stieler's (and the court's) felicitations to the happy princely pair in the audience, laud their virtues and attainments, and hope for happiness and success for their dynastic purpose: to rule a land of peace and plenty and to provide heirs who will insure political stability. While the first chorus (the prologue) also introduces the play and its characters, the final one breaks the illusion created in the play in order to reinstate the reality of the festive gathering. In this chorus, the nymph Lucina suddenly turns to the audience and spies the honeymooners:

Was Glantz ist hier?
Sitzt dort nicht Ludwigs Sohn/
Albert Anthon.
und seines Hauses Krohn und Zier/
die Roß' aus Barby . . . ?
(p. 139)

She then offers her congratulations in a monologue punctuated by Echo—an unfortunately clumsy attempt at another echo poem.

The middle choruses, on the other hand, form a theoretical defense of tragicomedy couched in Baroque concretization, to be discussed at a later point in this study. In the chorus to Act I, *Spitzfindigkeit* and *Ernst* argue, each trying to claim primacy in the play at the expense of the other. *Spitzfindigkeit* represents the aspects of comedy—wit, irony, and satire—whereas *Ernst* prefers to be allied with serious problematics and Nemesis. A chorus of fauns and nymphs at the end promotes love as a quality which binds and overcomes both. The chorus to Act II is a dialogue between *Melancholey* and *Freude*. They ultimately agree to divide the responsibilities in the play (*Melancholey* will claim Isabelle, while *Freude* will be Ernelinde's reward). The chorus closes with a song sung by shepherds and shepherdesses in which they laud acceptance of destiny and repeat the old topos about the court as the home of melancholy, the pastoral setting as the site of happiness.

Stieler's rendition of Cicognini's play is an entertaining heroic-gallant or romantic comedy with some serious and tragic undertones. But the merger of comic and tragic elements here is more complete than in the tragicomedies of Guarini and his followers, and thus somewhat disturbing. Instead of comic interludes or a comic subplot which provides a warped mirror image of the main plot, itself serious but with a happy ending, Stieler weaves the two inextricably. For instance, the announcement of the suicide of the despairing Isabelle is made by the comic nurse Empelonie, whose verbal vulgarity reduces the tragic impact ("und ist vor allen Sanct Velten mauß todt gestorben," p. 114). This odd ironization of the pathetic remains a chief trait of Stieler's own comic homunculus, Scaramutza, throughout the Rudolstadt plays and beyond to the tragedy of 1680, *Bellemperie*.

Ernelinde is designed as entertainment for marriage festivities, but it has serious intent, too, for it forms a sort of dramatized *Fürstenspiegel*, an educational tool to influence the behavior of princes. Specifically, Stieler teaches that princes should behave with sufficient concern for their state and for morality, rather than follow their passions into tyranny, folly, and sin. The opening lines, in a stark, abstracted prose reminding us rather of Expressionist dramas of this century than of Baroque ornateness, convey these problematics:

Heinr.	Ich bin König.
Isab.	Ich bin Königin.
Heinr.	Ich kan und will.
Isab.	Ihr kont nicht und must nicht wollen.

(p. 1)

Walter Benjamin uses these lines and a few following them as the tone-setting quotation for the chapter "Trauerspiel und Tragödie" in his *Ursprung des deutschen Trauerspiels* (1928),[12] and although he does not discuss the passage directly, the chapter deals with the problematics of kingship and tyrannical behavior as evidenced in Baroque tragedies.

In the following year, 1666, Stieler wrote *Die Wittekinden*, a genealogical play in honor of Albert Anthon's twenty-fifth birthday. The depiction of the count's heroic ancestor and the miraculous events surrounding the founding of the Schwarzburg principality—the receipt of the feudal lien directly from Charlemagne as a reward for service for the Christian Faith on the part of the newly converted Saxon warrior, the elder Wittekind (baptized name, Ludwig), and the divine vision which effected the conversion to Christianity of the younger Wittekind and his brother—portrays the divine sanction the dynasty had from its very outset. Wittekind's story, coupled with the series of illustrious ancestors presented in tableau "visions" at the end of the play, represented the dynasty in its entirety. Thus the play's content functions to express the basis for political stability in the principality: divine sanction and dynastic continuity in the person of the ruler, whose health, and thus the health of the state, is celebrated on his birthday.

The other major genealogical play of the period, Andreas Gryphius's *Piastus*, was written some six years earlier for an event of similar dynastic significance at the Piast court in Silesia. Scholars have assumed that *Piastus* was suppressed, since no evidence exists of its performance and since it was not published until long after Gryphius's death.[13] But the similarities between the two plays seem to lead to the conclusion that Stieler had either seen a performance of *Piastus*, read the play in manuscript, or at least heard a report about the way Gryphius had dealt with the subject theatrically. Stieler's work is expanded into a full-length play and adds comic elements, but otherwise conforms to the form and purpose of Gryphius's genealogical play.

Stieler's source for *Die Wittekinden*, as Höfer has shown (RF, pp. 91-92), is to be found in a genealogical chronicle of the origins of the Schwarzburg dynasty, Georg Rixener's *Genealogia sive geburtslini der aller ersten Graven zu Schwarzburg in düringen*. From this source, Stieler has taken the story of Charlemagne's conversions of the elder and younger princes named Wittekind, as well as the name of the elder Wittekind's second wife, Brechta of Blois. Höfer's discussion of Stieler's use of this story and the additions he made to it (pp. 92-96) is adequate, in spite of a number of negatively judgmental remarks, and it will not be necessary to repeat his analysis here. The topic was examined again in 1931 by Walter Wenzel,[14] but without adding anything of importance to Höfer's treatment.

In Stieler's play, the elder Wittekind ("der schwarze Ritter"), once leader of the heathen Saxons defeated and converted by Charlemagne, is now general of Charlemagne's armies fighting the Saracens in Spain. Despite rumors of his fall, Wittekind returns in

glory, and his sons, the younger Wittekind and Walprecht, convert
to Christianity due to a miraculous vision. The elder Wittekind
receives Anjou as hereditary duchy to be passed down to his children by his new wife Brechta; his sons Wittekind and Walprecht
receive the duchies of Schwarzburg and Gleichen. Rather than
merely presenting the glory and conversion of the illustrious
ancestors, Stieler adds elements which place the ancestor play in
the fabric of a typical Italianate comedy—an intrigue which
threatens the honor and happiness of the hero and a subplot concerning the wooing of the ubiquitous Scaramutza. The elder Wittekind, apparently a widower, has been given the hand of Brechta,
countess of Blois, as a reward for his services to Charlemagne, and
she loves him with a tender and chaste passion. The jealous
French noble Burckhardt, who tries to woo her in his absence and
is rejected, attempts to convince her that the hero is dead by
providing a poem full of such lies to the itinerant *Flugschrift* poet
Michele (singer of crude broadsheet songs on newsworthy themes
and events). Brechta believes the tragic "news" and falls into a
seemingly mortal decline rather than, as Burckhardt had hoped,
into his waiting embrace. Burckhardt's henchman Robert, who is
jealous of Wittekind's favor at court, goads the hero's sons into
uttering treasonous plots against the emperor—which he then
reports, causing them to be thrown into prison. Even Scaramutza,
who has the misfortune to be attacked by Burckhardt as he
attempts to enter his beloved Blonje's chamber for a midnight
rendezvous, languishes in prison. But Wittekind returns unan-
nounced and unlooked-for from his battles to effect the "cure" of
the joyous Brechta, the release of the prisoners, and the forgiveness of the repentant intrigants. The apparent tragic ending is
unmasked as a network of deception.

In the midst of this heroic-gallant comedy/genealogical play,
Stieler adds elements of the satirical comedy which arouse laughter
in order to cleanse the audience of the very faults at which they
laugh in others. Scaramutza woos Brechta's maid Blonje in a
delightful parody of the conventions of courtly love: he proposes
bed rather indelicately, she assumes an innocent and modest pose
but gives permission for a midnight rendezvous, he attempts to
enter her room by means of a ladder; he even wins her father's
permission to wed her by exaggerating his deserts as a cavalier,
whereas his behavior when he is assigned to be a messenger proves

his cowardliness and ineptitude. Courtly love and chivalric ideals are unmasked as empty formulas.

Aesthetic matters, too, receive a tongue-lashing in the play. The broadsheet poet Michele sings his folksy song to the derision of both Scaramutza (I, v) and Brechta:

> Was ist diß für ein heßlich Lied/
> Das mir die Ohren machet gellen?
> (I, xii)

Scaramutza terms Michele "Ein steiffer Dichter" (ibid.). But the aesthetic satire goes beyond mere criticism of the craft of professional "poets," for Stieler's real concern is one voiced by that most critical of commentators on poetry, Plato: "Poeten liegen gern" (p. 21), an accusation leveled (ironically incorrectly) by both Scaramutza and Brechta at Michele's first song, but forgotten when they are confronted by the second song, a fabrication about the supposed death of Wittekind written by Burckhardt, who has bribed the poet to propagate it. Only the loyal Pantalon doubts the second song (II, xiv), but he, too, is overruled by the poem's believers. Michele may be a poet of a different class than Stieler, but the self-irony is clear. Stieler, the court poet dependent on a patron for his material needs, must likewise fabricate in order to please, just as he has done in adding the romantic comedy to the portrayal of the count's ancestors and perhaps in flattering the count beyond his deserts. But if such subtle satire probably escaped his patron's notice, the words that Albert Anthon's secretary Stieler places in Scaramutza's brazen mouth could not. The braggart expresses those rebellious and disrespectful thoughts with which Stieler must have longed to confront his ill-wishers at court, but dared do only in the guise of the comic spirit of his creation:

> Jetzt lernestu mich kennen.
> Ich bin ein kluger Mann/
> Und/ die mich anders nennen/
> Die kommen übel an.
> Und daß du wissest/ wer ich sey/
>
> . . .
> So hör/ ich bin bald/ wie ein Secretar,
> Bey unsern Herren General,
> Dem schwartzen Ritter . . .

Dem Keyser dien' ich/ wann michs lüst/
Und wann er mirs belohnet.

(I, v)

When Scaramutza's listener, the poet Michele, notes that his motley appearance would hardly lead one to expect such a great personage, Scaramutza reveals his nature as that of a clown:

Du meinst/ daß ich bossierlich bin?
Das muß ich selbst gestehen . . .
Zu schertzen ist mein Brauch.

(I, v)

In his guise as court buffoon, Stieler attains the aesthetic freedom, or poetic license, to express those disrespectful thoughts which in any other context could mean his dismissal. That Scaramutza here, as in his other plays, represents the author, can be seen also in Scaramutza's jubilant lines when he has been successful in his wooing, for in them can be heard the fresh young voice of the Filidor of the *Geharnschte Venus*:

Juch he! wer wolte traurig seyn/
Wenn mich mein Schatz läst ein/
Wol durch ihr Kammerfensterlein/
Und schleust mich in die Aermelein/
Und gibt mir tausend Schmätzelein/
Das liebe Kammer Kätzelein?
Juch he! wer wolte traurig seyn?

(I, xiii)

A second comic figure enters Stieler's oeuvre in this play, Blonje's father Pantalon. And while he, too, may conceal Stieler's own disrespectful spirit (he mentions the unmentionable—sexual passion—when speaking with Brechta about her beloved fiancé, and is scolded for his presumption, I, xii), his contribution to the buffoonery of this play lies in his supercilious habit of adding a final "e" to all words at the end of verse lines except those which would grammatically possess one. It is possible that Stieler here brazenly satirizes the verbal habit, affectation, or French or Italian accent of some member of court present in the audience, a cruel but effective way to "cure" someone of a "vice."

These satirical effects which relate the play to the particular audience by means of self-irony and parody of specific individuals play with the essence of drama, and by extension, in seventeenth-century metaphysics, of life itself: the intricate interrelationship of appearance and underlying reality, illusion and the breaking of illusion, role playing and sense of individual identity. Stieler's ultimate tribute to his patron likewise uses the breaking of illusion and the destruction of the separation between play and audience, but with a political and polemical function in mind. The series of tableaus at the end of the play which "prophesy" the great rulers of the newly founded dynasty, Albert Anthon's ancestors, culminates in a bridge to the audience. *Fatum*, who narrates the tableaux, comments that she wishes the audience could see the ultimate product:

> Ach! soltestu ihn sehn/
> Die Augen würden dir für Freuden übergehn.
> Doch/ weil der Himmel mir
> Hierüber auch Gewalt gegeben/
> So wil ich dir
> Ihn zeigen/ wie er ist im Leben.
> Schau' hinder dich zurücke.
> Hier sitzt dein werther Sohn/
> Der Schönheit Glantz/ Albert Anthon.
>
> (III, xvi)

The final tableau is no *stummes Bild*, but the chief spectator himself, who thus is made an actor of the play, probably to his own delighted surprise. And as play merges with reality, so reality becomes aware of its nature as *Schauspiel* which presents the series of human events in acts and scenes upon the stage of history. Albert Anthon is assigned the political and dynastic role which he is expected to play in world events to come, appropriately enough, by his own court dramatist.

This tableau, with its use of illustrious ancestors in order to exalt and exhort the current representatives of a ruling dynasty, partakes of two traditional modes of presentation: the pseudo-prophecy and the ancestor cabinet. As in certain Jesuit historical plays and the historical tragedies of Lohenstein and Hallmann, the family tree of the current prince is the material in a pseudo-prophecy delivered usually to the dynasty's founder. Since the "prophetic" words concerning the intervening ancestors have already been "fulfilled" in history, those words of Divine Providence concerning future deeds of the current prince thus demand particular behavior from him to insure fulfillment of the remainder of the prophecy. But the bodily presentation of the ancestors here, unlike the merely verbal list in Gryphius's *Piastus* or Lohenstein's Dido-prophecy in his *Sophonisbe* (V, 77-186), also participates in another tradition popular in the sixteenth and seventeenth centuries throughout Europe: the ancestor cabinet, a room containing the portrait busts, statues, or paintings of real and legendary ancestors.[15] As a prince visits such a cabinet, he is supposed to muse on the deeds of his illustrious ancestors and consciously construct goals for himself which will necessitate that he model his behavior on theirs. Through these two mechanisms for the presentation of a dynasty in its entirety, as well as by providing the story of the founder of the dynasty as an exemplum, Stieler hopes to influence the actions of his prince, at the same time that he honors him.

The other play written for performance in 1666, *Die erfreuete Unschuld*, Stieler terms (like *Ernelinde*) a *Misch-Spiel*. It was designed to honor the count's sister Sophia Juliana on the occasion of her birthday, and apparently she or her brother requested dramatization of the particular story, as Stieler notes in the preface when he seeks to excuse the play's faults by complaining about the undramatic nature of the material. As Höfer has claimed, the source (not named by Stieler) is a novella by Matteo Bandello as translated into French by Pierre Boisteau.[16] But since Höfer neither explained the differences between the Italian novella and its French variant which led to his conclusion, nor compared either possible source with Stieler's play, it will be desirable to do so here.

The novella is the story of a duchess of Savoy who falls in love with a handsome nobleman of Spain, Mendoza, and who deceives her aged husband in order to visit him. After the Duke has fetched her back, he goes off to war, leaving her in the care of Count Pancalier. The Count tries to seduce her, and following her rebuff determines to get vengeance. He has his nephew found in her bedroom and accuses her of adultery. She is sentenced by the absent Duke to die at the stake unless a champion appears to defend her in a duel with her accuser. Her messenger to Mendoza to request his help is apparently turned down, but Mendoza travels in secret in order to ascertain her innocence and disguises himself as monk in order to hear her last confession. When he has heard it and is convinced that she is not guilty, he appears as an anonymous champion and defeats Pancalier, thus exonerating her. He slips away without revealing his identity. After receiving word of the death of her husband shortly thereafter, the Duchess returns to her home in England, where she and Mendoza inadvertently meet and, after initial misunderstandings—she still did not know he had been her champion—they marry.

Boisteau's version changes the spelling of the name of the hero of the piece from Mendozza to Mandozze (Stieler reverts to the Spanish spelling, Mendoza) and drops the Italian "i" at the end of two other character names, Appiani and Pancalieri (Stieler uses the French forms). The Duchess's lady-in-waiting is called Giulia in the Italian, Emilie in the French, Adelgunda in Stieler's German. And whereas neither novella provides a name for the Duchess, Stieler calls her Eleonora. The two novellas differ mainly in that a moral and religious tone is provided by the French adapter: citations of Biblical models for behavior decorate several speeches, prayers are quoted in their entirety. Most importantly for Stieler, the French novella has the Duchess not only repent of her disloyalty to her husband ("elle commença a se repentir," p. 126) and resolve to be true to him in the future after her return from Spain, but this version also has her view her illicit love for Mendoza as a sin for which she accepts her unjust execution as divine punishment, as she indicates in her confession to the "monk." The Italian version has her instead angry at her husband and melancholy about her lost love after her return from Spain; and her confessed sin is a lack of forgiveness for Mendoza who, she believes, has not come to her rescue. This change to a repentant Duchess in the French version clearly marks it as Stieler's source. And the French novella is also more readily adaptable as a drama, for it uses considerably more direct discourse, particularly in the final scenes—speeches which Stieler often follows very closely in his dialogue. In Stieler's dramatization the first third of the novella becomes exposition, indirectly relayed in a dialogue between Eleonora and her maid, while the rest of the novella becomes the three acts of Stieler's play—in the interests of dramatic compression and some modicum of respect for the dramatic unities, although the action of the play still extends over a year of time and spatially from Savoy to London. Stieler has added the comic subplot of Scaramutza's railings and wooings, as well as the choruses. He has also provided internal commentary by creating or expanding the roles of several charac-

ters who take Eleonora's side—the counselors Adolf and Burckhard, and the jailer Achastor. The prologue speaker, "Genius,"
speaks for Stieler (he may have been played by Stieler) as he
claims responsibility for any faults in the play or performance and
offers the modesty topos expected of authors. This prologue also
conveys birthday greetings appropriate to the occasion.

Like *Der Vermeinte Printz* and *Ernelinde, Die erfreuete
Unschuld* is a romantic or heroic comedy. Intrigue, disguises, and
deceptions form the complications and also contribute to their
solution; virtue and noble love are eventually triumphant; and the
various pairs of lovers from several social classes are united in
marriage at the end. But unlike the two plays of 1665, and like
Die Wittekinden, this play is not a situation comedy. The plot itself
is serious and, with one exception, humor does not derive from
situations in the main plot. Instead, satirical commentary about
society and art is provided almost entirely by the comic character
Scaramutza.

The lone exception is the parody of petrarchistic formulas in
Pancalier's declaration of love to Eleonora. The ridiculous wooer
uses popular clichés in his impassioned speech, and his metaphors
borrowed from the excesses of the "second Silesian school" become
pretentious nonsense in this prose context. The fact that the scene
ends in a predicament as dire for the heroine as any conceived by
Gryphian tyrants cannot erase the ridicule, but only add a certain
blackness to the humor. The resultant "gallows humor" is typical of
Stieler.

The rest of the scenes containing comedy belong to Scaramutza, although he is frequently paired with Pancalier, his master,
whom he teases and deludes unmercifully. He pretends to misunderstand Pancalier's instructions, he gives long rambling reports
when an exasperated Pancalier wants a short answer to some
pressing question, he twits his master with phrases in foreign languages known to him but not to Pancalier. This latter trait allies
him to Stieler himself, who was, by his own account in his later
handbook on the art of being a secretary, the resident expert at
foreign languages. Scaramutza directly accuses his master of guilt
in two sentences in English and French, respectively, which,
however, are lost on the monolingual Pancalier: "An impudent
man doth dailii persecute the innocent," and "Vous seres le
premier, qui en seres puny" (II, p. 3). When Scaramutza bears

messages from England for Pancalier, he places them in his smelly boot and expects his master to fish them out. Yet always he evades punishment, for this wily servant knows how to excuse himself with pretended stupidity or foolishness.

Scaramutza also brazenly criticizes the members of the courtly audience. He laughs at social-climbing courtiers and at parasites who only flatter the prince in order to fill their bellies. Once he even turns to the audience saying that he sees adulterers everywhere. In a scene with a doctor he parodies the pretensions of the learned by the use of Latin puns and purposely bad Latin. He even pokes fun at the author when he cites the tendency of secretaries to desire to rise higher up the ladder of the courtly hierarchy (I, p. 19). He provides aesthetic criticism when he announces the drastic change of scene which breaks the unities of time and place at the beginning of Act III and in III, iv, when he commissions a folksy love song from the court musician in honor of his Blandine, which she proclaims is so fine she will put it in her prayerbook.

The *Zwischenspiele* provide the clues for a theological interpretation of the play which conforms to fourfold Biblical exegesis. The existence of four distinct levels of interpretation, literal, tropological or moral, anagogical, and allegorical, allies this play to pastoral and allegorical comedy without weakening the entertainment value of the verbal humor or of the unravelling of the network of intrigue. In the interludes a dragon appears, accompanied by Gog and Magog and the Babylonian Whore, to persecute the personification of the Christian Church (also called Zion and Jerusalem). At last, in answer to her prayers, the archangel Michael, her spouse, appears with gleaming sword to drive off her persecutors.

The events depicted in the choruses are parallel to those in the plot of the comedy: Pancalier is the dragon, Eleonora is the persecuted Church, Mendoza her guardian angel and eventual bridegroom. Clues to the allegory appear even in the main text: Eleonora terms Pancalier a dragon (I, i), Mendoza is termed her "Heyland" (II, p. 19) and "Erlöser" (II, p. 11), and his battle with Pancalier is called "Gericht Gottes" (II, p. 19). Thus Eleonora's Christian virtue, on the moral level, is depicted as under siege by the Devil and defended by divine aid. The Babylonian Whore, the Devil's ally, represents the lust to which Pancalier tries to tempt her, or perhaps her earlier transgression; the maverick tribes Gog and Magog, associated with Babylon according to Ezekiel (38:39), attack Israel (Eleonora) by God's command as a punishment for past sins (her love for Mendoza), but Israel's (Eleonora's) eventual victory over them is a sign of divine forgiveness and favor (Ezek. 39:25-27).

Examination of the passages in the Book of Revelation dealing with the Whore of Babylon, however, leads to another level of interpretation, that conveying anagogical or final concerns. The Whore appears at the end of the world as representative not only of lust, but of the Antichrist, for her horns represent the kings who make war upon the Lamb (Christ). The beast upon which she rides is the apocalyptic dragon, also an image of the Antichrist, which will likewise make war on Christ. After the capture of the Antichrist at the hands of the hero/savior whose sword is the word of God,[17] the celebration of the marriage of the Lamb with his bride, the New Jerusalem, will take place. The parallels of the interludes, and by extension, of the comedy itself, to this set of passages then yields the following interpretation: Eleonora, the Church or congregation of Christ's followers, is attacked by the Antichrist at the end of time, but is rescued by the appearance of her divine and merciful bridegroom, Christ, with whom she then contracts the spiritual marriage which represents the union of God and mankind for eternity. It is the story of erring mankind, forgiven and defended by divine grace, and welcomed to its heavenly home after sin and travail on earth.

Yet one name chosen for the bride in the *Zwischenspiele*—"die Verfolgte Kirche" (the persecuted Church)—when taken together with the appearance of Gog and Magog in Turkish costume, may indicate yet another meaning, this one dealing with events in *Heilsgeschichte*, the story of the Christian institutions and their attempts to provide for the salvation of mankind. Eleonora's story would thus stand for the Christian Church under attack by the Turks in the Balkans and in the Mediterranean. The identity of the "savior" is probably, as in Lohenstein, the emperor Leopold (although his name is nowhere mentioned), since only two years earlier he had fought a decisive victory against the Turks in Hungary (the Battle of St. Gotthard on the Raab river). Anti-Turkish polemic frequently equated Gog and Magog to the Turks who were likewise considered a scourge of God and a sort of

Antichrist. Such imagery from Revelation and Old Testament prophecies dealing with the end of the world, when equated to the present conflict with the Turkish Empire, elevated a military situation to a cosmic event.

It was popular in the seventeenth century to prophesy the onset of the Millennial Kingdom promised in Revelation by means of various theological interpretations combined with mathematical computations. Germans who dabbled in this sort of speculation included Jakob Böhme and Johan Heinrich Alsted, although they set no dates for the cataclysmic event. However, Johannes Cocceius, a famous professor at the University of Leiden, named 1667 as the fateful year, while Comenius, who was also active in Holland, named 1672. Others in the early and mid-sixties, while less explicit, felt that the dawn of the Millennial Kingdom was imminent.[18] Perhaps the most famous computation of the date was made in 1642 by the Englishman Henry Archer.[19] He counted the 1260 years to elapse before the onset of the Millennial Kingdom from the fall (i.e., Sack) of Rome in A.D. 406, and thus arrived at the date 1666—the date of Stieler's play. While orthodox Lutherans denounced the millenarian hopes, and most millennialist tracts had to be published in the more tolerant atmosphere of the Netherlands, the chain of millenarians in seventeenth-century Germany extended from Johann Gerhard of Jena and Johann Valentin Andreae in the early decades of the century in multiple strands to Philip Jacob Spener, founder in the seventies of the Pietist movement—a movement which embraced the millennialist ideas. The intermediaries included the Pansophic and Rosecrucian writings associated with Andreae and his followers, as well as Philip Nicolai, Jean de Labadie, Jakob Böhme, Frederick Breckling, and Johannes Cocceius.

Among these millenarian accounts, Cocceius's version stands out as being perhaps the most similar to Stieler's in at least one respect: like Stieler's portrayal of events from Revelation, Cocceius's end of time is not limited to a thousand years, but is the eternal reign of Christ on earth. Thus Stieler's compression of events before and after the Millennial Kingdom and his lack of mention of a millennium, coupled with his conception of the end of time as a joyful event, is not an anomaly, but rather is representative of one direction in the eschatological theories and hopes of his century. An English millennialist work of 1642 also contains

concepts of the millennium very close to those contained in
Stieler's *Zwischenspiele*: Robert Maton, *Israels Redemption; or,
the Prophetical History of our Savior's Kingdome on earth, that is
of the Church catholique and triumphant, with a discourse of Gog
and Magog, or the battle of the great day of God almightie*. While
it is impossible at this time to demonstrate which of these or other
theories about an imminent Millennial Kingdom may have influenced Stieler, it seems probable that his use of the prophetic
events of Revelation in this play was hardly coincidental. It might
be further speculated, since Stieler shows little interest in millen-
nialism elsewhere in his writings at that time, that the impetus for
this usage came from his patron or patroness, as did the suggestion
for the source. That the court at Rudolstadt was probably involved
in a proto-Pietist movement is to be seen in the presence there of
Ahasverus Fritsch, "Hof- und Justiz-Rat" since 1661 after a stint
as tutor to Albert Anthon and his siblings beginning in 1657. He
is known to have been confidant and religious counselor of the
countesses Aemilia Juliana and Ludämilie Elisabeth.[20] In his book
on literary interest in millennialist movements, Dietrich Korn
refers to Fritsch as a representative of a reform movement which
was an important predecessor of Pietism—a movement which
longed with joyful expectation not for the millennium but for the
Jüngster Tag itself.[21] In the sixties to eighties Fritsch is known as
the poet of several books of ecstatic religious poetry, as well as of
treatises and a translation of the writings of the late medieval
mystic Johannes Tauler. In his *Teutscher Advocat* of 1678 Stieler
refers to Fritsch as a close friend and mentor: "Ahasv. Fritsch,
mein hochwehrter Freund und Gevatter,"[22] and the song book of
1679, a collection of religious songs and hymns on the theme of
penitence called *Der bußfertige Sünder*, is dedicated to Fritsch as
well.[23] The dedication to Fritsch, based entirely on the conceit of
"Fertigkeit," has a decidedly millennialist flavor, and once overtly
refers to the coming of the Millennial Kingdom. Fritsch is thus a
likely source of material or interpretation for Stieler's apocalypti-
cal *Zwischenspiele* to *Die erfreuete Unschuld*, as well as for the
forms taken by his later religiosity, as apparently developed
immediately following the death of his wife.

Such allegorical content might seem inconsistent with the aims
of comedy and with the joyful festivities of the occasion for
which the work was performed. But if one recalls the definition

of the purpose of comedy offered by Jakob Masen and Sigmund von Birken—to arouse hope and joy (*spes et gaudium, Hoffnung und Freude*)[24] in the audience—then what content could arouse more of these feelings than the announcement of the Millennial Kingdom, the thousand-year reign of bliss on earth. Stieler uses several devices reminiscent of the early *Fastnachtspiel*[25] or late sixteenth-century drama in an extraordinary departure from seventeenth-century illusionistic theater in order to make a firm connection between the reality of the play—the Millennial King-dom—and that of the audience—the birthday festivities.

Each *Zwischenspiel* ends with a well-known hymn praying for divine aid and giving thanks for it, and it would be fair to assume that the audience joined in the singing. The first, "Wo Gott der Herr nicht bey uns hält," can be found, for instance, in *Evangelischer Liederschatz für Kirche und Haus*.[26] Stieler specifies that only the first four verses are to be sung (I, p. 38). The sub-ject matter is that of the first *Zwischenspiel*: the enemies of Israel attack, and Israel must call upon God's aid. The second hymn, "Erhalte uns Herr bey deinem Wort," is by Martin Luther himself. Stieler meant for it to be sung in its entirety (II, p. 38).[27] This hymn likewise contains a prayer for Divine aid and is thus an appropriate choice for the end of the second act and second *Zwischenspiel*. It is interesting to note that Stieler is not the first dramatist to use this hymn in a dramatic chorus; Frischlin's *Phasma* of 1580 uses it in much the same way,[28] a fact which implies that this witty but unorthodox dramatist of the previous century may well have been influential for Stieler's own seemingly esoteric practices as a court dramatist. The third hymn is also by Luther: "Wär Gott nicht mit uns diese Zeit,"[29] of which Stieler specifies that only the final verse, beginning with "Gott lob und dank der nicht zu gab," is to be sung (II, p. 64). Each of these hymns makes the audience into a congregation, and the singing congregation into a persecuted soul who pleads for divine aid and who offers thanks for deliverance, thus implicitly equating the personal experiences of each worshipper with the vicarious experi-ence of a theater audience watching a representation of events on a stage.

Another link to the audience is formed when, at the end of the final act, Scaramutza's laundry girl Blandine emerges from the players to address the audience directly, inviting them to come up on stage to view Scaramutza's release from the dungeon. Although there is no overt invitation to the audience to attend the multiple wedding ceremony soon to take place, the announcement of the festivities was made both to the characters on stage and to the members of the audience. A parallel from one biblical account of the Millennial Kingdom comes to mind: "Blessed are those who are invited to the marriage supper of the Lamb" (Ezekiel 19:9). The implications are clear: this comedy expresses hope for eternal bliss and joy at its imminence in the spectator's present.

Dietrich Korn, in his fine survey on the theme of the end of the world as it appears in other poetic genres of the time (see note 21, above), rashly asserts, due to his ignorance of Stieler's play, "im 17. Jahrhundert ist kein Schauspiel vom Jüngsten Tage mehr geschrieben worden." He offers an explanation: "Bei den Protestanten mußte schon die mit dem Dualismus gegebene Scheu, das Heilige sinnenhaft zu machen, den Versuch einer Dramatisierung des eschatologischen Geschehens hindern, zumal das 'Schauspiel' nicht mehr wie im Mittelalter Gottesdienst, Ministerium war, an dem auch die Zuschauer kultisch handelnd teilnahmen, sondern ein Geschehen, dem der Mensch distanzierend und kritisierend gegenüberstand, das auch von den Akteuren weithin nicht mehr als Glaubensvollzug auferfaßt wurde" (p. 64). But *Die erfreuete Unschuld*, as has been shown here, exhibits precisely these "missing" possibilities for Christian drama: the play becomes almost a reincarnation of the religious drama of the Catholic past—the passion play—in which participants and audience together form a congregation that experiences the theatrical recreation of the cosmic events of human salvation as an act of worship, culminating as here, perhaps, in the singing of hymns. Korn goes on to lament, "Die Pietisten, bei denen das Thema wieder eschatologisch-aktuell wurde, schrieben keine Dramen" (p. 65). But in Caspar Stieler we see one writer of dramas who, in the climate of a courtly society which was influenced by a proto-Pietist movement, accomplished that very task.

For the count's birthday the following year (1667), Stieler wrote his first pastoral play, *Basilene*, as a prose comedy with verse choruses. In many ways this pastoral play is completely traditional, and thus it is easy to point out the resemblances of the structure, plot, individual scenes, and major motifs to those of one or both of the two most influential Italian pastorals of the previous century, Torquato Tasso's *Aminta* and Giambattista Guarini's *Il Pastor fido*.[30] Placing *Basilene* squarely in this tradition are its pastoral trappings, the inclusion of hunters, priests, and a satyr in addition to the shepherds and shepherdesses or nymphs, the multiple pairs of lovers who overcome all obstacles at the end, the intended allegorization of the love of the faithful shepherd (to be discussed below), and the use of choruses of shepherds or other onlookers of the action as commentary instead of *Zwischenspiele*. Certain scenes that are requisites of the pastoral play appear in *Basilene*: the chaste hunter or huntress rebuffs the wooer; an older friend or wise old woman tries to talk the unkind beloved into loving the wooer; the unrewarded lover despairs and threatens suicide; a lusty satyr attacks a shepherdess but is chased off by her lover; a maiden is to be sacrificed on the altar of Diana, but her faithful shepherd steps forward to take her place, and a curse is lifted from the land; multiple marriages are announced at the end.

But Conrad Höfer, who must be one of the few people to have read Antoine de Montchretien's pastoral play *Bergerie* (1601),[31] claims that this play, rather than *Aminta* or *Il Pastor fido*, must be seen as Stieler's direct source.[32] Although he surely goes too far in terming it the direct source, Höfer's claim of influence is well justified, for a number of characteristics of this French pastoral play that also apply to Stieler's *Basilene* are not part of the general pastoral tradition. Of those which Höfer mentions (pp. 97-98), only one seems conclusive: the substitution of an annual lottery to determine which maiden will be sacrificed that year, in place of the sacrifice as a seldom-invoked legal penalty for inconstancy, as in Guarini. Höfer does not discuss the significance of this shift in *Bergerie*, nor Stieler's possible reasons for following Montchretien. But this change is central to Stieler's conception, as will be shown below.

Several other features of *Bergerie*, not pointed out by Höfer, seem likewise to have influenced Stieler's *Basilene*. Most obvious is the fact that *Basilene* and *Bergerie* are both written in prose, with only verse choruses and a choral hymn to Diana, instead of remaining in the tradition established by Tasso and Guarini of using verse (usually free-form madrigals) throughout pastoral plays.[33] Another feature shared by *Bergerie* and *Basilene*, but different from *Il Pastor fido*, is that the female protagonist to be sacrificed is made the daughter of the priest who must wield the knife, an intensification of the pathos. Furthermore, she is now a huntress, dedicated to the Virgin Goddess Diana and a life of chastity, instead of affianced in an arranged marriage to a shepherd whom she does not love, as in Guarini. Stieler follows Montchretien in setting up a conflict between chaste hunters or huntresses and the ardent shepherds or shepherdesses who pursue them, allowing for both a metaphorics and a problematics of the hunt.

But Montchretien's *Bergerie* is a poor excuse for a play: it is theatrically ineffective, with so many unhappy pairs (he has doubled the already confusing proliferation in *Il Pastor fido*), and with such a variety of reasons for their unhappiness and of pathways to a happy conclusion, that it is difficult to keep track of them all. The speeches are too long and filled with clichés; adequate expression of emotions especially suffers from the use of commonplaces. In spite of the changes Montchretien has made in Guarini's plot, he does not create a unified thematics for the play. In fact, he has no central protagonists, and even the sacrifice scene is not focal; indeed, it is totally unprepared for in the play, and its outcome affects only one of the six pairs. He throws in a poetry contest which receives as much emphasis as the sacrifice scene; two of the pairs are involved in that staple of the commedia dell'arte, an "elective affinities" exchange of partners; several unhappy lovers are lost in the shuffle and don't participate in the multiple pairing at the end of the play.

It speaks well for Stieler's talents that he was able to see *Bergerie* as a source of ideas, in spite of its faults, and that he was able to make of this incredibly weak drama an effective stage play and an aesthetically pleasing text incorporating significant psychological, sociological, philosophical, and religious content. Stieler reduces *Bergerie*'s six pairs of lovers to three and eliminates the convolutions of plot—lovers' triangles and quadrangles—which require several exchanges of partners in both *Bergerie* and *Il Pastor fido*. He further structures his pairs by making their stories variations on a single plot: each pair is made up of a chaste hunter and an ardent shepherd. At the top of the theatrical (and social) hierarchy stand Basilene, daughter of the head priest and devotee of Diana, and the noble shepherd Filidor, descendant of Hercules, who woos her in vain. Parallel to this couple, but on a lower social niveau, are the servants: Labelle, who follows her mistress in the hunt, and Scaramutza, who opens the play by breaking her *Jagdzeug* into tiny bits in order to divert her from the hunt and its requisite chastity. The third pair involves a reversal of gender: the chaste hunter Oridor is pursued by the ardent sister of Filidor, Melinde. Each pair is joined together by means of a different device: Basilene admits love for Filidor only after his offer to replace her on the sacrificial altar causes the goddess Diana to exhort her to love; Labelle, already wavering, gives in to love when Scaramutza rescues her from the clutches of a lustful satyr; Oridor falls in love with Melinde after he has wounded her, thinking her a deer. Within all this variety, Stieler has expounded upon a single theme: the victory of love over chastity as a blessing for society.

Complementary to this theme is another, which provides both an additional structural pattern and an additional nexus of meaning for the play as a whole. Stieler's play, extending and expanding upon a blind motif in *Bergerie*, not only sets up two conflicting groups of people, hunters and shepherds, but also views them as progressive stages in human history. Hunting is the inferior pastime or occupation both because, in its insistence on chastity, it does not adequately provide for the continuation and stability of the society, and because it involves the warlike spilling of blood. As the seeress Empuse explains to Basilene,[34] mankind had to hunt in its earlier, more imperfect state of existence, but since Pan introduced pastoral culture, such a life-style was no longer acceptable:

> Seit dehm/ daß unser Gott Pan in dieser Arkadien die Schäfer Ordnung auffgerichtet/ und die Hirten auff der Schalmey unterwiesen/ steht das gantze Land im güldnen Frieden/ die Felder Blühen daher/ wie ein Paradieß. . . . Siehe liebe Tochter! das sind die reichen Früchte der angenehmen Ruhe. Das unsere Vorfahren hingegen bey dem wilden Leben/ absonderlich aber der unruhigen Jagd/ sich mit eicheln und dem Blute der wilden Thiere ernehren und in den Bergen zerstreut wohnen musten. (Fiii)

She points out that such violence as is to be found in the hunt will corrupt the behavior of the hunters towards their fellow human beings, thus endangering the very fabric of society. This cruelty appears in the play in Basilene's contempt for Filidor's feelings—a figurative wound which nearly drives him to suicide—and Oridor's physical wounding of Melinde.

Associated with the persistence of some members of the society in this destructive pursuit is the curse of Diana and the human sacrifice it demands—the only shadow on the idyllic existence in a Golden Age in Arcadia. As I and others have shown,[35] the plot of Guarini's *Il Pastor fido*, and of its German translation by Hofmannswaldau, at least, are elaborately cloaked allegories for *Heilsgeschichte*, the progress of the human race towards universal salvation. The pivotal figure in this fiction, as in the Biblical presentation of world history, is a Good Shepherd who, out of love, offers himself as a sacrifice for the sins (or Original Sin) of the reluctant human soul or Church, whose initial resistance is indicative of its fallen state. The result in *Il Pastor fido*, as in the New Testament, is the end of the Age of Law (a reference to the Ten Commandments and other laws in the Old Testament) and the onset of the Age of Grace. A parallel, and symbolic shift in the practice of worship is the New Testament ban on blood sacrifices. In *Basilene*, the curse of Diana, parallel to the "curse" of Original Sin, is lifted by the self-sacrificing actions of another "Great shepherd of the sheep" (Hebrews 13:20). In *Basilene*, Stieler, following Montchretien, has eliminated the allusions to Original Sin and the Law, but has replaced them with a more metaphorical presentation of the ages in the progress of human salvation: hunting and gathering must yield to agriculture, violence and bloodshed must make way for peace and tranquility, asocial selfishness must give way to love and marriage. The coldhearted hunters who have wounded their wooers, whether figuratively (with Cupid's arrow and their own scornful words) or literally (Oridor and Melinde), must be converted into lovers and true shepherds themselves; those wounded will be healed by love. The Old Testament ethic has been overcome by that of the New Testament, blood by grace and love. Such an interpretation of a story involving a hunter and a shepherd in the Old Testament—that of Esau and Jacob—is made by St. Augustine in his *City of God*: Isaac is tricked into blessing the younger of his twin sons, Jacob, "a plain man, dwelling in tents" who kept sheep, instead of his elder son, Esau, "a cunning hunter" (Genesis 25:27). Augustine interprets this neglect of the elder son by showing that Esau represents the earlier Chosen People, the Jews, while Jacob represents the Christians

who are later preferred by the Lord (Book XVI, Chapter 37).[36]
Stieler has made creative use, building on unexplored motifs in
Bergerie, of the potential for allegory in the traditional opposition
of hunters and shepherds in Christian theology and in pastoral
drama in this schema. *Basilene*, seemingly a romantic comedy in
pastoral guise, is actually an allegorical presentation of Christian
truths.

It is interesting to note that Stieler seems to have gone out of
his way to hinder or delay recognition of the eternal model, possibly a sign that he may have considered the allegory in Guarini's
pastoral too lightly cloaked. He has changed the names of the
characters to make them less significant and thus eliminated a
major set of clues to the meaning. He even gives the faithful
shepherd his own pen name, Filidor—perhaps a further distraction
and veil designed to increase the audience's pleasure in its ultimate
discovery. The addition of comic scenes and characters to the plot
provides further diversion from the serious contemplation
demanded for allegorical exegesis. And, in a departure from earlier appearances of Scaramutza in Stieler's plays, this priest's servant utters statements which would shock or at least irritate the
audience. He blasphemously claims priestly authority, smokes in
the sanctuary and calls it incense-burning, and has no respect for
divine ceremonies. To her father's horror, he chases Basilene with
the sacrificial sword, relishes the thought of the bloody human
sacrifice, and speaks of slaughtering, cooking, and consuming the
girl. This black comedy or gallows humor will increase tension in
the audience, not cause a relaxation as with comic relief, and this
tension, too, may serve to conceal what the play would reveal.

Stieler's *Basilene* has an occasional function—to honor the
Schwarzburg count, his patron, on his birthday. This function is
fulfilled in part by specific laudatory references in prologue and
epilogue, but the play is not satisfied to merely flatter the prince
and wish him a happy birthday. Thus the laudatory passages and
their message are united to the thematics of the play: the prologue
speaker Mars, god of war, claims he appears because March, the
prince's birthday month, is named for him, but he announces that
he now directs his efforts toward the East (the Turks); Irene, goddess of peace, takes his place as epilogue speaker. The two can
parallel the progression of the ages of mankind delineated in the
play, blood and violence replaced by peace, harmony, and love.

But they also refer to the political actuality: a healthy, vigorous prince who has hopes to continue his dynasty through royal marriage (love), rather than by war and conquest, provides for a land graced by peace and harmony. Albert Anthon's birthday is not a private celebration, but a public observance of an occasion that is for the public benefit; as occasional literature, then, and as comedy, Stieler's *Basilene* appropriately offers hope and joy (*spes et gaudium*).

The final Rudolstadt play, *Der betrogene Betrug*, was performed to celebrate the birth of the Schwarzburg heir in November 1667—some seventeen months after Stieler's departure from Rudolstadt. It is not known whether Stieler wrote the two plays of 1667 before he left for Eisenach or sent them to Rudolstadt from his new residence; but earlier doubts as to their authorship, totally dependent on the fact that Stieler was no longer in the services of the Schwarzburg count, no longer come into question. The plot of this play, which Zeman singles out (with *Der Vermeinte Printz*) as Stieler's finest comedy, seems to have little connection with the event for which it was performed, unlike the other five plays. Don Ferdinand, already wed to Victoria in Toledo, abandons her and travels to Madrid, where he is to wed Elvira. Victoria discovers his intentions and sets out to deceive this bigamous deceiver. She disguises herself as governess to Elvira and thus manages to thwart Ferdinand's marriage plans by revealing his deceits to the intended second bride. But she also deceives him into reconsummating their own marriage by making him believe he has a rendezvous with Elvira. Ferdinand returns to Victoria, Elvira marries the man she really loves (Don Alexandro), and even the servants Scaramutza and Lisille are planning a wedding at the end of the play. Surrounding the three acts of this romantic comedy is the four-act mythological masque of Jupiter's seduction of Danaë in a rain of gold.

The source of the main plot is a novella titled "A Trompeur, Trompeur et demy," which is recited by a character in Part I, Chapter 22 of Paul Scarron's novel *Le Romant Comique* (1651),[37] as Stieler indicates in the preface to the play.[38] Höfer has capably compared the plot structure of the play and its source,[39] showing that, for the purpose of complying with rules of dramatic structure, Stieler has incorporated the first part of the story, which took place the previous month in another location, into the opening monologue as reflections, thus allowing dramatic compression according to the unities of time, place, and action, and providing for the exposition in a succinct fashion. Höfer also mentions the additions of the comic characters Scaramutza and Lisille, and briefly discusses their function in the play. However, several additions to Höfer's account of the relationship of *Der betrogene Betrug* to its source need to be made here. There were minor changes in character names: Ferdinand's assumed name Lopes de Gongora becomes Franciscus de Gongora in Stieler's text, and Elvira's beloved Don Diego is changed to Don Alexandro, while Stieler's text provides Victoria with an assumed name, Eleonore, which is never mentioned in the novella. One character, the old retainer Beatrix, is eliminated, perhaps to make room for Scaramutza and Lisille in the plot of the play.

Most interesting in a comparison of the two works are Stieler's techniques for turning narrated events into dramatically effective scenes on stage. Much that is presented with narrative obliqueness and understatement in the novella is turned into lively scenes on stage—for instance, the presentation of Ferdinand to Elvira as her bridegroom, and the final confrontation and reconciliation of Victoria and Ferdinand. Other dramatic scenes are based on conversations only described by Scarron's narrator, but made into effective dramatic representations by Stieler. Whenever possible, Stieler has followed direct discourse very closely, but he resists dialogues containing long speeches, and tends to break up those recounted by Scarron into a quicker-paced pattern of statement and response. And Stieler adds an element of subjectivity to the objective portrayal in the novella when he adds monologues in which major characters muse aloud about their thoughts and feelings. Thus Stieler focuses his play on emotion and characterization in a way which is totally alien to the novella source, and in so doing, deepens the story's meaning and effect. A further example of Stieler's tendency to add typically German metaphysical weight to the rationally presented French moral tale is his introduction of a religious tone to the final scene in which Ferdinand accepts the validity of his marriage to Victoria (to be discussed below).

As Stieler's title indicates, this play revolves upon the theme of deception and its overthrow. Ferdinand thinks to deceive his wife and his new betrothed, but is instead deceived; Danaë's father Acrisius thinks to deceive Fate, which had decreed that his daughter's son would kill him, by confining her in a cruel prison where she will have no chance to fall in love, wed, and bear a child, but instead Jupiter's deceptive disguise penetrates the prison, and the divine lover impregnates her with the fateful son. The deceptions which are evil and must be overcome, Ferdinand's bigamy and Acrisius's attempt to cheat destiny, are defeated by counterdeceptions which rely on disguise. Victoria changes her name and her social class, and her new garments and position as a servant in Elvira's household make her real identity impenetrable to others; even though she faces Ferdinand himself, he cannot recognize her. Venus, to help carry out the destiny the fates have decreed, disguises herself so cleverly that not only is Acrisius blind to her real identity, but her father Jupiter himself cannot see through her rags and wrinkles. Jupiter, who appears at first as a shower of gold to Danaë, is also not recognized: her "Hilf Jupiter" (p. 27) is ironic, and not until he reveals himself to her in her dream does she realize she has been ravished by a divinity: "Ach Jupiter" (p. 27). Deceivers and innocents alike are deceived in the eternal tragicomedy of the dichotomy between appearance and reality, between façade and essence. But in the end the veils are lifted to reveal Divine Providence as the ultimate helpmate of virtue and right.

This play, although superficially a romantic comedy, is, like Gryphius's *Verlibtes Gespenste*, a conversion drama. Ferdinand's hidden evil is discovered by the abandoned Victoria, who curses him as "du vermumter Vertumnus, der sich in einen Engel verstellet/ und das gantze Hellenheer in seinem Hertzen beherbergen darf" (p. 2). His lowest moment comes when he coarsely derides Victoria's widowhood, desiring a virgin for his wife instead: "Sie mag hinfahren. Ich habe mir nie vorgenommen eine Wittbe zu heyrathen. Jungfer Fleisch ist niedlich. Die Pfütze/ worinn ein ander gebadet/ mag ich nicht aussauffen" (p. 54). Victoria's actions, seen by a thankful Elvira and her father as a manifestation of Divine Providence (p. 40), culminate in the conversion scene. Victoria accuses Ferdinand of perfidy, he is admonished to repent, he confesses his guilt and repents of it, he pleads for forgiveness and is ultimately forgiven by the woman he had most wronged, his wife.

In this play marriage is not the *unio mystica* of Christ as bridegroom with his spouse the human soul, but the earthly manifestation of divine grace and forgiveness. As Victoria redeems her wayward husband and returns him to their marital union, she has provided for his spiritual redemption as well, in rescuing him from sin and in offering him forgiveness. Just as Christ lowered himself by being born a lowly human being in order to redeem the human race, so Victoria has lowered her social class and received the derision of her servant and the duress of serving another with equanimity in order to redeem Ferdinand. Her actions are an allusion to Jesus' sermon in the Temple of Jerusalem (Matthew 23:12 and Luke 18:14): "Wer sich selbst erniedrigt, der wird erhöht."

The interlude also seemingly deals with adultery: Jupiter must quickly woo and win his human paramours in order to escape the wrath of his wife, Juno, queen of the gods. Yet this motif is a blind one in the *Zwischenspiel*, for Jupiter's roving eye has positive results. Instead, the meaning of this masque must be viewed from the perspective of traditional allegorizations of this tale from Ovid's *Metamorphoses*, most of which view the shower of gold as Divine Love miraculously achieving union with the soul. Divine Providence, in the guise of the chief Roman god, fulfills the oracle of Fate by breaching the prison walls to provide for the birth of a culture hero who will battle tyranny, evil, and vice and punish the blasphemous man (Acrisius) who has tried to resist destiny.

The prologue and epilogue of the play provide commentary on the function of this theatrical performance and, by extension, all such occasional literature. The *Vorredner* is the poet Horace who brings the antique gods with him out of Hades, like Orpheus leading Eurydice, to entertain the courtly patron. The relationship of poet and patron emerges: Stieler's patron's fame will live on eternally in the poet's praises, just as Horace's patron (Augustus) is famed partly due to his poetic expression. The play should attack vice by arousing laughter at it and should demonstrate the virtuous way (p. 2); but it should also entertain, celebrate the joyous occasion of the birth of the heir, and arouse pleasure and joy ("Lust und Freud," p. 3). The mythological representatives of poetic inspiration, Apollo and the Muses, appear as the epilogue, and they provide well-wishes from the author and his actors for the health and future of the newborn heir. The ode to the infant Ludwig Friedrich plays with the name of the child by allying his

future with peace (*Friede*). In the botanical image of flowers and
seeds, it alludes to his place in the dynastic continuum. Thus
Stieler's hopes for those necessities of political stability, peace and
continuity, form the framework of his congratulations to the
proud parents. The appropriateness of the *Zwischenspiel* for this
occasional function is clear, since it is the story of the origins of
the hero Perseus, whose birth metamorphoses into that of the
Schwarzburg infant in the epilogue. But the body of the play, too,
has some bearing on this function, for it celebrates the victory of
divinely ordained marriage over all perils. Dynastic marriage has,
in real life, provided the heir who will, it is hoped, bring continuity and peace to the principality and secure it from the chal-
lenges of others. The play celebrates the birth of an heir directly
in the *Zwischenspiel*, and glorifies the dynastic marriage from
which this child derived in the play itself.

Yet humor is not lacking in this play. It has two main sources:
dramatic irony or situation, and the prattling of the servant
Scaramutza. In the case of the former, humor occurs when the
audience, knowing Victoria's counterplots, watches Ferdinand fall
unwittingly into her trap. Scaramutza's humor has two sides. He
teases his mistress Victoria about her loss of relative status in her
disguise, behavior which earns him angry words and blows—slapstick; and he uses a series of delightful sexual double entendres in
wooing Lisille, which she artlessly—or artfully—claims not to
understand. But it is in general a more refined humor than
Scaramutza's scenes in Stieler's other plays, and Scaramutza and
his Lisille achieve in their love and wedding plans at the end a
measure of real dignity. Scaramutza, who can see through the
deceptions of his masters, can also boast of an ethical nobility
which elevates him above Ferdinand. And this natural nobility is
rewarded with marriage, without forgetting the material necessities
for sustaining a family—a point which Stieler, not privately
wealthy and totally dependent on the generosity of his patrons,
well understood. Beneath the safety of the disguise of Stieler's fool
there lurks the author himself, poking fun at his noble patrons
who have the power to order him around and who must be asked
for permission when their employee wishes to marry. By the time
this play was performed in the Schwarzburg residence, Stieler had,
accompanied by material signs of his old patron's best wishes, fled
to the more lucrative position in Eisenach.

But his legacy—the six Rudolstadt plays—is a set of romantic or heroic-gallant comedies of great theatrical effectiveness which constitutes an anomaly in its own century and in the entire history of German literature. In these six plays Stieler has also provided unique evidence about the nature and function of courtly theater. Each of the plays not only contributed to the festivities of the courtly context of its first performance, but also derived a part of its significance from the cause for celebration. While *Die Witte-kinden* directly celebrates dynastic continuity on the occasion of the ruler's birthday, other plays do so indirectly, and the theme is provided more by the context of the performance than by the material of the plot or its treatment (*Der Vermeinte Printz, Ernelinde, Der betrogene Betrug, Basilene*). *Der Vermeinte Printz* further participates in political diplomacy in its rejection of the Salic Law, while *Ernelinde* and *Der betrogene Betrug* offer moral lessons particularly appropriate for the princes upon whom political stability relies. *Basilene* links peace and dynastic marriage as the basis for political stability, while *Der betrogene Betrug* bases it upon peace and the children of such a dynastic marriage. *Die erfreuete Unschuld* lauds political stability based on virtue by equating it to the ultimate political stability: Christ's Millennial Kingdom, which many of Stieler's contemporaries considered imminent. Since the occasion and the audience of the first performance must be considered to have contributed some of the meaning of each of these plays, it would be impossible to fully understand them without some knowledge about that context.

All of the Rudolstadt plays, with the exception of the transla-tion *Ernelinde*, add scenes or even a subplot concerning the bold servant Scaramutza to an extant romance-language plot. This comic character, a wise fool, may even have been played by Stie-ler in the performances. Certainly he reflects the author's own jaundiced views of courtly society, politics, and intrigue. Into the mouth of this fool Stieler has placed words he could never dare to speak himself to his patron's face, unless he himself had been court jester—a role quite out of keeping with Stieler's sense of his own dignity and the dignity of his position in the court bureau-cracy. But from behind the mask of his homunculus, Stieler bra-zenly satirizes what he sees around him, protected by the aesthetic freedom of play-acting. While the rest of the characters in the plays are trapped in the courtesies and courtly phrases which constrain the author himself in his role as secretary, Scaramutza speaks, in Stieler's own Erfurt dialect, those scornful and derisive phrases to his social betters which Stieler might have loved to utter, and to the girls he wooed those vulgarly sensual phrases with which the young Stieler of the *Geharnschte Venus* had felt at home. Scaramutza's significance will be discussed more fully in chapter 9, below.

Why should the members of the courtly audience have enjoyed being the butt of such satire? If they did notice it, and did not intentionally overlook it for the sake of the pleasure aroused by the play as a whole, then it must be assumed that they were capable of enjoying some measure of objectivity about their self-imposed social constraints and the artificiality of social position in the old feudal hierarchy—an intellectual capacity sometimes ascribed to eighteenth-century courts, but somewhat surprising in a century when absolutistic rulers took themselves very seriously. In any case, Stieler's patron and courtly audience in Rudolstadt may be said to have contributed more to these plays than is normally the case, and it is to their credit that what can be ascribed to them speaks of their virtue, tolerance, and humility.

5

Later Dramatic Tests and Activities

The severance of ties with Stieler's Rudolstadt patron in 1666 did not mean a total retirement from theater, although in his *Sekretariat-Kunst* the aging bureaucrat and author expressed his opinion that the requirement of such activities by his employer was beneath the dignity of the position of secretary.[40] Several plays of the Rudolstadt cycle, in fact, postdate his formal employment there, although it cannot be ascertained whether Stieler had finished them and left them with his former employer or whether he wrote them after his departure—on request or in appreciation. To this group I will now add *Melissa. Schäfferey. Anno 1668*, a previously unknown play which I attribute to Stieler; as will be argued below, the event it celebrates is more likely connected to the Rudolstadt court than to the courts of the Saxon dukes who were his employers from 1666 to 1676. In 1669 Stieler translated the famous *Il Pomo d'oro* libretto from the celebrations for the marriage of the emperor Leopold I at the request of the Saxon duke Johann Ernst; in 1680 he published two new plays in Jena, *Bellemperie* (from Thomas Kyd's *Spanish Tragedy*) and *Willmut* (an original allegorical play). In 1683 he rewrote Christian Weise's prose comedy *Die triumphirende Keuschheit* as an opera libretto titled *Floretto*, which he apparently reused the following year in modified form in one of two productions he produced in Weimar and for which he penned the requisite courtly *Zwischenspiele*. And in 1685 he gave drama great scope and the highest ranking in his *Dichtkunst*. It could even be argued that his pen name in the *Fruchtbringende Gesellschaft*, "der Spahte," is an anagram for his identity as writer and producer of plays, "Thaesp" or "Thespa"[41] (for Thespian).

Melissa. Schäfferey. Anno 1668 exists as an *unicum* in the collected volume of Baroque plays at the library of the University of Halle.[42] The copy contains only the simple title, genre, and vague date, and does not indicate author, publisher, printer, or publication date. Only one early bibliographer has recorded the work: Gottsched in his *Nöthiger Vorrath* of 1757-65, vol. I, p. 223. And Gottsched recounts nothing more about the work than what is found on the title page. The director of the library in Halle is of the opinion[43] that the publisher is quite likely J. C. Neuenhahn of

Jena and that the printer might be Caspar Freyschmidt of Rudolstadt—names which are those connected with Stieler's Rudolstadt plays. But no previous attempt has been made to ally the play to Caspar Stieler's oeuvre, or, indeed, to deal with it at all. The work is a short pastoral verse drama, apparently a libretto for a *Singspiel* or *Singendes Zwischenspiel*. It is only forty-two pages long. A three-page mythological prologue precedes the action, and short (one-strophe) choruses close each act. They are printed as part of the text, as in *Basilene*, rather than separately at the end of the entire play.

Although neither author nor publisher is identified on the title page, certain characteristics of the printing, language, and content of the piece make Stieler the most likely author. Apart from its position in a collection which includes other Stieler plays, and its typeface which appears to be the one used by Stieler's publisher of the Rudolstadt years, the superficial appearance of the layout allies it to the Rudolstadt plays: the simple title composed only of the heroine's name and the genre reminds one of *Basilene*, Stieler's other pastoral play, while the brevity of the "Inhalt," the list of characters as "Personen," the indication of place given at the end of the introductory material as a simple but complete sentence ("Der Schau-Platz ist ein Lust-Wald"), the placement of most stage directions in smaller type in the margins, the terms used for act and scene, and the rationale for the scenic divisions— all these details also characterize the other Stieler plays.

Examination of style, dialect, and vocabulary offers more secure evidence of Stieler's authorship. The separation into high and low styles for various classes of characters is characteristic of Stieler, and even though Scaramutza does not appear in this play, the low-life characters Hyccas and Piphynx, who as cowherd and goatherd stand far below the status of the shepherds, speak in what is unmistakably Scaramutza's style; not only do they use the same colorful variety of coarse vocabulary, with dozens of synonyms for half-wit and rogue, but Hycca's pert speech wooing Melissa could pass for one made by Scaramutza to one of his "Wäschermädgen":[44]

> Du bist so gar zu fein!
>   So gäthlich/ wie ein Mäußgen;
> So niedlich/ wie ein Zeißgen;
> So klug/ als wie ein Füchßgen;

So schlau/ als wie ein Lüchßgen.
  So blank/ wie meine Blässe;
So frisch/ wie Borren-Kresse;
So schlang/ wie eine Tanne;
Ey nimm mich doch zum Manne!

                    (p. Cij)

The cleverness of low-life speeches is augmented in *Melissa* by
the delightful usage of exclusively barnyard metaphors by the
wretched cowherd, as in the following declaration of his love:

Du weist/ wie du durch unverhofften Fall
Mir meines Hertzens Stall
Mit Krippen und mit Rauffen
Zu Brand gebracht. . . .

                    (p. Ciij)

The "high style," used by Melissa, Meliboeus, Amyntas, and the
chorus, on the other hand, points ahead to the somewhat more
"Baroque" and bombastic style of Stieler's later plays.

One of Stieler's most prevalent and obvious speech habits
permeates this play, as it does the Rudolstadt plays and the plays
of 1680: the interruption of separable-prefix verbs by another
word (or words) in positions where there would normally be a
single unit, as on the first page: "Der jähling auf- kan -schwellen"
(p. Aij). In this short play the habit appears six times, whereas
other plays of the period not by Stieler might exhibit one instance,
if that, for purposes of versification. Further preferences for
certain words or spellings, many already listed by Höfer and
Köster in their analyses of the Rudolstadt plays and the
Geharnschte Venus, likewise appear here: *abe* for *ab*; *nd* rhyming
with *nn*; *eigen* rhyming with *eien*, *iegen* with *iehen*; use of the
dialect "e" lost in High German in such words as *Hertze*, *sehre*,
Herre; *eilft-* for *elft-*; *mpt* for *mt* and *md* for *m*; *-gen* for *-chen*;
and the various vowel deviations from High German. Several local
idioms and pronunciations noted by Höfer for various Rudolstadt
plays reappear: *löffeln*, *mein Tag* (*sein Tag*, etc.), *spaat* for *spät*,
kunt for *konnte*. As Köster and Höfer have shown for other Stieler
works, these speech habits which creep into at least the humorous
speeches point clearly to Thuringia and, specifically, Erfurt, as the
home of the author.

The versification, too, allies this work to Stieler's. From a
century when stilted trochaic songs or ponderous iambic Alexan-

drine verses predominated, Stieler's comfortable shorter iambics delight our ears; but while Höfer has noted the tendency to four-beat iambics in other works, in *Melissa* Stieler uses the Italian madrigal form of irregular line lengths appropriate to the pastoral drama. In fact, this may be the first German play in which iambic *pentameter* is the predominant verse form. The brief choruses, on the other hand, use the hymnic dactylic rhythms preferred by the later German writers of iambic pentameter tragedies. The apparent instinctive ease in versification, the bold tone, the inventiveness of the rhymes so visible in this play were noted by Höfer as characteristics of versification in the Rudolstadt plays.[45]

Melissa's author, like Stieler, seems exceptionally skillful at selecting dramatic moments, weaving an intricate plot, and creating believable and quick-paced dialogue—the keys to theatrical effectiveness, as Stieler himself points out later in his *Dichtkunst*:

> Ein Aufzug, der sich dehnt, erwecket gern Verdruß,
> wie lange Reden auch. Zumal, wann einem muß
> allein man hören zu. Es muß da seyn ein Leben.
> Zur Lust und Munterheit sind Predigten nicht eben.
> Redt einer nur allein, der mach' es kurz und gut.
> Ein ander lös' ihn ab. Geschwinder Wechsel tuht
> ein großes zu der Lust. . . .
>
> (pp. 79-80, lines 2675-81)

In II, v, for example, he exhibits the false accusations made against Melissa on stage in a witty and action-packed scene rather than in the form of a report or narration of the occurrence, as many authors of the period would undoubtedly have done. It is easy to imagine possible stage business and acting styles on the basis of the text—the sign of the experienced all-round Thespian.

Less tangible, perhaps, is the virtual sameness of views of love and the human condition—views which are relatively rare in seventeenth-century Germany—recognizable in *Melissa* and Stieler's earlier works. There exists in all of Stieler's works before 1668 an optimism about the possibility of human happiness and a respect for romantic love which far outstrips the demands of the romantic comedy genre—views which find their culmination in this play. Marriage is neither the appropriate reward for ethical behavior (as in Gryphius's *Horribilicribrifax*, for example), nor just a standard ending, but apparently the very pillar of stability, both social and political, an attitude perhaps attributable to the

effect of love and marriage on Stieler's own life.[46] Stieler's preference for an assertive woman at the center of the action, relegat-
ing men to a secondary or somewhat passive role—apparent in
Melissa as in the Rudolstadt and Weimar plays—may likewise have
its roots in his personal life. Other common tendencies which seem
to emanate from a single personality are the curious admixture of
reverence and irreverence for authority and the oblique but biting
social and aesthetic satire.

A further parallel between *Melissa* and the Rudolstadt plays
is the use of personages from pagan antiquity. Several of the earlier comedies utilize Roman divinities in choruses which comment
on the plot or on the applicability of the play to its festive context. These gods function much like personifications, since they
tend to act not as believable deities, but rather as representatives
of the qualities traditionally associated with them, e.g., Jupiter as
political wisdom, Mars as war and disquiet. In *Melissa*, as in *Der
Vermeinte Printz*, the supernatural prologue sets the stage for
activities in the human sphere by presenting in dialectical form a
discussion of the major theme. Juno, goddess of marriage, claims
precedence over Venus in matters of chaste love. As in Birken's
Latin allegorical play of 1652, *Psyche*, Venus's son Cupid is
eventually chased from the stage as representing an invalid perspective on love. But of the plays of 1665-68, a pagan deity
becomes a physically present party to the action of the plot only
in *Melissa*. Cupid takes part in a number of scenes in which he
argues with Melissa in an attempt to elicit her worship or in
which he plots to punish her for her disrespect towards his power.
Indeed, he is the villain of the piece, and his disgrace and exile
from earth at the end of the play constitute an analog for the
deserved fall of a Baroque tyrant at the hands of divine inter-
vention in contemporary tragedies. However, such use of pagan
deities as characters is traditional in the genre to which *Melissa*
belongs: the pastoral *Singspiel* (e.g., Opitz's *Dafne*) as opposed to
the pastoral drama (e.g., Guarini's *Il Pastor fido*).

In 1668, the year recorded on the title page, Stieler would
have been in his second year of service to the ducal brothers of
Saxony-Weimar in the town of Eisenach, a time when he might
well have tried to solicit the particular favor of his patrons by
designing a festive *Singspiel* for them. On the other hand, the
year 1668 was significant for Stieler's literary career in that it was

the date of his application and admission to the *Fruchtbringende Gesellschaft*,[47] an event which might have called upon Stieler's talents for further proof of his abilities in the form of a new literary creation. The fact that the only surviving copy is preserved in Halle, seat of the head of the society, would tend to support such a surmise. It is certain, however, that *Melissa*'s date (whatever it might mean—date of completion, performance, presentation, or publication) precedes Stieler's admission into the society, for all his works subsequent to admission, beginning in 1669, carry his newly assigned pen name, "der Spahte," while *Melissa* mentions neither author's name nor pseudonym.

Each of the Rudolstadt plays, on its festive title page, lists the dynastic occasion in the royal family which gave the play its raison d'être. Since the only extant copy of *Melissa* contains no such festive title page, similar information is not available for its purpose and production. But the contents of the play clearly mark it as a "marriage play," that is, a play designed to be performed as part of marriage festivities. However, examination of the family history of Stieler's new patrons, the ducal brothers of Saxony-Weimar, eliminates the possibility that the play was written for any such function for them: indeed, no marriages took place during that decade or the next, and funerals were by far more numerous than such happy occasions as births.[48] It would appear that Stieler did not write the play for his new patrons, if, as I surmise, it was a marriage play. Instead, it might be possible to place it as the last of the Rudolstadt plays, and the third to be sent to his former patron after arriving in Eisenach (or left behind at his departure in 1666), in company with *Basilene* and *Der betrogene Betrug*. While it is true that no princely wedding was celebrated there in 1668, either, one had been in the works for several years. Albert Anthon's sister Ludaemilie Elisabeth had long been destined for her cousin, Christian Wilhelm von Schwarzburg-Sondershausen, when she finally agreed to a 1672 wedding date.[49] Since plans could well have been underway in 1668 or even 1666 for the expected event, it would not have been unlikely that Stieler would have provided the play ahead of time. The documents which itemize elaborate plans for the wedding include the information that there was to have been a performance of a "Comoedie." Certainly the fact that the typeface seems to point to Stieler's Rudolstadt publisher would make this surmise a real possibility. It would also explain why no specific occasion found its way to the title page, since the wedding of 1672 never came about.

The frustrations of the search for the festive occasion also plagued research into possible sources. Since the play belonged to the type of the Italianate pastoral *Singspiel* (e.g., Opitz's *Dafne*), it seemed logical to assume that a Romance-language source might be found—an opera libretto from Vienna or from one of the Italian courts so fond of opera. Aside from the negative finding that no *Melissa* preceded it as opera or play, however, the results of a long search were in vain. It is always possible that the play has as its source a work with a totally different title (just as *Basilene*'s title gives no hint of its connection to any of its sources), but neither the plot nor the characters were known to the experts in seventeenth-century Romance literatures whom I consulted as informants. I thus tend to think that in this play we have Stieler's second original drama text (*Die Wittekinden* is the first). Like that play, of course, it has sources and relatives: the plot outline (lovers, separated by complications, are reunited at the end) is the staple of the diet of the romantic comedy, as of the pastoral play; similar motifs and/or forms appear in Opitz's *Dafne*, Harsdörffer's *Seelewig*, Gryphius's *Gelibte Dornrose*, and Stieler's earlier *Basilene* and later *Willmut*. However, *Melissa* contains neither the erotic playfulness of *Dafne* and *Il Pastor fido* or its German translations, nor the moralistic anti-eroticism of *Seelewig*, but seeks the middle ground where the sensual is acceptable only under the aegis of appropriate and loyal love culminating in marriage—love with the stamp of divine and social approval. Several of the character names are derived from Latin literature, both antique and modern, and from the Italian pastoral tradition.[50]

The plot is a variation on the usual pastoral themes: the shepherdess Melissa has angered Cupid by insisting that Juno, goddess of marriage, alone deserves her thanks for the chaste love shared by Melissa and Meliboeus. The jealous love-god separates the two lovers and tries to destroy their love, first by temptation and then by slander. But the wise ruler of the land, Amyntas, intercedes to help reunite the true lovers, and Cupid is driven out in disgrace. Particularly interesting is the fictional hierarchy modeled on seventeenth-century social realities: shepherds and shepherdesses as a noble class above the goatherds (Piphynx is a kind of bureaucrat delegated authority by Meliboeus, like the upper middle-class bureaucrats of Stieler's ilk), and far beyond the permissible aspirations of the cowherds (Hycca's illicit love for Melissa). Harsdörffer's musings in his *Frauenzimmer Gesprächspiele* (1644) on the types of *Hirten* that may appear in pastoral literature[51] may have been a source. The Nürnberg guru of all pseudo-shepherds in seventeenth-century Germany lists four types—"Kühhirten," "Schafhirten," "Geißhirten," and "Seuhirten"— and while he does not structure them into an explicit hierarchy, he does indicate that *Schafhirten* are to be preferred because their animals are the nicest and because they have less work to do. It is a short step from this rationale to a complete class structure, as in *Melissa*.

Like a Christian martyr, Melissa is tormented by a besotted suitor and the temptations of sensuality, but remains steadfastly faithful to her chaste and sanctified love. Her righteousness in the midst of degradation and despair, coupled with the *deus ex machina* figure, the ruler Amyntas who comes to her rescue, combine to bring about the happy ending. Any allegorical significance the play might have intended is to be found in this analogy to the temptations and ultimate salvation of the human soul: Divine love (*caritas*) reigns victorious over love of the world (*amor*), marriage as the earthly cipher for the *unio mystica* is triumphant over blind passion.

Der göldene Apfel, *Freudenspiel*, Stieler's translation of Francesco Sbarra's Italian-language libretto for the grandest grand opera of the century, *Il Pomo d'oro*, was not published in the seventeenth century and exists only in a single manuscript copy at the Zentralbibliothek der Deutschen Klassik in Weimar.[52] This manuscript, as Zeman has pointed out, is completed in a calligraphic style characteristic of presentation copies; Stieler's handwriting appears in the occasional corrections superimposed on it.[53] On the title page Stieler uses his newly acquired pen name, "Der Spahte," for the first time in connection with a dramatic text, thus securely identifying him as the author. This title page also explicitly indicates the patronage: he had translated *Il Pomo d'oro* "auf empfangenen gnädigsten Befehl des Durchleüchtigsten Fürsten und Herrn, Herrn Johann Ernstens, Hertzogens zu Sachsen" (Duke Johann Ernst of Saxony-Weimar), one of the four ducal brothers who were Stieler's current employers.[54] The date is also given: 1669, only a year after the first performance of the opera in Vienna and two years after the first publication of the libretto. There is no indication on the title page that Stieler's text was performed, or even designed for performance, in Weimar or Eisenach.

Sbarra's original libretto, set to music by Venetian master Marc Antonio Cesti and with sets created by the famous stage engineer Ludovico Burnacini at enormous expense,[55] was designed as the culmination of perhaps the most elaborate courtly festivity ever: the celebration of the marriage of the Holy Roman Emperor Leopold I to his cousin, the Spanish heiress Margareta of Spain, which was to reunite the two Habsburg dynasties and their holdings—including the wealthy Spanish possessions in the New World—under the aegis of the Empire. A marriage of such import, seen as the acme in a long series of significant dynastic marriages of the House of Habsburg,[56] warranted the tremendous outlay in expenditure and energy, spread over a two-year period from 1666 to 1668, for the succession of festive events. Other festivities, which began even before the arrival of the new empress in December of 1666, included the ballet "Concorso dell'Allegrezze universale" by Heinrich Schmeltzer, "Cibele et Atti, Dramma per musica" by Antonio Bertali, "La Monarchia Latina trionfante, Festa musicale" by Antonio Draghi and Schmeltzer, the horse ballet "La Contesa dell'Aria e dell'Acqua" designed by Sbarra with music by Antonio Bertali, the fireworks display "Von Himmeln Entzindete Und Durch Allgemainen Zuruff der Erde sich Himmelwerts erschwingende Frolockungs-Flammen," and numerous other performances of various kinds.[57] The performance of the opera *Il Pomo d'oro* was apparently delayed by problems in construction of the theater until the summer of 1668, when it was staged on the occasion of the Empress's birthday.[58] This performance, some eight hours long, was divided into two sections given on consecutive days.[59] If there were other performances, they have not been reliably documented.[60] Yet this one performance was destined to a fame unequaled by any other opera of the time: contemporaries and eye-witnesses marveled at it; copies of the two festive publications of the libretto, complete with engravings of the twenty-three scene sets, can still be found in libraries once connected with important courts all over Europe;[61] descriptions of its excellence and splendor continue to crop up in histories of the period written fifty to eighty years later, including flagrant exaggerations which are probably indicative of the magnitude of popular interest in it.[62] The Emperor himself expressed his amazement and pride: "Ist gewiß ein Stück gewest, desgleichen wenig gesehen worden sind."[63] Sigmund von Birken mentions the opera in his *Teutsche Rede-Bind- und Dicht-Kunst* of 1679 as a good example for the use of a *Vorspiel* before a play,[64] thus placing the libretto in the canon of works to be emulated. And Stieler's translation into German was not the only one: another appeared anonymously in 1672 in Nürnberg.[65] The score, minus Acts III and V, is preserved in the library in Vienna.[66] Although the opera has never been revived for the stage, it has been published, complete with the Vienna score, by Guido Adler,[67] and excerpts have found their way into performances and even recordings.[68] The composer Marc Antonio Cesti is now recognized as an important figure in the history of opera.

Its importance for contemporaries is further demonstrated by the fact that three major motifs used in this opera, and/or in other imperial wedding festivities of these years, find frequent reuse in other literary works honoring this imperial marriage and later events important to the House of Habsburg. Daniel Casper von Lohenstein's "Judgment of Paris" *Reyen* in *Cleopatra* was written before the famous opera libretto, but must have taken on a new level of meaning in its later editions.[69] His *Sophonisbe*, which has its genesis during the years of the festivities in Vienna, makes both overt and covert references to the wedding and its imagery. The "prophecy" of Dido refers to the wedding (the Turks will tremble "Wenn der Löwe wird die Löwin Spaniens ihm legen bey," V, 182, p. 338) as does the fourth *Reyen* (IV, 625: "Perle" is a reference to Margareta), while the second *Reyen* revives both the imagery of the four elements found throughout the festivities (to be discussed below) and the story of Jason and the Golden Fleece (from the *Contesa dell'Aria e dell'Acqua*). The fourth *Reyen* connects Leopold, as Hercules, with both the golden fleece (IV, 621-24) and the golden apple (615).

The imagery from *Il Pomo d'oro* found reuse in other imperial polemic as well. In a description of Leopold's third marriage (1676), the motif of the three goddesses is employed in an emblem in which the hand of God offers the imperial globe ("Reichsapfel") to three women, presumably consecutively, as representatives of the three empresses so honored by Leopold.[70]   And a celebratory publication for the coronation in 1690 of this third wife (Eleonora) as empress, along with her son as Roman king, describes Eleonora as all three goddesses in one, with the virtues of each, and then extends the image to state that she is "dreyfach Erbenreich gekront"—a reference to her three children who are Leopold's only surviving heirs.[71]

Sbarra's *Il Pomo d'oro* uses the story of the Judgment of Paris, who must offer the golden apple to the most beautiful goddess, to honor the recently wed imperial couple. The apple thus becomes the *Reichsapfel*, symbol of empire. Although the apple is tossed among the gods by the personification of discord, and desire for it by the three rival goddesses (Juno, Pallas Athena, and Venus) brings about a disruption of peace and tranquility, the resultant disunity is only temporary in this version. When the warring goddesses turn eventually to Jupiter for a solution, he offers the apple instead to the new empress, Margareta, as most worthy—a judgment with which the three goddesses are satisfied. The tragic results of Paris's choice—his own adulterous flight with Helen, Menelaus's queen, and the destruction of Troy at the hands of the furious Greeks after seven years of war—are avoided, and peace and tranquility are restored. As in the famous ditty, "Others may conquer by war; you, blessed Austria, by marriage,"[72] the clever politics of dynastic marriage can alter the disasters of legendary and historical models and provide a sort of ultimate "happy ending." Here, the apple of discord becomes the apple of concord, symbol of the *pax romana* the Holy Roman Empire wishes to impose on a pan-Christian Europe, and the imperial marriage is elevated to a symbol of the peace, stability, and dynastic continuity expected as a result of the union.

Had Sbarra contented himself with spectacular dramatization of the plot and polemical intent described above, the result would have been similar to many short mythological masques of the sixteenth century, or perhaps to Lohenstein's "Judgment of Paris" *Reyen* in *Cleopatra*. But Sbarra has enriched his libretto with a romantic pastoral subplot, a problematics of licit and illicit love, a cosmic context (the four elements), and a dense layer of satirical and comic material. The subplot concerns Ennone (Enno), a nymph whom the shepherd Paris abandons in order to woo Helen. Ennone and Paris swear eternal love in a typical opera love-scene;

when Paris leaves her, Ennone falls into depression and despair. But she is finally rewarded with the love of a faithful shepherd, Aurindus, who had wooed her in vain before Paris's faithlessness to her. In a typical use of pastoral motifs, their rustic and virtuous bliss is contrasted with the corruption of court as exemplified in the bickering of the gods and in Paris's adulterous pursuit of Helen.

The behavior of Paris under the influence of Venus and of the beauty of Helen works as a more implicit contrast to the imperial marriage, as well: Paris is an exemplum *e contrario*. This prince, whose duty is to marry according to principles of virtue and dynastic interests, instead chooses to enter into an adulterous union which will bring about the destruction of his country and his dynasty. His behavior is set up as the opposite to that of Leopold, who has married entirely in accord with virtue and dynastic interests, with his duty to his family and country, and with political wisdom. Illicit love is rejected, licit love is applauded in this paeon to what was seen as the most important dynastic marriage of the age.

That the meaning of this marriage extended beyond the more prosaic hopes for political unification and an heir can be seen in the imagery of cosmic forces which permeate Sbarra's text, and indeed, all the texts designed explicitly for the wedding festivities. Just as the four elements provide the underlying unity between the equestrian ballet and the fireworks display (each event conjures up two of the four elements, air and water, fire and earth respectively), so too does Sbarra's *Il Pomo d'oro* introduce these primary building blocks of the cosmos into the struggle among the three goddesses for supremacy. Juno calls upon Eolus, the god of winds (= air), Pallas Athena employs the heroes (= earth), and Venus counters by bringing the sea-god Neptune and his demigods (= water) into the conflict. When Juno tries to involve the element of fire, however, she is thwarted by his refusal—indicative, perhaps, of the altered ending of the story in which no Troy will burn. The opera ends with a ballet of the three elements which did get involved: "Der Geisterlein in der Lufft/ Der Helden auf der Erde/ Der Sirenen und Tritonen im Meer."

Most interesting is the addition of comic characters, particularly Filaura, Ennone's old nurse, and Momus, court fool of the gods. Their interspersed scenes or parts of scenes equal, both in length and in significance, the dramatic action in the two plots. Filaura's comic scenes serve mostly to lighten the mood when Aurindus, the love-sick shepherd, is on the stage. She teases him unmercifully about his affliction and thus serves to undermine any tendencies toward melodrama; but she also represents in its worst light the materialistic worldview of the court as she derides his hopes for Ennone's love solely on the grounds of his poverty. Her speaking name sums up her vice: love of gold. Aurindus's name, on the other hand, is indicative of true personal worth; he is the representative in the play of the Golden Age. Filaura serves as a parody and thus a critique of the pretentious, avaricious courtier, a type which must have plagued the court in imperial Vienna, as elsewhere. But her coarse language and earthy constructions were a source of hilarity, as well. She is a stock comic figure, derived from the commedia dell'arte, whose counterparts also appear, for instance, in Gryphius's *Seugamme*, Cicognini's (and Stieler's) *Ernelinde*, and Shakespeare's *Romeo and Juliet*.

Momus is also a stock figure derived from Italian and ancient comedy; his name is Greek for "scold," and this is his dramatic function. With fool's license he laughs at the foibles of the gods and criticizes their vices, just as a Shakespearean fool points out the weaknesses of his royal master. Momus laughs at Neptune's preference for wine over water, his appropriate element, and calls Mars the god of good eating since he understands feasting better than making war. This fool punctures their vanities, openly disapproves of their ridiculous feuding, and exposes the vices of the supposed hero of the piece, Paris. But he also prevents the suicide of a despairing Aurindus and succors a swooning Ennone. The combination makes him the true force for ethical behavior in the play. He describes his satirical function in the play himself:

Io son Momo
Galanthomo,
Dico mal, ma dico il vero.

(Momus ist ein Biedermann
der da kan,
reden wahr, und drüber schertzen.)
(V, ii)

He goes into more detail about his profession in a dialogue with Paris (I, xii). Many of his speeches are directed not to the characters, but to the members of the audience, and he thus establishes a rapport with them, letting them in on his jokes and causing them to ally themselves with his ethical stance and thus to retain their objectivity about the events on the stage.

A third comic character is introduced in only a single scene: Charon, ferryman at the River Styx, laments that business is slack, and rejoices when he hears of the war caused by the bickering of the rival goddesses. When the Furies wish to cross, however, he pretends not to recognize them (for they never offer him any gratuities) and refuses at first to ferry them across, arousing their ire. This stock scene of a servant refusing to recognize, and serve, his master or superior derives from Roman comedy and the commedia dell'arte, although its use of Charon as the rogue is unusual, and a twist in the direction of gallows humor.

Sbarra employs several motifs from traditional Habsburg polemic in order to honor the dynastic marriage. Twice—once in the prologue as the backdrop for the allegorical figure of the Glory of Austria and again upon the gift of the golden apple to Margareta—the motif of a room lined with the images of the illustrious ancestors of the imperial house is used as a traditional representation of dynastic stability and glory.[73] The triumphal procession in the twelfth scene of act four likewise has its antecedents in Habsburg polemic and, indeed, in honorific imagery all over Europe since the Renaissance.[74]

In connection with the patronage of this opera and the other wedding festivities, it is interesting to note that the Emperor Leopold was personally involved as creator and participant, and not only as patron and audience. As he often did for musical performances at his court, he supplied some of the compositions for the set pieces himself;[75] he rode in the equestrian ballet and probably danced in some of the other ballets presented in honor of his own marriage, along with the nobles of his court. These festivities in Vienna under the patronage of Leopold provide perhaps the highest form of the sort of performance art that blurs or even obliterates the boundaries between participants and spectators, allowing the illusions of art to provide a playground for the celebrants which was not only vicarious. Art and court, artist and audience all blended into a cohesive whole.

Stieler's translation of the famous opera at the specific request of Duke Johann Ernst reflects the desire of middle German courts outside the sphere of influence of the Italian language to catch a glimpse of this glorious event for themselves. The translation retains the honorific passages which connect the opera to the imperial marriage, only consolidating the speeches of some of the individual provinces in the prologue into more generalized groupings of Austrian possessions and adding the identification of his own patron in an appropriately honorific way. Little else has been altered to any great extent: in terms of characterization, plot, scenes, and speeches, the translation is a faithful rendition of the Italian into idiomatic German.[76]   The translator seems to have complete understanding of his Italian original: the only possible error I could find was the omission of alimentary tract humor in one speech (I, x), but even this was likely intentional. The comic scenes, especially, have been translated in a creative and idiomatic fashion, not unlike that in Stieler's other translation, *Ernelinde*, which was, as noted above, actually used in several volumes of Grimm's *Deutsches Wörterbuch* as an outstanding source for colloquial expressions.

From the perspective of a study on Stieler, the most significant aspect of this work is its versification. Comparison with metric forms that dominate in Stieler's original verse dramas (*Die Wittekinden, Melissa*, the various *Zwischenspiele* and choruses) reveals that Stieler must have been working here under some sort of constraint. For instead of using his usual predominantly iambic madrigal verse with a few passages of dactylic in joyful scenes, Stieler here turns to a mixture of meters in which trochaic and dactylic are foremost in the madrigalic sections, although not to the exclusion of iambic or even more irregular meters, and the strophic sections are much less *Lied*-like than in his original works. It is easy to see, by comparing Italian and German versions, that the source of this incongruity lies in an attempt to follow exactly the metric scheme of his original in almost every speech—a conclusion which naturally leads to speculation that he may, in spite of Höfer's doubts,[77] have designed *Der göldene Apfel* as a singing translation. Aside from the speeches of Juno to Paris, which Stieler places in almost the only Alexandrines in his entire dramatic oeuvre, while the originals contain four-beat verses seen by Wellesz as "archaizing,"[78] there are few discrepancies in number of lines or in meter in the entire text, and most of those occur in the madrigalic speeches of the comic characters.

The translations of the ariose passages, including all of Enno's speeches and the arias by serious and comic characters, fit the surviving music by Cesti, although Stieler's verses often provide new text for each musical phrase, rather than utilizing repetitions of lines to be emphasized as in the original (e.g., I, xi, pp. 72-74). The latter example, in particular, could be used as evidence that Stieler had a copy of the score, not just of the libretto, before him as he worked. I consider it quite possible that Stieler intended his text as a *Singspiel* in the more modern sense: spoken passages would alternate with musical presentation of ariose and aria sections which could well make use of Cesti's score. Such a translation would represent a departure from previous procedure in translations of opera texts—Opitz's "translation" of Rinuccini's *Dafne* had to be set to new musical compositions, as did the adaptations of Italian operas by Harsdörffer and others. The fact that Stieler accomplished this difficult task in a text which closely reflects the content and tone of the original, and which never sounds stilted or forced, speaks for his exceptional ability as a wielder of words. Even when he is compelled by metrical constraints to abandon his preferred, and presumably natural verse form (the iambic), the words, rhythms, and rhymes seem to flow effortlessly from his pen. Other typical features that mark Stieler's language in all his works occur here, too: the appearance of earthy, even coarse colloquialisms in the comic scenes, the preference for the insertion of a word or phrase between a separable-prefix verb and its prefix, the use of some of the same favorite words and phrases (e.g., "ein Herz so hart wie ein Kieselstein," "karten," "Pol," "Rivier," "löfflen") and of the same spelling habits and dialect sounds (e.g., "eu" for "ie"), and a love of malapropisms and puns as sources of verbal humor.

There can also be no doubt of Stieler's authorship of the two plays of 1680, *Bellemperie* and *Willmut*, for he affixed his pseudonym "der Spahte" to them as well. Less certain is the event for which they were composed and the context intended for their first performance. Although they were published in Jena, where Stieler had spent the two years from 1678 to 1680, Zeman connects them[79] to Stieler's new position in Weimar (1680-84) where he was not only secretary, but also apparently director of the court theater. I consider it possible that he wrote the plays in order to help him gain the Weimar post, or possibly to initiate his directorship there with new and original works from his own pen. No record of such a Weimar performance survives, nor is there a festive title page to allude to such a performance. Although half of the extant copies of each play are bound alone, it is apparent from the preparatory word "Willmut" at the bottom of the last page of *Bellemperie* that they were intended to be bound together, as in the copies at Yale and Coburg. However, the fact that the pagination begins anew for *Willmut* allowed for separate binding. Other than the assumed performances in Weimar, *Bellemperie* and *Willmut* appeared on stage in Meiningen in 1682 and in Görlitz in 1684-85.[80]

Bellemperie is Stieler's first and only tragedy, in spite of the implicit promise in the collective title of the Rudolstadt plays fifteen years before. It is the fifth continental version of Thomas Kyd's popular revenge play of 1587, *The Spanish Tragedy*,[81] and, as Stieler himself states in the "Veranlassung zu diesem Trauerspiel," his version is a drastic revision of the anonymous Dutch *Don Jeronimo* of 1638.[82] Rudolf Schoenwerth has explained rather minutely the relationship of Stieler's *Bellemperie* with its direct source[83] by comparing the two plays scene by scene, but it remains to recognize Stieler's improvements and to analyze the reasons for the changes he has made.

The princess of Castille, Bellemperie, loved Horatio, son of a high-ranking courtier, and was secretly betrothed to him. But her brother, in order to clear the way for her marriage to his friend and ally, the prince of Portugal, has teamed with this suitor to murder her beloved. Bellemperie and Hieronimo, father of her murdered fiancé, plot a bloody revenge which will not only end in the deaths of the two murderers and their fathers at the hands of the avengers, but in their own suicides as well. The vengeful deeds are carried out during a play within the play in which the two guilty murderers and the two avengers are the chief actors, while the two royal fathers (kings of Spain and Portugal) constitute the courtly audience. The plot of the tragedy within the tragedy is a typical martyr-tyrant play set in the Turkish Empire: Perseda, a captive Christian (played by Bellemperie), is wooed by her captor, Solyman (played by Bellemperie's real suitor, the prince of Portugal). Her Christian fiancé, Erastus (played by Bellemperie's brother) is stabbed to death by Mustafa (played by Hieronimo), after which Perseda stabs Solyman, then kills herself.

Instead of play-acting these three deaths, however, Bellemperie and Hieronimo really carry them out.

The most obvious change, as Schoenwerth has pointed out, is the new title and the concomitant alteration in focus for the whole in favor of the female protagonist. Not only does Bellemperie gain in importance at the expense of Don Jeronimo/Hieronimo, but her character grows, too, in strength and interest. Instead of a passively, if steadfastly loyal woman in mourning for her murdered beloved who must be led to aid in the revenge, she becomes the primary intrigant who evolves the plot, assigns the roles, and carries out her vengeance and suicide with horrifying speed and vigor. She is both the coldly calculating intrigant who never wavers in her grisly self-assigned task, and the fiercely passionate avenger whose thwarted love has turned to murderous hatred against those, including her own brother and father, who have done her wrong. In a series of effective scenes, Stieler pits her two aspects against one another, as she struggles to hide her hatred and pretend her compliance with her brother's wishes—a hypocrisy necessary for the completion of the plotted vengeance. This preference for a bold and active heroine at the center of the plot is a hallmark of nearly all of Stieler's dramatic output.

As Schoenwerth notes, Stieler relegates the actions of his source's first two acts—including the plotting of the princes and murder of Horatio—to background material presented in the preface and as narrated exposition in his own first two acts. But Schoenwerth does not seem to notice that this alteration considerably strengthens the play by focusing attention on the truly dramatic events of Bellemperie's vengeance. Stieler's version begins *in medias res* with a call for vengeance on the part of Horatio's ghost (not unlike the start of Shakespeare's revenge play, *Hamlet*). This compression of the action likewise brings the play into conformity with Aristotle's (and Scaliger's and Stieler's own of his *Dichtkunst* of 1685) dramatic unities of time, place, and action—in this case, particularly, a real improvement in the plot structure.

In order to further enhance the theatricality of the piece, Stieler also adds a number of new dramatic scenes. One of the most interesting and effective of these is that between Bellemperie and Lorenzo (prince of Portugal, Horatio's murderer, and now the new fiancé forced upon her by her brother) in which they

exchange assurances of their mutual love. While Lorenzo is prob-
ing to discover her true feelings, she is cleverly concealing them
beneath double entendres and the appearance of compliance (II,
vi). Stieler has also added several scenes which tend to augment
the role of the ghost of Horatio—an alteration which Schoenwerth,
from the perspective of his own century, views as seriously
weakening the audience's respect for the play. But for the less
jaded audiences of the seventeenth century, which seemed never
to tire of the appearance of ghosts and apparitions, whether on the
itinerant stage, in the Jesuit theater, or in the works of the famous
Silesian dramatists, Stieler's additions would have been welcome.

But as Schoenwerth has also pointed out, by far the most
numerous and most effective of the scenes added by Stieler are
those in which his homunculus and mouthpiece, Scaramutza, that
brazen servant, twits his social betters and woos his favorite maid-
servant, Gillette. These comic intrusions in the high tone of the
German *Kunsttragödie* (a tone present in spite of Stieler's use of
prose) perhaps may remind us of the *Hanswursterei* of the itinerant stage attacked so viciously by Gottsched in the next century,
but they are probably needed in so heavy-handed and grisly a
play (again, one is reminded of Shakespeare, this time of his
theatrically effective use of comic relief). This Scaramutza, more-
over, is no slapstick comedian of the alimentary-tract variety. He
is a witty and clever character whose ironic comments destroy
pretensions, break theatrical illusion in order to show that life
itself acts out roles, and offer political satire. After the bloodbath
ending the tragedy within the tragedy, Scaramutza steps to the
front of the stage to claim the vacated thrones of the two kingdoms, Castille and Portugal. A buffoon would govern them better
than rulers who put themselves above justice and the law.

Schoenwerth does not comment on the differences he notes
between the endings of the two plays. But in fact, Stieler's ending
constitutes a total reworking not only of Hieronimo's role, but also
of the intended interpretation. In the Dutch version (as in Kyd's
original), Jeronimo is taken into custody and threatened with torture by the two royal members of the audience after the deaths of
the two princes and the princess during the performance. After
gestures of defiance and another murder at his hands (the Spanish
king), he commits suicide, leaving the Portuguese king alive to

moralize on the misuse of power and the certainty of Nemesis. But Stieler has compressed the final murders into the play within the play, blurring the distinctions between inner and outer play at the end, for Hieronimo informs the kings right at play's end of the deaths and then promptly kills them (both of them—Scaramutza is left to moralize instead of the Portuguese king), after which he commits suicide. Thus the attenuated denouement is curtailed, and the stunning precipitousness with which Nemesis carries out her revenge is heightened. Furthermore, with Scaramutza—still in his costume for the internal play—leading the way, the actors rise from the dead to form a Dance of Death, which stresses the absolute merger of both plays at the end. The significance of these features initiated by Stieler will be further discussed below.

As in his Rudolstadt plays, Stieler also added verse *intermezzo*-style choruses to follow each act of *Bellemperie*. The Roman deities and personified abstractions (e.g., *Ehrgeitz*) discuss the thematics of the first and second acts in a dialectic designed to generalize and moralize, while the epilogue is spoken by triumphant Nemesis alone, who directly admonishes the audience against vice and sin and warns of certain retribution. These *intermezzi* firmly link *Bellemperie*, like Stieler's earlier plays, to the Italian theatrical tradition, but also to the *Kunsttragödie* of the Silesians.

As a tragedy, *Bellemperie* breaks new ground for Stieler, but in spite of a change in genre, the play retains most of Stieler's hallmarks: the intrusion of Scaramutza and his various paramours into the serious action, the use of prose in the acts and verse in the choruses (only *Die Wittekinden, Melissa, Der göldene Apfel*, and *Floretto* are written entirely in verse), the division into three acts, the separation into high and low styles on the basis of the social class of the speaker. Other than the gruesome subject matter (which, by the way, also appeared as a subplot in *Ernelinde*, and which always threatened the happy endings of the others), the most easily noticed difference is that Stieler seems to have replaced his former reliance on *Kanzleisprache* for the elevated speeches with the less officious but more flowery and possibly even more artificial language of the mannered late Baroque (e.g., Lohenstein, Hofmannswaldau).[84] The style of Stieler's *Bellemperie* belongs neither to that of the verse *Kunsttragödie* nor to that of the prose *Trauerspiele* of the schoolmen, but remains his own concoction of them, together with the more lively and theatrically effective style of the itinerant stage. Stieler's stylistic influences, like his literary sources, are merely raw materials which he will smelt and refine into his own highly individual creation. In *Bellemperie*, his choice of subject matter, too, constitutes an anomaly in German Baroque tragedy. For instead of the tyrant-intrigant-martyr triangle in any of its permutations, Stieler follows an English and Dutch tradition also loved by the continental itinerant stage in choosing to write a revenge play. In place of a passive martyr who resists the tyrant and his evil courtiers only by refusing to do the demanded actions, Stieler turns his martyr, Bellemperie, into the intrigant who will carry out divine retribution against the "tyrant" who caused her to suffer. The oppressor's Machiavellian manipulations are usurped by the innocent martyr and used as weapons against the tyrant; the martyr-turned-avenger commits suicide in the ultimate rejection of earthly happiness. Nemesis, apparently a pagan guise for Divine Retribution, seems victorious, yet there is no Christian humility, passivity, or optimism at the end. In committing suicide, Bellemperie is her own victim, just as she previously succumbed to her own passions and emotions. So while retribution is one result (inherited from Stieler's source), death is the other—and the author's most original contribution to the material.

Death is Stieler's final word in this macabre play, for the internal and external plays merge at the end, after the epilogue spoken by Nemesis (which logically ends either or both), in the Dance of Death. The dancers are the actors playing the dead protagonists of the external play who were to have only pretended to be killed during the internal play. Perhaps in an allusion to the famous German predecessor of the motif of the play-within-the-play, Gryphius's *Herr Peter Squentz*,[85] Stieler has his actors resurrect at the end. But their *Totentanz* does not, like the end of the internal play in *Peter Squentz*, break the theatrical illusion for satirical and comic reasons, but rather in order to drastically affect the audience. For the Dance of Death is a traditional motif[86] not only predicting the impending death of the individuals who see it or are drawn into it, but also proclaiming the mortality of all—a *memento mori* whose sources lie in medieval folklore and the periodic scourges of the plague (The Black Death). If, as for the happier dances closing sixteenth-century theatrical performances during Carneval, the audience was drawn into this dance, the effect could be a truly devastating experience of one's own transience.[87]

Because of this *danse macabre* that ends both internal and external plays and constitutes their complete merger with each other, and possibly with the reality of the audience as well, Stieler's use of the motif of the play-within-the-play is the most novel of the German seventeenth century. But even before the Dance of Death, the internal and external plays have merged, for the vengeful killings perpetrated by Bellemperie and Hieronimo coincide with the murders to be acted out in the illusion of the internal play. As Perseda "kills" Solyman, Bellemperie really kills Lorenzo; as Mustafa "kills" Erasto, Hieronimo really kills the Castillian prince. The internal audience (and probably the external audience as well) has to be told that the illusion has become "reality," that the dead protagonists of the internal play are also dead in the reality of the external play. To this point, Stieler has merely followed his source, and while we might speculate that this astonishing manipulation of illusion was what attracted him to the material, the novelty of *Bellemperie* does not lie here. Rather, Stieler's contribution lies in the manipulation not just of the levels of illusion, but of the emotions of the audience. The audience, which, according to Aristotle's theory, has experienced tragic pleasure upon viewing tragic deeds it knew to be imitations not affecting its own safety, is put through an experience parallel to that undergone by the internal audience. Death and Nemesis refuse, in Stieler's play, to stay safely up on stage, but instead intrude into the reality of the audience. Just as the kings found, to their horrified surprise, that the events were real and that the murderers from the illusion of the playlet were about to become their own murderers, so, too, does the exterior audience lose its sense of separateness from the exterior play as the actors rise from the "dead" to begin a Dance of Death which beckons to and perhaps ultimately includes themselves. A more powerful *memento mori* in a theatrical experience is scarcely to be imagined.

The companion piece to *Bellemperie*, *Willmut*, has an original plot—at least insofar as it has no single source. Willmut, a rash and headstrong young prince, chafes at the restraints his parents have placed on him. He refuses to marry the princess they have chosen for his bride, the virtuous Allguda von Seelewig, and instead sets out to woo the seductive Scheinguda. Eventually brought to his senses by his wise advisers, he comes to agree freely with his parents' wishes.

The play is a dramatized allegory, and as such belongs to a dramatic genre which was very popular in the seventeenth century. Stieler's own depiction in his *Dichtkunst* of 1685 of this type of drama, which he terms "Allegorien," provides a useful definition.[88] He begins by describing the freedom of the poet of this genre to create story, setting, and characters out of his own imagination, then insists that they must still be plausible, i.e., realistic. The play must both please (*delectare*) and teach (*docere*). And above all, the allegorical drama must contain a hidden meaning:

> Zumal, wann drunter ist was heimlichs zuverstehen,
> so Allegorisch heißt. Die Wahrheit will verbildet
> und ümgekleidet seyn, verzuckert und vergüldet.
>
> (p. 55, lines 1712-14)

The names of characters in such plays ought to aid interpretation, and thus they should be formed from German words (e.g., Gottlieb = love of God, Reinhart = purity). *Willmut*'s predecessors in this genre include Jakob Masen's *Androfilo* of 1648 (translated by Sigmund von Birken and published and performed in 1656), Birken's own *Psyche* (Latin 1652; translated and published in his *Rede-Bind- und Dicht-Kunst* in 1679), and Georg Harsdörffer's pseudo-pastoral opera, *Seelewig* (1644), which gave its name to Stieler's heroine. Less famous allegorical plays abound among Jesuit dramas, courtly *Festspiele*, and school plays of the seventeenth century; their common hallmark is the transparent meaning of the names of the characters.

These "sprechende Namen" are also one aspect which differentiates allegorical drama as a separate genre from tragedies or comedies which have allegorical (hidden, usually religious) significance (e.g., in Stieler's own oeuvre, *Die erfreuete Unschuld*, *Basilene*, and possibly *Der betrogene Betrug*). The distinction is one of primary intent and focus: the allegorical play uses characters as personifications of abstractions, and their deeds and interactions add up to a moral or religious precept, while the tragedy or comedy with allegorical significance portrays real personages and real events (whether historical or based on a fictitious source) at the same time that it perceives and latently demonstrates the underlying analogy to personages and events or processes in *Heils-*

geschichte. Certainly there exist many borderline cases (an excellent example is Jakob Bidermann's *Cenodoxus*), but *Willmut* is a clear exemplar of the allegorical drama as defined by Stieler. However, even *Willmut* contains elements of the other genres: the characters and plot of a *Heldenspiel*, the satire and wit of a *Lustspiel*, to use Stieler's own terms from the *Dichtkunst*.

Although *Willmut* is Stieler's attempt at a new genre of comedy, his usual traits still make their appearance. The play consists of three prose acts, with verse prologue and epilogue (this play has no choruses between the acts). The characters who present this verse material outside the main action are Roman deities as personifications for their traditional functions and meanings. And not only does Scaramutza appear, up to his old tricks as usual, but the division into appropriate high and low styles for the two social classes, nobility and servants, is maintained.

In his "Vorsprache an den Leser," Stieler claims that the meaning of the tale will be clear to all those who have a sense of "Sittenkunst," and that the prologue and epilogue will help the reader/audience to understand the play. But the author here analyzes the meanings of the names of the characters to be certain that their significance will not escape the reader. The names of the king and queen, Adelheld and Redawinne, stand for understanding and reason, Willmut's name for the will (voluntas), his bride Allguda von Seelewig for the supreme good (summum bonum), the seductive Scheinguda for the apparent good (bonum apparens) whose servant is Wunne, lust (voluptas). Willmut's three servants, who influence his original choice of vice and lust, represent his senses and sexual appetite, while the loyal advisers who come to his rescue are Kührmann, the free will, and Wahlbrecht, correct choice.

The prologue speaker, Hercules, calls on the audience to discover the hidden truth in the play: "Greift nach dem Kern/ dem Absehn vom Gedicht!" (p. 12). In the epilogue Mercury, god of the mysterious, again calls upon the audience to allegorize the plot:

Merket auf/ was vor eine Lehre
solche Schau euch erteilen will.
Ich/ Merkur/ Tolmetsch tunkler Sachen/

bin allhier/ euch zu tuhn Bericht
und den Kern schalenbloß zu machen/
den versteckt dieses Kunstgedicht.

(p. 145)

He then proceeds to analysis and allegorization, which is completely superfluous by this time, even to a modern reader: Willmut as mankind has freedom of the will to choose wisely (heavenly orientation) or ill (earthly orientation); after first plunging into error, he listens to reason and ultimately makes the choice which will be rewarded with eternal salvation.

But even in *Willmut*, Stieler leaves something for the reader/audience to decipher on the basis of well-known traditions: the reason for the choice of Hercules as prologue speaker. Although never mentioned explicitly in this play, the most popular story about Hercules in the seventeenth century, Hercules at the Crossroads, comes immediately to mind. In this often allegorized parable, Hercules arrives at a crossroads where two women point the way toward opposite paths. One, usually called Voluptas, possesses alluring beauty and promises him much pleasure and good fortune along her broad and easy way; the other, variously dubbed Virtus or Religio, appears stern and forbidding, and promises much toil and suffering up her narrow, uneven path to the summit. Hercules correctly chooses the difficult path of virtue. Many depictions of the tale also show the ultimate rewards: Heavenly grace at the end of the difficult path, the fires of Hell at the end of the easy one.[89] Although Willmut does not choose literally between two roads, he does choose between two women who are directly analogous to those who confront Hercules, and in doing so, he certainly selects from between opposing ways of life—the allegorical significance of the crossroads, after all. Thus the parable of Hercules at the Crossroads is evoked in the minds of the spectators as a parallel to the play they witness; it is not necessary for Stieler to present the pagan analogy visually or verbally (as Lohenstein did in his *Sophonisbe*),[90] since he knows it to be well known to his audience. And it does leave the connoisseurs among them a mental exercise of the sort so much loved in the seventeenth century.

Although both Willmut and Hercules stand for mankind, a popular use of the Hercules parable—as a mirror for princes—may also be implied in the juxtaposition of the two stories.[91] Willmut,

who is, after all, not *Jedermann*, but a prince and heir of a kingdom, could be seen as a model for the behavior of princes in general, or even for the actions of a particular prince, the son of
Stieler's new patron, Wilhelm Ernst of Saxony-Weimar, who would
come into his inheritance in 1683. For what is best for the individual—the *summum bonum*, virtue, salvation—is also what is best
for the Christian state. A virtuous prince provides not only for his
own salvation, but for the physical and spiritual well-being of his
subjects as well.

Potentially somewhat alienating in this allegory is the intrusion of Stieler's omnipresent dramatic homunculus, Scaramutza,
whose slapstick humor performs with its usual genial coarseness
and whose illusion-breaking techniques continually remind the
audience that they are watching a play. But even Scaramutza
receives an allegorical identity—*Wahn* (delusion)—an ironically
appropriate significance for the fool who creates and breaks illusions and at the same time demonstrates mankind's foibles. Thus
Scaramutza, who appears in romantic comedy, pastoral, tragedy,
and allegorical drama in Stieler's works, can be seen as the comic
(in the wider sense of theatrical) spirit *per se*, the epitome of contemporary theater and dramatic creation. By extension, since life
is a stage and men and women merely players, he represents the
essence of human existence: appearance, delusion, illusion.

Stieler's last known involvement with theater occurred in
1684. In discussing two festive theatrical performances that took
place in Weimar in October and December of that year, Conrad
Höfer comes to the conclusion that the anonymous *Zwischenspiele*
created for two pre-extant dramatic texts and published in com-
memorative editions by the court printer were written by Caspar
Stieler.[92] Furthermore, he concludes that Stieler himself, then
employed in Weimar as secretary to the Dukes, had revised the
plays to be used and probably fulfilled the function of producer
and director.[93] These performances and their newly created *Zwischenspiele* have received cursory treatment in studies on Stieler[94]
and Thuringian theater,[95] and brief mention in a number of
studies on music and musical theater of the Baroque.[96] All of
these discussions depend almost entirely on Höfer's more exhaus-
tive study.

On the nineteenth of October, 1684, according to the festive
title page of the published *Zwischenspiel*,[97] a performance of "dem

theatralischen Schauspiel" *Krieg und Sieg der Keuschheit*, accompanied by the "Musicalische Freuden-Feyer," was part of the birthday celebration for one of the reigning dukes, Wilhelm Ernst, "Herzog zu Sachsen/Jülich/ Cleve und Berg." The performance took place "Zu Weimar auf dem Fürstlichen Gartenhause," which Frenzel has identified as the "Grünes Schlößchen"—a small palace in the gardens—and described in his account.[98] Although the title page indicates that the play and its *Zwischenspiel* were "aus unterthänigster Schuldigkeit glückwüntschend vorgestellet," no author or director is named. Conrad Höfer bases his attribution of the *Zwischenspiel* to Stieler on opportunity and on his own intuitive sense of Stieler's style. In 1914, when Höfer's study appeared, the text of the play *Krieg und Sieg der Keuschheit* was represented in the Weimar collection by an "Argument," which can not be found today. On the basis of this plot summary, Höfer determined that the *Schauspiel* in question must have been Christian Weise's first known dramatic work, *Die triumphirende Keuschheit* (1668), but that it had been slightly altered for the present event in ways which clearly carried the stamp of Caspar Stieler: the assumed name of the protagonist was changed from Floretto to Filidor, Stieler's pen name from his youth and name of the protagonist of another Stieler play, *Basilene*; and the comic characters Pickelhering and Ephialtes became Stieler's trademark fool and clown, Scaramutza and Pantalon.[99]

Christian Weise's play must have been widely known, for it was contained in his popular volume *Der grünenden Jugend überflüssige Gedancken*, which had already appeared in five editions by 1684.[100] *Die triumphirende Keuschheit* would have been an attractive text for Stieler, if he had been seeking a play to his own tastes and did not have the time or inclination to write one himself for the occasion, for the plot and treatment in both stem from the same European tradition of heroic comedy as his own creations from the Rudolstadt period. In fact, one could easily demonstrate the likelihood that Weise was greatly influenced by Stieler's comedies of the sixties for this play, at least. Several episodes may even have been modeled on similar ones in *Ernelinde* and *Die erfreuete Unschuld*. In the first scene in Weise's play, for instance, the veiled declaration of love of the lady of the house to her servant (I, i) echoes that of Ernelinde in Stieler's play (I, x). Similarly, the way Weise makes the change of thwarted love into hate plausible enough to cause Clarissa to accuse Floretto of wrongdoing and bring about his imprisonment reflects the parallel scene in *Die erfreuete Unschuld* (I, ii). The alternation of scenes between the wooing of high-born and low-life characters, the use of a romantic plot to carry a serious, even religious significance, and, above all, the use of colorful colloquialisms in the comic speeches, all closely ally Weise's first play to Stieler's Rudolstadt oeuvre. An astonishing number of these slang expressions are, in fact, to be found in Stieler's texts as well, and can be shown to be typical not so much of Weise's home dialect, as of Stieler's.[101] Naturally, the fact that the protagonist Floretto is actually a German count from Saxony would also have been an attraction in choosing an appropriate text for a festive occasion at a Saxon court.

Die triumphirende Keuschheit (and *Krieg und Sieg der Keuschheit*) tell the story of a German nobleman, Graf Heinrich von Sachsen, who, as a result of adverse fortunes of war, becomes the slave ("Knecht") of an Italian nobleman. The wife of this Italian master, Clarissa, becomes enamoured of Floretto (or Filidor), as Heinrich chooses to call himself, but the protagonist resists her seductions, remaining true to his master and to his chaste love for Clarissa's cousin Belisse, niece of the king. With all the fury of a woman scorned, Clarissa accuses Floretto-Filidor of rape and adultery and contrives to have him thrown into prison. But due to his fame as a musician, he is fetched from his cell to sing for the king, whose melancholy is cured by his sweet song. His innocence is recognized, along with his talent, and the play closes with his admission of his true identity and his marriage to Belisse. As several scholars have already pointed out, Weise's plot is a modernization and reworking of the biblical story of the chaste Joseph who resists the blandishments of Potiphar's wife (Genesis 39:7-45).

Another possibility that Höfer has not explored is that the text of *Krieg und Sieg der Keuschheit* might not have derived directly from the Weise play, but from an anonymous opera libretto based on Weise's play—*Floretto*—set to music by Nicolaus Adam Strungk and performed at the Hamburg opera house in 1683.[102] The opera is a fairly close reworking of Weise's prose comedy, retaining even the names of the main characters (except for "Pickelhering," which is changed to "Jucundus") and much of the language, but changing the entire text to an operatic mix of madrigalic and strophic verse. Music historian Hellmut Christian Wolff is impressed by the results: "Der Hamburger Bearbeiter ist leider nicht bekannt, er war ein äußerst witziger Kopf" (p. 61). Wolff describes the madrigalic portions: Weise's "realistischer Stil wirkte so stark auf die Oper aus, daß der Rezitativ-Text und die Partien der komischen Personen oft sehr frei-rhythmisch geführt sind und fast in Prosa verfallen" (p. 61). That *Floretto* may have been the play in question for the Weimar performance in 1684, rather than *Die triumphirende Keuschheit*, is shown by the fact that a copy of *Floretto* is still to be found in the library there.

Perusal of the text of the opera libretto *Floretto* leads to an even more exciting possibility, for the "witziger Kopf" who had adapted Weise's prose play for the operatic stage was no "Hamburger Bearbeiter" (as an analysis of his language will show, below) but a Thuringian. Furthermore, *Floretto* was almost certainly published by Johann Müller, "Fürstl. Sächs. Hof-Buch-drucker" in Weimar, the same one who identifies himself on the title pages of the two Stieler *Zwischenspiele*, since the elaborate capital letters are identical. The versification closely resembles that in *Melissa*, *Der göldene Apfel*, and the *Singende Zwischenspiele* to *Der betrogene Betrug*, particularly the madrigalic recitative portions with lines of irregular length closely following the patterns of natural speech, while at the same time limiting themselves almost entirely to iambic rhythms and utilizing a variety of rhyme schemes. Three lines even employ Stieler's characteristic separable-prefix verb unnaturally split around another word or words. These and other indications of similarity to Stieler's works will be detailed below. In my estimation, Caspar Stieler himself, not some anonymous Hamburger, is the most likely "Bearbeiter" of Weise's prose comedy for the Hamburg operatic stage. That the sole printing of the libretto occurred in Weimar would be attributable to the fact that Stieler was already settled there by the time he received the request or completed the commission to versify and adapt the play.

As mentioned above, the highly ornate capital letters used for the larger typeface that appears in all titles for the preparatory material and for act and scene numbering divisions are exactly those which appear throughout in the *Zwischenspiele* texts (which are printed entirely using the larger typeface). These ornate capital letters in both texts exhibit complex patterns of spirals and cur-

licues within the normal letter shape which make possible the
statement that they are indeed absolutely identical. The likelihood
is thus very great that *Floretto*, like the 1684 *Zwischenspiele* texts,
was printed in Weimar by Johann Andreas Müller, official court
printer. There is no reason to assume any date of publication other
than 1683, the year the libretto was performed as an opera in
Hamburg. Stieler's presence in Weimar as court secretary beginning in around 1680 provides a ready explanation for the publication of the libretto in Weimar, rather than in Hamburg.

Comparison between the physical arrangement and layout of
this operatic text and other theatrical texts by Stieler reveals a host
of striking similarities. The title, altered to the name of the prin-
cipal character, reminds us of the two plays closest to this in time,
as well as of *Melissa*. The *dramatis personae* page resembles that
of most of Stieler's dramatic texts, with its division into Roman
and Gothic type for Romance- and Germanic-language material,
its manner of identifying characters, and its title ("Persohnen des
Sing-Spiels"). The division into not only the acts inherited from
Weise's play, but also the scenes (and their basis in entrances and
exits of characters) typical of Stieler is significant, as is the
nomenclature involved: "Handlung" and "Aufftrit" for act and
scene, respectively, as in *Melissa* (other Stieler plays use "Auffzug"
or "Eintritt" to designate a scene; for plays where Weise does number scenes, he uses the form "Erste Handlung, erster Aufftrit," as
here). There are also differences in the character of these divisions
from those in Stieler's other dramatic texts. Unlike *Floretto*, which
has both act and scene in the nominative case (like Weise) and
which lacks definite articles, most Stieler plays use a genitive case
(e.g., "Erster Handlung") for the act designation and/or utilize
definite articles (e.g., "Der ersten Handlung"). And although
Floretto follows its prose source in using "Andere" meaning second
(act or scene), the rest of the numbers are spelled and pronounced
with precisely the idiosyncracies normal for Stieler (although
Weise's are nearly identical): "Vierdter," "Siebenter," "Neundter,"
"Zehender," "Eilffter." As in *Die Wittekinden* and all later
dramatic texts of Stieler, the abbreviated names of the speakers/
singers appear set off from the text in the left margin, while the
many stage directions, more frequent in Stieler's texts than in
those of his contemporaries, appear in the right margin. Although
some of these are in Latin ("ad spect.") or French ("a parte"), and

instead of "Schauplatz" he uses the term "Theatrum" for stage sets—not usual in Stieler's works—such shifts could well have to do with the norms for Hamburg opera texts. Unlike Weise's dramatic texts and like those of Stieler (and Gryphius), the text is followed by the word "ENDE."

Unlike any other dramatic text by Stieler, *Floretto* contains a distinction between recitative verse (madrigalic verse, made up of different and irregular line lengths without repeatable patterns; see the discussion in the *Singspiel* chapter, below) and strophic verse in the way it appears on the page: strophic verse, usually titled "Aria," appears in larger type, and any repeating strophic units are numbered. Thus, unlike *Die Wittekinden*, the *Singende Zwischenspiele* to *Der betrogene Betrug*, *Der göldene Apfel*, or *Melissa*, this libretto conforms to the Italian form, standard since Monteverdi early in the century, in which the operatic text and setting utilize both types of verse and distinguish clearly between them.

The most convincing evidence of Stieler's authorship of *Floretto* is to be found in an examination of the language and of the techniques of versification. Aside from a single line of *plattdeutsch* ("Ey dat kömmt rar," IV, iv), the language of *Floretto* does not allow placement of its author in Hamburg, but instead stamps him unequivocally as a product of the Middle German region of Thuringia and Saxony. Of the Thuringian and Saxon dialect words, phrases, and sounds cited first by Köster and then by Höfer[103] in their identifications of the Filidor who penned *Die geharnschte Venus* and the Rudolstadt plays as Caspar Stieler, this text written from twenty to twenty-five years later contains an astonishing number. Very noticeable is the tendency to rhyme *eu* with *ei* (e.g., *neigen, beugen*), although the characteristic silence of the "g" in such words, as pointed out by Höfer, is never apparent in *Floretto*. As in Stieler's other works, an extra *e* is extremely frequent, both in final position on such words as "Hertze" or "alleine," and also within words, as in "erfreuete." "Uff" tends to creep in for "auff" in a noticeable proportion of all instances in *Floretto*, as in other Stieler works. Certain favorite words or phrases of Stieler crop up here: "steup," "juch hey," the derogatory terms "Rabenaas," "Holtzbock," "grobes Schwein," "das Mensch," "garstiges Thier," "Lümmel," etc. The barnyard imagery used so prolifically in *Melissa* in context with the lowly cowherd Hyccas recurs here in the language of Jucundus, particularly in his dealings with the love-lorn

Melane who is pursuing him. The derogatory name "der hölzene Peter," used in *Floretto* I, vii, and in *Die erfreuete Unschuld* (19), is specifically Thuringian in origin. Some of Stieler's favorite curses make their appearance in *Floretto* as well: "Sankt Velten," "zum Hencker." On the other hand, some Stieler favorites seem to have changed slightly, and could speak for different authorship: "heint" instead of "heunt" for "heute abend," "Sein Lebtag" instead of "sein Tag," etc. One characteristic made much of by Höfer in identifying Stieler's handiwork, the splitting up of a separable-prefix verb by some other word or words (otherwise rare outside of the verses of Simon Dach and other poets of the Königsberg circle) occurs only three times in this text (while there are numerous instances of the normal, linked form), but this number is not surprising when one compares usage in *Floretto* with that in the other later texts designed to be sung (notably the choruses of *Bellemperie*).

One only needs glance at the other early texts of the Hamburg opera (those before ca. 1690) in juxtaposition to the text of *Floretto* in order to be struck by the excellence and ease of the versification in the latter, particularly for the dialogues designed to be performed as recitative. In chapter 7 on Caspar Stieler and the German *Singspiel*, the question of the development of such madrigalic versification in Germany and Stieler's place in that development will be dealt with at length; suffice it to say here that no other author in Germany at this date was writing, or even could write, the wonderfully natural recitative verses that appear in *Floretto*. The strophic material, too, lends itself to musical presentation: the strophes are short and simple, most of them either the bar form always favored by Stieler, or the fashionable Italian da capo aria format. In spite of the strophic repeatability of most of them, only a few sung by comic servants have the internal regularity of the German *Volkslied*; the others utilize the irregular line lengths and odd rhyme schemes of madrigalic verse within each strophe. The effect, as will be discussed in the *Singspiel* chapter below, is one of enhanced emotionality and expressiveness.

In the "Vor-Bericht" to *Floretto*, at the end of a plot summary similar to those often bound with Stieler plays, the introducer of the libretto declares: "Die *Invention* dieses Singspiels hat man von einem bekannten und berühmten Manne zum teil geborget/ zum teil nach Erfoderung [!] des Singspiels geändert; Der geneigte

Leser wolle ihm auch gefallen lassen/ daß man/ üm das Stück etwas beliebter zu machen/ bemühet gewesen/ solches mit etlichen wenigen Intrigen und Maschinen zu vermehren." There can be no doubt that the "bekannter und berühmter Mann" from whom the plot and much of the language was borrowed was Christian Weise; the more extreme anonymity of the indefinite "man" who adapted Weise's text could well be attributed to Stieler's continuing reluctance to connect his name or official pseudonym with dramatic texts, and perhaps also to the natural supposition that Stieler, always hard up for enough funds to provide for his large family, adapted this play for financial reasons only. What was not borrowed—what was altered for reasons of the musical presentation and what was altered to make the result "beliebter," or more accurately, to reflect Stieler's concept of good theater—merits a close examination here.

The most obvious change for purposes of musical presentation is, of course, the translation into verse of the prose dialogues. Other alterations which probably derive from the operatic genre of *Floretto* are the addition of scenic effects dependent on machines (particularly flying deities and apparitions) and the apparently elaborate stage sets which change frequently (made possible in late Baroque opera theater by the development of multiple curtains and scrims, as well as stage flats, etc.). A necessary requisite for "grand" opera by this date was the inclusion of scenes of great pomp; in *Floretto*, an entirely new emphasis was needed in order to incorporate such scenes: a military conflict and involvement in them by some of the central characters. Rodomann and Justinian thus become generals who confer with the king and his advisors in several new scenes of "state" (II, vii; III, ii; III, ix) and who lead a triumphal procession following the battle (III, i); we hear of the king's only son and heir who dies in the battle, precipitating many of the events on stage. The sudden and somewhat unbelievable ending, in which Floretto is made ruler, probably also conforms to the norms for grand opera in the Italian style, although one wonders whether constraints of time might not also have been responsible for the brevity and abruptness of the final act (Weise's was of normal length).

But most of the changes bear the stamp of Stieler's own preferences or make the play better conform to the comic genre in which Stieler finds himself most at home: the heroic or romantic comedy, sometimes called the "Intrigenlustspiel." In *Floretto*, the romantic and "heroic" elements are enhanced in that Belisse, especially, is made a more central character, and the love she shares with Floretto is portrayed more explicitly and extensively, including several totally new scenes (II, iv, and III, vi). Belisse's position at court is also better defined, and helps to prepare for Floretto's astounding climb to power in the final scenes: rather than just a distant relative to the king and Justinian's sister, she becomes in *Floretto* the only child of the king's brother and the choice of the king for a bride for his only son. Solo scenes with Belisse or Floretto receive a new depth and emotionality in the operatic version, as the protagonists lament their separation and Floretto's servitude and imprisonment. And not only their speeches of love, but also those of the love-struck Clarissa and even Melane indulge in the traditional Petrarchisms of love poetry, just like those of lovers in Stieler's other dramatic texts.

Weise's play *Die triumphirende Keuschheit* contains a good deal of historical and political content, for he sets the events in the period of the thirteenth-century conflict between King Charles of Anjou, King of Naples, who claimed much of Italy for himself and France, and the German Holy Roman Empire, which had claimed the kingdom of Naples for nearly fifty years. In Weise's story, Graf Heinrich was captured while fighting for this German imperial interest and was enslaved, since he had kept his identity a secret in order not to betray the German side in the conflict. The proclaimed marriage at the end between Belisse and Heinrich is thus a paeon to peace in Weise's version—perhaps an expression of Weise's hopes for peaceful resolutions of contemporary conflicts with French and/or Italian foes. In *Floretto*, however, this historical and political content is diffused: King Charles is a generalized king of Sicily—a popular place for romantic plots—at some generalized time in the eternal present; the French characters at his court, who in Weise's version helped to specify the historicity of the background events, have lost that designation and become merely "foreign" courtiers; and "Graf Heinrich von Sachsen" becomes the more fictive-sounding "ein sächsischer Fürst/ Heinrich genant." The praise of "Teutscher Treu" in this scion of a Saxon royal house is gone in the operatic version designed for performance outside Saxony. And the background conflict, in Weise between German and Franco-Italian forces, shifts to an invasion of Sicily by Saracens, a staple of the romance plot, whether in a novella or in a heroic comedy.

But at the same time that the drama has been made less historical and political, it has also become less improbable. The king, instead of being driven mad by a spider bite and cured by dancing a tarantella to Floretto's divinely inspired music, as in Weise, is here depicted as crazed by his grief and guilt-feelings at the death of his young heir in the battle. His madness, more like that of Shakespeare's Lear, for example, is portrayed on stage in a new scene (III, xv). Floretto's music now causes the king to swoon and fall into a healing sleep of forgetfulness and purification. Floretto's reaction to Clarissa's blandishments indicate that he is troubled by temptation, unlike Weise's chaste protagonist or his biblical prototype, Joseph.

The roster of characters in Floretto has also shifted in a manner perhaps appropriate for Stieler. Belisse's nurse (a comic archetype from the commedia dell'arte tradition) has been replaced with "Arpe, ein Hexe," a figure more likely associated with romance; Pickelhering, an appropriate name for an alimentary-tract clown, has undergone a name change to Jucundus, indicating perhaps that his jocular function is not dependent on excesses in eating and drinking or on scatological humor. Jucundus depends here on his wit and his irreverence, on his pretentious Latinisms and his affectation of cavalier status in order to make the audience laugh, like Stieler's homunculus Scaramutza and similar characters. There is no longer an ugly old wooer for Ephialtes (father of Pickelhering/Jucundus), but only Clarissa's maid Melane, a young but unlovely wooer of Ephialtes's son. Her scenes with Ephialtes seek his help in her campaign to marry Jucundus, and thus resemble the scenes in other Stieler plays where Scaramutza appeals to Pantalon, perpetual father of the girls he woos, for aid or permission. Added to Weise's cast of characters is a totally new group entirely typical of Stieler: personifications and deities who affect the outcome ("Die Liebe," "Die Wollust," "Die Keuschheit," "Nemesis," three evil spirits, and Apollo).

It is interesting to note the major changes made in 1684 which Höfer extrapolated from the Argument to *Krieg und Sieg der Keuschheit*: Jucundus became Scaramutza and Floretto became Filidor. If Stieler was, as I have postulated here, the author of *Floretto*, and if *Floretto* was indeed the theatrical piece reused in

1684 under the title *Krieg und Sieg der Keuschheit*, then how can
we account for the appearance only in the version of 1684 of Stieler's alter ego and one-time alias? I believe that such self-
referentiality could only have been appropriate in a court performance where the members of the audience knew the author
personally and could appreciate the in-jokes inherent in such
usages. Thus, for his anonymous submission to the Hamburg opera
from a distance and presumably for remuneration, Stieler retained
his full anonymity; while for a local production before his patrons
and fellow courtiers, colleagues, and friends, he would naturally
inject his personality into the event in a self-conscious way which
would be obvious to his audience—just as he did in all of his
theatrical works designed for performance at court. The new title,
necessitated by the name change of the protagonist, might well
have also been designed to protect him from any repercussions, if
he had made any agreements for exclusive use with the Hamburg
opera, a commercial enterprise; on the other hand, the new title
would also show, in its reuse of the key term "Keuschheit," Stieler's knowledge that Weise's play formed the primary source for
Floretto.

The version called *Krieg und Sieg der Keuschheit* produced in
1684 in Weimar was given a *Vorspiel* and five choruses. As noted
above, these accompaniments for the festive occasion were printed
by Johann Andreas Müller, court printer, in honorific format,
with a large and decorative typeface, and with several pictorial
ornaments. While the typeface is that of titles in *Floretto*, thus
indicating that they were all printed by Müller, the difference in
the decorative ornaments and title, and the fact that they were not
bound together, probably indicate that these *Zwischenspiele* were
printed at the time of the performances they honor, whereas
Floretto may well have been printed a year or so earlier. The *Vorspiel*, sung by Apollo and the nine Muses, begins with a strophic
"Freuden-Lied" in trochaic meter which announces that peace now
blesses the land, after bitter warfare, allowing for a new flourish-
ing of the arts. There follows a conversation in madrigalic verse in
which the Muses explain to a curious Apollo the reason for their
joy: peace has replaced war, wisdom and beauty now rule, the
new prince encourages the arts, his birthday is a day of celebration for his land. They all join together then in a strophic song in
joyful dactylics praising the Duke and wishing him well on the

occasion of his birthday, accompanied by the appearance of a cloud with flaming letters proclaiming "VIVAT WILHELMUS ERNESTUS." The *Vorspiel* concludes with Apollo's announcement of the "Lustspiel" to follow and, as spokesman for the participants, he expresses their wish to please. It is probably significant that Apollo is also a character in *Floretto* (III, xviii), but not in Weise's *Die triumphirende Keuschheit*.

The remainder of the especially printed text contains only the choruses, each consisting of a single strophic song, to follow their respective acts. The first three comment on the preceding action in a manner typical of many seventeenth-century German choruses, while the fourth urges *Kunst* and *Wissenschaft* as appropriate and valuable activities and interests for a prince, and the fifth "singet die Keuschheit Triumph," first in the iambic verse most typical of Stieler and then, in the final strophe, in jubilant dactyls. A portion of this final chorus also reminds the Duke of the advantages of his patronage of the arts:

So bringet die Kunst/
Huld/ Ehren und Gunst.
Wer die will genießen/
Mus jene begrüßen.

In my estimation, only the *Vorspiel* and the third, fourth, and final choruses are from Stieler's pen; the first two are poorly constructed verses in trochaic meter, exhibiting little facility in either versification or rhyming and containing neither the freshness nor the concreteness of Stieler's own language. Some other contributer to the festivities—perhaps even a member of the ducal family—is probably responsible for the portions not by Stieler.

The second theatrical performance in Weimar in 1684, as documented by the title page of the festive pamphlet containing, again, only the *Zwischenspiel*[104] for the play, was the "Freuden-Spiel" *Die erlösete Treue und Unschuld*, accompanied by the "Glückwüntschende Winter-Lust," on December 28 upon the occasion of the birthday celebration of Duchess Charlotte Marie, "Gebohrner und vermähleten Hertzogin zu Sachsen/ Jülich/ Cleve und Berg," the young cousin and wife of Wilhelm Ernst. As for the October event, the title page reports that this performance took place in the "Gartenhaus" ("Grünes Schlößchen"), and no author is named. Although there was no "Argument" surviving even in 1914 for the play *Die erlösete Treue und Unschuld*, Höfer was able, on the basis of names and other allusions in the published choruses, to identify it as the opera *Die beschuldigte Unschuld oder Filopiste aus Thessalien*,[105] set to music by Philip Stolle, and performed in Halle in 1665 and again in 1674 on the occasions of the birthdays of other Saxon duchesses.[106] Höfer feels it likely that Stieler altered this text too for the Weimar occasion, probably adding Scaramutza and changing the names of some of the other characters (p. 9).

The opera is a pastoral *Singspiel* with stereotypical elements reminiscent of Guarini's *Il Pastor fido* (constant lovers, evil seducers, mysterious oracles, and a happy ending complete with a marriage),[107] but it also owes its existence to a tradition of historical and quasi-historical portrayals, so popular at the time, of princesses (or, less often, princes) on the fringes of Europe taken captive by Muslim potentates (including Lohenstein's *Ibrahim Bassa*, Gryphius's *Catharina von Georgien*, and the play-within-the-play in Stieler's own *Bellemperie*). According to Höfer (p. 9), the choruses are not entirely original, but are instead poetically superior adaptations of those included with the opera. He feels that the entire opera text may have undergone similar improvements at Stieler's hands. Unlike the play for the October performance, this text demands balletic elements, and belongs to the tradition of *Sing-Ballette* made popular in Dresden and Wolfenbüttel in the fifties and sixties.

The *Zwischenspiel* "Glückwüntschende Winter-Lust" consists, like "Die musicalische Freuden-Feyer," of a *Vorspiel* and strophic choruses to follow each act (in this case, three instead of five). The *Vorspiel*, which contains both madrigalic and strophic verse, is a *Streitgespräch* on the topic of the four seasons, and the chief protagonist and victor in the argument is, appropriately for the date of the performance, Bruma, goddess of winter. The scene is set "In einer mit Frost und Schneeüberzogenen Gegend"; musicians dressed as "Halcionen"—ice birds—provide instrumental music as a sort of overture. The three goddesses who represent the growing seasons—Flora, Ceres, and Pomona—berate Bruma for the barren winter landscape, but must yield in the end to her own claims for recognition. Not only does winter participate in the biological cycle in a productive, if largely invisible way by providing a period of rest and rebirth, but it also has a claim to fame as the season for the birthday celebration not only of the Savior, but also of the Duchess for whom this performance is designed. The *Vorspiel* closes with a strophic choral birthday greeting for the duchess, in which the formerly bickering goddesses join together, now completely in agreement.

In this prologue, also, the typical characteristics of Stieler's personal style and his talents appear exhibited to greater advantage than in the choruses. One need only remark the original rhyme-words, the particular use of deities as personifications, and the cleverly structured arguments. As in the *Zwischenspiel* to *Der betrogene Betrug*, Stieler here creatively expands the metaphor of the *Stammbaum* in lauding the basis of political stability in dynastic continuity, explicitly in the polemical sections, but already implicitly in the arguments of the four seasons: although the winter has apparently destroyed every green and growing thing, the family tree of the Saxon dukes continues to blossom and bear fruit. The Duke and Duchess are celebrated as "hohe Sachsen-Reiser," whose virtues "grünen" and whose fame remains "unverwelckt" (p. 6).

Another typical sort of Baroque chorus appears in this *Zwischenspiel*, this one based more on Greek tragedy than on morality plays: the captive Thessalonians lament their fate in the first chorus, express hope for rescue in the second, and sing their jubilation in the third. These choruses, unlike any others by Stieler, and like the very similar ones by Gryphius in *Catharina von Georgien*, are adorned with traditional metaphors, adages, and emblems, based mostly on seasonal themes and imagery. The first two choruses sound so conventional that it is difficult to see Stieler's hand at all; the third, however, abandons the plaintive trochaic meter and shifts to a clever use of dactyls in lines of varying lengths to express the joy at the happy outcome. In this third chorus, too, metaphorical links are set up with the seasonal thematics of the *Vorspiel*, offering a sense of unity and completion, and some typical characteristics of Stieler's language surface at last: concrete imagery, colorful colloquialisms, creative choice and use of words, bold rhythmic patterns, gems of folk wisdom, together with a classical allusion.

Höfer has speculated about the nature of the performance by extrapolation of scraps of information in the texts and by interpolation of documentary evidence about other courtly theatrical performances of the times. Thus he assumes the participation of

courtiers, and even members of the ducal family, in the performances, including perhaps women, particularly as singers and dancers, but probably also as actors and actresses (pp. 4 and 10). He
supposes, in the case of the opera *Filopiste*, that musical presentation of the piece in its entirety was attempted, and that, lacking
sufficient musicians in Weimar, the musicians were borrowed from
Weißenfels, along with the text (p. 9). The more recently published information correcting Höfer's (see note 106, above) would
tend to eliminate Weißenfels as such a source. Frenzel has shown,
in any case, that the establishment of a *Hofkapelle*, perhaps
capable after all of performing an opera, took place no later than
1683 when composer Johann Samuel Drese can be shown to have
been in place as *Kapellmeister*.[108] This fact, together with the
probability that not Weise's prose comedy but the verse opera text
derived from it was used in the earlier performance that year,
makes possible the tentative conclusion that the theatrical performances produced by Caspar Stieler in Weimar late in 1684 were
not spoken plays with sung *Zwischenspiele*, but German-language
operas in the grand style, representing developments in German
comic and musical drama that stretch from the sixties in middle
Germany to the previous year at the Hamburg opera. But whether
we view the performances as steps in the development of theater
or of opera in Weimar, it is clear that the departure of Stieler the
following year brought any possible further development to an
abrupt halt.

It might seem strange that the last dramatic texts attributable
to this talented Thespian are not plays, but only their accompaniments—preludes and choruses. Such a judgment as is implied in
the "only," however, would show a lack of understanding of
theater and its context in the German seventeenth century. While
the "main attraction" was the action of the plot and the dilemmas
of sympathetic characters, then as now, in the German Baroque
the *Zwischenspiele* provided a framework which largely determined the aesthetic, ethical, and social effect of the performance
on its audience. In court theater of the time, especially, this frame
was an integral part of the structure of any dramatic event, for
the *Zwischenspiele* were responsible for expressing, and even
creating, the relationship between poet and audience, between
theatrical performance and festive context, between the themes of
the literary text and the dynastic occasion which the piece

celebrated. It was only in the *Zwischenspiele* that text and context could intersect in a restatement of the solidarity of the social group which included not only the courtly audience, but also the performers, dramatists, and producers of plays for such amateur theatricals. A play without such a framework would have been, in fact, completely unsuitable for performance at court. Stieler's final theatrical contributions thus clearly serve to connect him with court theater and to give him a label he never apparently wanted: court dramatist.

III

IN THE GREEN ROOM

Discussion

"Fette Suppen und hohe Sprünge":
Questions of Patronage and Occasion

Caspar Stieler may have written the poems of *Die Geharnschte Venus* for his own enjoyment and in order to achieve some recognition as a poet, but most of his remaining literary works, including poetry and drama, were written either for a festive or solemn occasion, often at the specific request (read: behest) of some courtly patron, or in order to catch the attention of a potential patron when the poet found himself temporarily without a post. When Höfer titled his monograph on the Rudolstadt comedies "Die Rudolstädter Festspiele," he was referring not to their literary genre, but to their occasional origins and intentions: their title pages tie them explicitly to specific courtly occasions. Some of Stieler's most important poetic works, then, could appropriately be termed examples of occasional literature. But the appellation "occasional literature" has fallen into disrepute, as has, perhaps not coincidently, the social hierarchy which made it possible. The fact remains, however, that much of the literary production of the seventeenth century in Germany participated in this mode, and without any negative connotations attached at the time. Stieler expends several hundred lines of his own *Dichtkunst* on instructions for finding inspiration when writing poems for various occasions.[1] Like Birken before him,[2] he sees occasional poetry as a set of natural genres which express themes of universal significance.

A large proportion of the poems and performances created for such occasions in the seventeenth century has undoubtedly been lost to us, for many probably existed only in the memories of the presenters, handwritten on scraps of paper discarded after the performance, or extant even at the time only in sketches or outlines. Indeed, it is cause for amazement that so much has in fact survived through three centuries to be of interest to us today. This survival can be explained quite simply by the custom of the time to record and publish, in honorific pamphlets handed to the prince and perhaps disseminated among his relatives and fellow princes, the words and images of the various art forms involved in those festive occasions at court, works that were designed as single performances to occur only during the particular celebration or solemnity: temporary architecture, triumphal processions, costumes, fireworks, pantomimes, poems, and plays. Collections of such honorific poems for a single event and descriptions, often illustrated with lavish engravings, of some visually marvelous performances can be found in virtually any library once associated with any of the seventeenth-century German courts, whether as small as Rudolstadt or as grand in scale as Vienna; many of these also found their way outside the German-speaking world proper to courts in Paris, St. Petersburg, Poland, or the Vatican. Many records were undoubtedly preserved as part of the heritage of the particular princely house which created and maintained the library.

But there is another, and perhaps more important, reason for the survival of many of these records of festivities from a bygone age. Festive and solemn occasions at court, after all, were observances of the archetypal episodes in human existence: princely births, birthdays, marriages, and funerals can represent the events common to the biological existence of each of us, and are therefore carriers of universal themes. These occasions, all of which, when they occur in the life of a prince, are also of importance to the continuity and stability of the polity, participate likewise in the common themes of man's political existence. Several other kinds of events important to the state were also graced by countless occasional poems, plays, triumphal processions, fireworks displays, and so on: victory or peace celebrations, the signing of treaties, the visit of royalty, even the arrival of diplomats and trade envoys. The events celebrated are idiosyncratic, yet the primary themes are part of universal human experience. The idea that occasional literature is necessarily time-bound or trivial is completely untenable.

It is undeniable that much occasional poetry is of little interest except to the historian, yet some literary works written for the purpose of presentation at a particular occasion have value as literary works in their own right. One thinks here, for instance, of Hallmann's fine pastoral *Adonis und Rosibella*, written for the second marriage of the emperor Leopold I, or Gryphius's festive plays *Piastus* (celebration of the birth of an heir) and *Majuma* (written for the coronation of Ferdinand IV). Several acknowledged masterpieces of the period were written to honor royal marriages or were altered in order to do so (Lohenstein's tragedies

Sophonisbe and *Ibrahim Sultan*; Gryphius's double comedy *Verlibtes Gespenste/Die gelibte Dornrose*). The number of funerary and marriage poems included in recent anthologies of Baroque lyric gives further support for this contention. Stieler's chief dramatic works—the Rudolstadt plays—belong in this group as well.

Poetry—and that included the writing of plays—was the recreation of the leisure classes in the seventeenth century and the avocation of many educated bureaucrats and teachers. It did not provide a source of income. Indeed, aspiring poets without financial independence had to find some gainful employment, some salaried post which would not only support them and their families, but also, in some cases, provide funds for publication of their works. The courts no longer supported poets solely in return for entertainment and homage, as in the Middle Ages.[3] Now it was expected that a poet could make himself useful to a princely patron or to a municipal government as adviser, secretary, treasurer, lawyer, scribe, clerk, reader, librarian, tutor, musician, or chaplain—or in a post combining a number of these functions, such as Stieler had in Rudolstadt. Alternatively, a poet or dramatist might find monetary support and an outlet for his talents as teacher or rector in a school, or as a pastor of a church. Even in Vienna, noted for its artistic patronage, poets and dramatists (primarily librettists during the reign of the musical emperor Leopold) had other, non-literary tasks as well—composing histories, polemical pamphlets, or genealogies, for instance.

Even for the creative individuals supported more directly by princes in return for their painting and sculpture, architecture, stage sets, or musical compositions and performances, dependence on patronage was a reality. Few could afford to rely on sporadic commissions and temporary employment. The most famous singers, dancers, painters, architects, and composers were likely to prefer the security of an extended relationship with a particular patron. Like many young educated men of his time, Caspar Stieler in 1662 needed both a patron and a secure position. Aside from his obvious qualifications—education, a great variety of experiences, similar posts in the past, and a facility for foreign languages—the ultimate advantage in obtaining the position in Rudolstadt may have rested on his poetic abilities. As was often done in that period, his job application was in the form of an honorific poem

which praised his potential patron at the same time that it showed
off his own poetic and scholarly talents.[4] The two plays of 1680,
Bellemperie and *Willmut*, may possibly have served the same
function, as Stieler was apparently between posts when he wrote
them.[5]

Patrons of the arts in the seventeenth century had more to
gain from their poets than fulsome praise and frivolous entertainment. In the post-medieval period, beginning perhaps with the
emperor Maximilian I, princes grand and petty alike realized the
utility of the arts in the promotion of their images as wise and
benevolent rulers; as heroic defenders of the fatherland and the
Faith; as purveyors of peace, prosperity, and stability; and as
magnificent personages whose settings proclaimed them as somehow larger than life.[6] The pretensions of the Habsburgs to power
and influence beyond their hereditary lands were the first impetus
to this application of the fine arts; as the minor German princes
began to try to model their behavior and their images on those of
the great absolutistic princes of the day, especially on Louis XIV
of France, they, too, found the arts to be an ideal vehicle for the
promotion of a desired image. Count Albert Anthon of Schwarzburg-Rudolstadt, in his own small way, was to use Stieler's
dramatic talents to enhance his image based on the models he had
found at the greater court of the Dukes of Braunschweig. He thus
applied his theater to a demonstration of his own importance
within the microcosm of the small principalities of Saxony and
Thuringia. In Stieler, a master of Horace's twin thrusts of comedy—enjoyment and usefulness—Albert Anthon found the ideal
object of his patronage.

Stieler's relationship with his Rudolstadt patron is fairly well
documented in the prefaces to the plays of that period and in various comments in his later handbooks,[7] as well as in the archives
in Rudolstadt. In his preface "Dem Lesenden" he seems to blame
the choice of a story unsuited to dramatic presentation for his *Die
erfreuete Unschuld* on the wishes of those who have the power to
command; in the preface to *Der Vermeinte Printz* he indicates that
his activities as dramatist derive from his wish to please and obey
his patron rather than from any self-interest: "Alleine bezeuget er
(der Dichter) hiemit öffentlich/ daß ihme kein einbildischer Lob-
kützel die Feder zu dieser Schrifft geschnitten. Der unterthänige
Gehorsam/ womit seinem Herrn er verpflichtet/ ist der Flügel

gewesen/ auß welchem sie gewachsen." And while Stieler's praise
of Albert Anthon in the plays written for him is conventional,
both in content and (for the most part) in presentation, glimmers
of the true relationship between author and patron can be inferred
from the freedom with which Stieler apparently feels comfortable
to criticize, satirize, even parody the courtly society of which he
was at least a peripheral member, not to mention the various jokes
and tricks he plays upon the princely patron himself, as we have
seen. Far less can be deduced about his relationships with later
patrons, which probably lacked the intimacy and personal sympa-
thies of the Rudolstadt years.

Courtly patronage and a remunerative position which allowed
time for his other writing were not the only sorts of patronage
sought by Stieler. In 1668 he sought and gained admittance to the
"Fruchtbringende Gesellschaft."[8] The newly discovered play
Melissa, which I have ascribed to Stieler, bears the date of the
poet's application and admission to this *Sprachgesellschaft*. As
discussed above in the section on that play, it is possible to see it
as a part of that application. Like the genealogical poem Stieler
offered in 1661 to the new Count Albert Anthon, *Melissa* may
have been offered to the nominal head of the society, Duke
August von Sachsen-Weißenfels, as proof of his abilities. The fact
that the only extant copy is to be found in Halle, seat of this personage and of the society, could be seen as supporting evidence
for my hypothesis. Membership in this famous *Sprachgesellschaft*
was a sort of honorific patronage which, while it provided no
direct financial support, supplied the sort of recognition and
recommendation necessary to gain both remunerative posts and
publishers willing to venture their own capital on Stieler's books.
In later years, this recognition and the huge body of publications
that it fostered were to lead to Stieler's ultimate goal: life as an
independent free-lance writer, liberated both from the time-
consuming labor in the chancelleries and from the necessity to
perform at the behest of his patrons. Unfortunately for the
admirers of Stieler's poetry and plays, this free-lance writing took
almost exclusively the form of handbooks on Stieler's various areas
of expertise and, in later life, the revised editions of the most
popular of these. If Stieler wrote his plays only at the command of
patrons or in order to honor present or potential patrons, then
their occasional function is not an encumberance, but their very

raison d'être. And although a cycle of poems unconnected to the fate of a dynasty and a country often found its way into print at little or no cost, even the small-scale patronage of a count whose lands extended less than 300 square miles was necessary to provide both impetus and resources for the creation of a theatrical performance. Drama cannot exist without the theater, and the theater was, for most of seventeenth-century Germany, an ephemeral institution that existed only in the context of a significant occasion.

Caspar Stieler and the German "Singspiel"

In the "Vorrede" of *Die Geharnschte Venus*, the poet places himself among the various composers of musical settings for the songs with great modesty: "Die übrigen übelklingenden [Melodeyen] schreibe ich mir selber zu/ als die ich nach meiner Einfalt gedichtet/ nur vor mich und wehm sie gefallen."[9] Köster and Höfer use this comment to attribute those eighteen compositions signed with the initials "C.S." to their identification for "Filidor der Dorfferer,"[10] although Theobald Raehse in his 1888 edition of *Die Geharnschte Venus* used the same comment to secure his attribution to Jacob Schwieger (two of the compositions were initialed "J.S.").[11] Musical historian Kathi Meyer (later Meyer-Baer), who wrote the essay on the musical settings for Höfer's 1925 edition of *Die Geharnschte Venus*,[12] agrees with the composer's modest stance for the most part, seeing in the eighteen musical compositions with Caspar Stieler's initials signs of a decided dilettantism. She cites in this context the "Ungleichheit ihrer Stilart und ihres Wertes" (p. 187), but also notes, "Dem Herausgeber Stieler ist ab und an neben zahlreichen dilettantischen Fehlgriffen ein frisches Tanzliedchen gelungen" (p. 192). She discerns no pattern in the distribution of the texts among the various composers, but in fact there is one such overt pattern in the first four of the seven "Zehen": the first song of each is set to a Stieler composition (his other fourteen compositions, however, are scattered in I, III, IV, VI, and VII).

While the musical settings for the *Geharnschte Venus* are still extant, due to the fact that they were published with the texts in the 1660 edition, little other music composed by Stieler seems to have survived.[13] Yet Stieler's name and pseudonym (and those of Schwieger or Bleyer, to whom his works have variously been attributed) appear ubiquitously in the studies on seventeenth-century music in Thuringia and Saxony as the librettist/composer of *Singspiele*—by which is meant the six Rudolstadt comedies, although *Willmut* is also mentioned by one historian as an example. Some use Höfer's monograph *Die Rudolstädter Festspiele* as their source.[14] Nevertheless, they seem to be ignorant of the fact that the drama texts are written primarily in prose, for they refer only to the verse interludes set to music. Engel, for example, describes one play: "'Die erfreuete Unschuld' stellt die Knechtung der Kirche und ihre Befreiung durch den Fürsten Michael dar."[15] Gülke thinks the comedies as a whole are mythological.[16] Several mention Stieler's activity as producer of a comedy with original musical interludes and an opera with original additions in 1684,[17] apparently on the basis of Höfer's study, "Weimarische Theaterveranstaltungen zur Zeit des Herzogs Wilhelm Ernst."[18] All these treatments by music historians are brief and scanty, yet they universally seem to see in Stieler's Rudolstadt and Weimar plays with musical interludes the roots of musical drama and even opera, at least in Thuringia and Saxony.

Most music historians, beginning with Otto Kinkeldey in 1914 in his introduction to a volume on the works of a later Rudolstadt *Kapellmeister* and composer, Philipp Heinrich Erlebach,[19] erroneously believe Georg Bleyer to have been at least the composer of the musical settings, if not actually the author of the texts of the Rudolstadt plays. A study from the pen of an important Germanist, Willi Flemming, in his "Einführung" to the *Oratorium, Festspiel* volume of the DLE series, *Barockdrama*,[20] also explicitly attributes the texts of the plays to Stieler's replacement in Rudolstadt. But Flemming's attribution and the surmises of the music historians were decisively refuted in a major article published in 1941 by Conrad Höfer, "Georg Bleyer, Ein thüringischer Tonsetzer und Dichter der Barockzeit."[21] Höfer not only disproves Bleyer's authorship of the plays, but also shows that the probability that Bleyer had composed the music for the four plays of 1665-66, at least, was nil.[22] Furthermore, Höfer unearthed documents which showed that Stieler's tasks as "Cammer-Secretarius" in Rudolstadt included musical duties. The existence of a "Capell-Direktor" as such cannot be shown until the fall of 1666,[23] when Stieler had already departed, and, after all, with the multiple talents of Caspar Stieler, perhaps none was needed. The list of members of the court *Kapelle* for the wedding of 1665 in Rudolstadt, according to a document published by Peter Gülke, was headed by the "Herr Cammer Secretarius," not a "Capell-Direktor"—evidence that the secretary did indeed fulfill the duties of this post at that time.[24] Yet, like Gülke, all recent music historians seem to have overlooked Höfer's study, and thus continue to attribute the music, at least, to Bleyer.

If Stieler wrote 18 of the 70 compositions setting his songs of *Die Geharnschte Venus* to music and had duties in Rudolstadt that included those of *Kapell-direktor*, then it is logical to assume, as Höfer and others since him have, that Stieler may well have provided some of the musical settings for his *Zwischenspiele*; at the very least he would have been well qualified to choose a composer and oversee the work of setting the texts, much as he did in the edition of *Die Geharnschte Venus* for the other 52 songs. Yet the appearance of these compositions can only be guessed at, based on the evidence of the texts.

All of Stieler's dramatic texts utilize musical presentation to some extent; three of them may have been entirely set to music, and one, *Floretto*, certainly was, while the others used music only in the choruses or *Zwischenspiele* and in occasional songs which are imbedded in the prose text as part of the plot. Stieler seems to have been equally adept at madrigal and strophic (*Lied*) versification. Musically, madrigal verse (a topic to be discussed in greater detail at a later point) would normally have been set as recitative—"a type of vocal writing, normally for a single voice, which follows closely the natural rhythm and accentuation of speech, without being governed by a regular tempo or organized in a specific form," according to the *New Grove Dictionary of Music and Musicians*.[25] This musical presentation encouraged freedom of interpretation and a certain "studied negligence in singing."[26] Strophic verse, on the other hand, was normally set as an "aria" ("a closed form, usually strophic, for one or more voices, with or without instrumental accompaniment")[27] or, in Germany, a "Lied" (a secular solo strophic song which was a "careful synchronization of musical and poetic prosody").[28] But distinctions in the seventeenth century were not so clear as such definitions might imply: lyrical sections in recitative passages can be described as "arioso," and strophic verse can be set in a manner which ignores repeating patterns or is interpreted with great freedom of expression and tempo.

As is usual in Italian musical dramas of the seventeenth century, madrigal verse predominates for dialogue and action in Stieler's verse dramatic scenes, while strophic verse is used primarily for solo reflections or prayers and for choral summations or reactions to the action. As Höfer noted in 1904, Stieler seems to exhibit a preference for iambic versification,[29] but dactylic and trochaic meters also appear (usually only in strophic verse, although, as discussed above, following Sbarra's metric scheme in *Il Pomo d'oro* Stieler uses a great deal of dactylic verse in his translation of that libretto).

But unlike his *Geharnschte Venus* and a later song book, the texts of Stieler's dramatic works contain no musical notation, and the scores have apparently not been preserved in any form. Furthermore, few of his texts even contain directions on the format of musical presentation, content merely to indicate by "singt" or "singend" that the verses below are to be presented musically. Some do not even so direct, although the preparatory pages indicate that the character who presents the verses is a singing character (without, however, identifying the voicetype). In other cases it is fair to assume that the verses, since they occur in what he terms the "Singende Zwischen-Spiele," were very likely sung. One drama, *Die erfreuete Unschuld*, contains fairly elaborate instructions on the presentation of the musical *Zwischenspiele*, however, and although quite different in format from any other Stieler play, it may provide some extrapolations to be applied to the others.

Four of Stieler's theatrical texts are totally in verse, and they may have been intended to be set to music in their entirety. *Die Wittekinden*, termed by the author "Singe- und Freuden-Spiel," is written almost entirely in iambic madrigal verse, usually three to five beats per line. Even the choruses following acts one and two (the Furies; the Fates) and the allegorical figures Superstitio and Veritas, who appear at the beginning of the first act in a sort of "Vorspiel," use madrigal verses. In fact, the only strophic versification in this play consists in two imbedded "Zeitungslieder," both sung by the streetsinger Michele. However, the first—a poorly constructed jingle in "Knittelvers" (pp. 6-7)—arouses the critical disgust of two of the listeners on stage, and is obviously parodistic of the lowest form of "occasional" poetry, the broadsheet ditty. The second is a well-formed lyric in iambic pentameter written by a courtier, who hires Michele to sing it (pp. 53-54). Ironically, the poorly executed words convey the truth, while the well-constructed lines of the courtier contain dangerous falsehoods. The singer is interrupted by the expressions of alarm of his credulous listeners during the seventh four-line strophe of the latter. Another type of music makes its appearance after the final act, although no musical directions are included: the play ends with a ballet in which dancers represent the major towns of the principality.

Although Kinkeldey expresses the opinion that only the *Zwischenspiele* of *Die Wittekinden* were sung[30] (plus, presumably, the imbedded songs), his assumption clearly is untenable. Not only are the scenes with Superstitio, Veritas, the Furies, and the Fates not termed "singende Zwischenspiele," as in the other plays; they are not even set off from the rest of the text in any way. They are merely numbered scenes in the same verse form. Furthermore, since they are considerably shorter than the *Zwischenspiele* of the other plays, they could hardly warrant the generic tag for the whole piece, "Singe- und Freuden-Spiel," shared with no other Stieler play. Indeed, it is probable that *Die Wittekinden* was sung in its entirety, an operatic *Festspiel* not unlike two plays by Gryphius of the previous decades, *Majuma* and *Piastus*.

Another dramatic text almost certainly by Stieler that is written totally in verse is *Melissa. Schäfferey. Anno 1668*. While there is no explicit indication that any of it was to be sung, the work consists of an iambic madrigal verse form similar to that in *Die Wittekinden* (although more lines are of the five-beat variety), and it also has two imbedded songs. But this play adds a few lines in dactylic madrigal verse in the choral reflections on the preceding action, and a finale in regular four-beat dactylic verse. One of the songs is a solo by the protagonist in trochaic meter with strophes containing five pentameter lines followed by a four-beat (or fourteen-syllable) line. The other song, sung by the chorus of shepherds just prior to the finale, combines four three-beat lines and two refrain-like four-beat lines in each strophe, and may have been a bar song. *Melissa* is a short pastoral drama of the sort often set to music in the Italian tradition. Among the ancestors of this text, for purposes of making suppositions about its musical setting, one might number not only Cavalieri's *Rappresentazione di Anima e di Corpo* and its German descendant, Harsdörffer's *Seelewig* of 1644, but also Rinuccini's opera *Dafne* of 1597 (adapted by Martin Opitz in 1627 in his opera in German madrigal verse), Agostino Agazzari's *Eumelio* of 1606, and their derivatives—all of which were presented musically in their entirety.[31]

Among examples of Stieler's madrigal verse, *Der göldene Apfel* shows the most variety, usually in emulation of the Italian original, as discussed above. The lines range from one to five beats, and mix a great deal of dactylic verse in with the trochaic and iambic meters. Sometimes the metric system even becomes regular for a time, although never overtly falling into strophic units. While Höfer felt that the translation was not intended to be a singing text,[32] Stieler's versification usually follows the Italian rhythms exactly, so that large portions of the text could conceivably have been sung to the original music by Marc Antonio Cesti,[33] especially where Cesti's recitative setting gives way to that termed by musical scholars "Ariettenhaft" or "arioso." I consider it probable that, in Stieler's translation, the dialogues were either recitative or even merely spoken, while the reflective monologues became musical solos, set like gems within the text, perhaps utilizing Cesti's own notation. That Stieler here uses verse forms otherwise alien to his work (he elsewhere almost never mixes trochaic and iambic verse forms in a single set of lines, and he rarely uses dactylic verse in his plays except as choral exclamations of triumph and joy) is certainly indicative of the fact that some sort of constraint to follow the metrics of his source existed—a constraint it is probably easiest to locate in a pre-extant musical score.

The libretto for the comic grand opera *Floretto*, which I also attribute to Stieler, as discussed above, was without doubt sung in its entirety. It follows the Italian pattern established by Monteverdi of recitative dialogue punctuated by arias whose form and settings were in contrast to the madrigalic verses around them. Most of these are solo arias by major characters in the serious primary plot or in the comic subplot, sung by a single character alone on the stage, either expressing emotions or reflecting on events. Several involve the deities or personifications of emotions from the eternal framework speaking to each other or directly to the characters; several juxtapose arias—usually metrically related if not identical—by two different characters in a sort of duet. However, two voices sing together only in the finale, which also includes several lines of choral ensemble. Of the fifty-three arias (all titled "Aria" and set off from the madrigalic dialogue with a larger typeface and often with indented lines to reflect internal structural patterns), twenty-five are in one of the traditional formats for the German *Lied*, the bar form, while ten are of the Italian "da capo" type which repeats the first line or two, perhaps with slight variations, at the end of the song. One aria combines these two forms in a tour de force of metric complexity. And the seventeen others exhibit a variety of patterns, from simple, regular folksong strophes to madrigalic ariose passages resembling those in Cesti's *Il Pomo d'oro*, for example. Many of these arias use trochaic verse as a contrast to the iambic madrigalic verses around them, although quite a number use iambic rhythms or both trochaic and iambic (in different sections), and many utilize dactylic feet for some of the lines, usually those at the end of the strophe.

Typical examples of the da capo and bar-form arias in this text are those of Clarissa and Floretto in adjacent scenes (I, iv, and I, v); Clarissa's reads as follows:

Floretto mein Leben
Dir bin ich ergeben
Dein liebliches Wesen
Hab ich mir beständig zu lieben erlesen/
Vergnüg mich im Hertzen
Mit spielendem Schertzen
Ergetze die Brust
Mit süssester Lust.
Floretto mein Leben/
Dir bleib ich ergeben.

In contrast to Clarissa's frivolous and licentious dactyls in da capo structure, Floretto's mournful trochaic verses in a bar-form *Lied* express his sobriety and virtue, as well as his unhappy situation:

Hab ich den nicht gnug verlohren
Himmel/ da die Freyheit hin
Ach! wozu bin ich erkohren
Ach! wer tröstet meinen Sinn
Furcht/ und Schrecken Angst/ und quälen
Wil mich Armen gar entseelen.

From such simple and regular structures to the freedoms in the ariose "aria" by Floretto in II, xiii, the arias in this libretto represent the entire spectrum of possibilities in use at the time. Clarissa's brief, but complex bar-form da capo aria in V, iv, in which she expresses her joy at being forgiven, may serve to demonstrate the virtuosity of the versifier:

Nun leb ich von Hertzengrund wieder erfreut/
Weg Jammer und Plagen/
Weg Zagen/
Ich liebe/ ich lebe nun gänzlich erneut/

Ich flehe/ begehre/
und ehre
Den Printzen/ als der mich von Lastern befreit/
Drüm lieb ich/ und leb ich von Hertzen erfreut.

Not only does this ending pick up and repeat, with variations, the first line of the aria, but it also varies that line in such a way that it becomes an echo of the first line of the second metrically identical section of the bar form as well. The extreme shifts in line length, reminiscent of the metrical freedoms of madrigalic verse, create an aesthetically pleasing tension in that they appear in a repetitive and therefore tightly structured metrical scheme; similar tension is produced in the enjambment which links the repeating pattern of the bar with its non-repeating summation—a particularly compelling instance of enjambment since all other lines in the strophe end in a punctuating slash or period. Repetitions of "ich" and "weg" promote a sense of parallel structure, a further instance of variety within regularity in this short text.

Although both serious and comic characters utilize bar form, folksong, and even da capo arias, those of the comic characters—servants and other "simple" folk—generally use simpler forms, as in the contrasting arias of the king and his "lustiger Diener" Ephialtes both on the same topic, the onerous aspects of responsibility and power (II, vii and ix). Both arias are six-line, four-beat bar-form songs, but that of the king shifts from trochaic to dactylic meter for the final two lines, while that of his servant remains trochaic throughout. The language choice in each, of course, also reflects the social status of the speaker. The songs of Jucundus, especially, use low-life vocabulary in order to produce their comic effect, as in the three-strophe bar-form "aria" he claims to have found in a cheese wrapper (he himself terms it "ein Liedchen") that he sings for his father (IV, v). Such use of an imbedded comic "Liedchen," the singing of which was called for in the text, appeared also in *Die Wittekinden* and *Melissa*, as mentioned above. Unlike the later operas in Hamburg, *Floretto* does not take advantage of the spectacle of the military triumphal march to create a choral piece, and even the choral lines at the end of the opera are only intended to be sung by the few characters on stage; there is obviously no chorus for crowd scenes or choral renditions.

Most of the aria texts in *Floretto*—the bar form and many of those in the "unclassified" category—closely resemble forms found already in Stieler's *Die geharnschte Venus*, and they could well have had settings not unlike those in the song cycle of two decades before. Some, however—many of these either da capo or ariose forms—seem to exhibit a brevity and elegant simplicity which would lend themselves to the sort of elaboration and reuse of textual elements seen, for example, in German in the settings of arias from Opitz's *Judith* by Appeles von Löwenstern, to be discussed below. The usages of contemporary Italian opera in Vienna and Venice might also help in reconstructing the sorts of settings likely to have been used for the ariose and da capo texts.

Floretto's madrigalic text for dialogue portions, designed to be set as recitative, is the work of a practiced master of the form. The line lengths range from two to six beats, with most having three, four, or five beats. With very few exceptions, it is entirely iambic (in a few passages it lapses into dactylic rhythms, with *Auftakt*, and occasionally a line of apparently trochaic verse is slipped in—but only after a feminine rhyme at the end of the previous line). For the most part, the versifier avoids rhyming two lines of the same length, and although there is a great deal of pair rhyme, especially in comic scenes, the rhyme schemes in the loosely structured madrigals often show amazing variety, complexity, and irregularity. Rhyming pairs are frequently split across boundaries between two different speakers or even scenes, and often connect a madrigalic passage to the aria set within it. A typical example might look like this: ABBACCDEFEFDGH/new scene, new speaker/HGIIJJ, etc. (p. C3v). Sometimes a rhyme word appears as far as ten lines apart from its partner. In addition to all these methods of imitating the effect of the orphaned line ("Waise") that is requisite in Italian madrigals, the versifier of *Floretto* also employs true *Waisen*—nearly unknown in German madrigalic drama texts before this date. (Stieler had done so previously only in lyric madrigals.) The unrhymed or seemingly partnerless lines are often emphatic exclamations which are thus further highlighted by their divergence from the rhymed verses around them; quite a number of them begin scenes, creating an aural suspense which is never gratified. In several scenes, on the other hand, the rhyme schemes become exquisitely structured, as in II, vii, where the rhymes of the four answering lines of

Rodomann to a statement made by the king create an exact mirror image (ABCD/new speaker/DCBA). The line lengths, however, work against this structure (6-4-4-5//3-3-4-3), thus preventing the virtuosity of the rhyme scheme from detracting from the sense of natural speech in this scene. Hellmut Wolff has already pointed out the relative excellence of this libretto, in comparison to others of this early period in the Hamburg opera, and has praised its free-rhythmic naturalness.[34] The *Zwischenspiele* which Stieler created for the performance of this text at court in Weimar in 1684 will be treated separately, below.

But even the dramatic texts not intended as operas rely heavily on musical presentation for portions of the performance. A *Zwischenspiel* to one of the prose dramatic texts could stand alone as a self-sufficient musical masque: the *Danaë* appended to *Der betrogene Betrug* is as long as *Melissa* and does not relate to the comedy it punctuates in any obvious way, although it does tie the performance as a whole to the festive occasion, as discussed above. This "Singendes Zwischenspiel," as Stieler terms it, uses iambic madrigal verse throughout, with two- to five-beat lines, although the majority consist of only three beats. It must certainly have been sung in its entirety.

Der betrogene Betrug also has verse "Vorredner" and "Schluß-redner" parts to frame the whole, and directions by Stieler make it clear that these roles were to be sung. Horatius enters the stage before the play, "folgende Arie singend." The "Arie" is a four-beat iambic song with eight-line strophes which gradually disintegrate, so that strophic boundaries are lost by the end. The same gradual loss of strophic boundaries also occurs in the song of the "Schluß-redner," Apollo, likewise four-beat iambic, but having four-line units mingled in with the eight-line units. His song is followed by a "Wiegenlied" with refrain sung by a chorus of the (obviously nine) Muses. This four-beat trochaic song is clearly derived from folk forms.

The first of the Rudolstadt plays, and the first dramatic text attributable with any certainty to Stieler, *Der Vermeinte Printz*, has a "Vorredner" whose lines are four-beat iambic without strophic divisions. This *Vorspiel* and the "Singende Zwischenspiele" in the mythological sphere are plot carriers, related to the main action through parallel, contrast, and cause-and-effect. The *Zwischenspiele* are primarily madrigalic, consisting of iambic lines with three, four, or five beats, although several passages consist of regular three-beat iambic lines. Only the final chorus contains strophic versification: Hymen sings a *Lied* with four, four-beat, iambic lines per strophe, while Sibylle's has six-line strophes. A dialogue before the finale shows a variety of verse forms, including the madrigal, while the finale itself is a *Tanzlied* in dactylic verse.

The companion piece of 1665, *Ernelinde*, has a madrigal "Vorredner" part containing in the middle an inset three-strophe song in four-beat iambic, six-line strophes. The first two "Singende Zwischenspiele" consist of madrigal solos or duets followed by a strophic iambic choral *Lied*; the final one has instead a madrigal echo song at the end.[35] *Bellemperie* (1680), Stieler's only tragedy, displays not only madrigalic "Vorsänger" and "Schlußsängerin," but also *Zwischenspiele*. These madrigal verses are mostly iambic, but one passage contains a great many dactylic sections, and in general, these verses show the most variety among Stieler's madrigalic production outside the Sbarra translation of 1669. *Bellemperie* ends with a "Totentanz" ballet, as discussed above. The companion piece, *Willmut* (1680), has only a "Vorsänger" and a "Nachsänger" as a frame for its prose text. Their verses, not divided into strophes, are regular iambic pentameter ("Vorsänger") and five-beat trochaic with a caesura after the first two feet ("Nachsänger"). In *Basilene* (1667), following traditions for pastoral plays, there are choruses instead of *Zwischenspiele*, and all are strophic. The "Vorredner" Mars, identified as having a "Baßstimme," sings a *Lied* with eight iambic lines exhibiting a regular pattern (5-3-5-3-5-4-5-4); the "Schlußredner" Irene dances in as she sings an iambic pentameter song with six-line strophes. The choruses sing a variety of song forms, all in iambic meter.

Most unusual in Stieler's dramatic oeuvre is *Die erfreuete Unschuld* (1666). The "Vorredner" part is again iambic pentameter, and there are no overt indications that it was to be sung (although I find it likely that it was). But elaborate instructions on the performance of the *Zwischenspiele* are provided. Each *Zwischenspiel* was a combination of pantomime (of an event from the Book of Revelation, as discussed above) and music, partly instrumental and partly vocal. The original vocal parts are strophic religious songs, apparently all sung to the same tune since each strophe in the entire sequence exhibits the same metric pattern—six lines, of which the first five are iambic, the last partly dactylic. All have four beats except the first line, which has three. Stieler provides instructions for the music by naming the voice of the singer or singers and the accompanying instruments (the minimum necessary group of musicians for the performance consists of one bass, two tenors, two altos, and two sopranos; five viola da gambas, four violas, four violins, and a theorbe or bass lute). As Kinkeldey has noted, "Man staunt über die Mannigfaltigkeit der Leistungen und wundert sich, wo die Instrumentisten herkamen."[36] Each pantomime and vocal rendition of the strophic text is followed by the instruction that an appropriate well-known hymn be sung. Stieler gives the first line or title of each hymn, plus some indication about which verses, but leaves the texts up to the memories of his singers (and audience, and even reader). The first *Zwischenspiel* is offered here in its entirety as an example:

Stummes zwischen Spiel
Die Erste zwischen Handlung
Der erste Aufzug

Der hellische Drache steiget aus der Erde/ und speyet gegen die vier Theile der Welt/ zum Zeichen seines brennenden Zornes/ Feuer und Schwefel aus. Da in zwischen mit einem starcken Singe Basse/ den fünf Violdigammen begleiten/ folgende Worte gesungen werden.

Verfolgte Kirche/ wache!
Es meldet sich der grimme Drache.
Der Hellen Abgrund steht entdeckt.
Das Tiehr/ so Gifft und Schwefel leckt/
Steigt aus dem finstern auf die Erden/
Und wil vor Gott gehalten werden.

Sein Molchgespey und Geifer
Schießt mit geglühtem Zornes Eyfer
Auf Osten/ Süden/ Nord und West.
Die Funcken/ die sein Wühten bläst/
Bedrohen gar der Sterne Zinnen/
Und dencken Sion zugewinnen.

Der zweyte Aufzug

Die Babylonische Hure tritt mit einer dreyfachen Krohne in geschminckter Larve und geiler Tracht tantzend auf/ und fält/ nachdem sie des Drachen gewahr wird/ vor ihm nieder und behtet ihn an. Hierzu wird von einem Lieblichen Alte/ mit zu ziehung vierer Bratschen diese Ode gesungen:

Ihm folget die Entwichte/
Mit geilgeschmincktem Angesichte/
Der Hurenbalg von Babylon/
In Lucifers gedritter Krohn!
Ihr Gang begleitet zu der Helle
Und ist bemüht auf Tod und Fälle.
    Jetzt neigt sich die verruchte.
Sie kniet nider/ die Verfluchte/
Und behtet an das Wundertiehr.
Die keinen Zepter scheut alhier
Und wider Gott gedenckt zusiegen/
Darf zu der Schlangen Füßen liegen.

Der dritte Aufzug

Die Verfolger der Kirche/ Gog und Magog/ (deren jener
vom Haubt biß zu Fuß/ gewapnet: dieser aber in einem Tur-
ban und Türkischen Kleide sich vorstellen/) treten dürstig
auf den Platz/ und nach dem sie von der Huren mit
Schmeichelgebehrden gelocket werden/ verbinden sie sich
mit ihr und dem Drachen/ durch einen Eydschwur. Bey
dieser Handlung werden folgende beyde Verse mit einem
Tenor und vier discant Geigen beweglich abgesungen:
    Gog/ Magog/ ihre Lieben/
So mit ihr Hurerey getrieben/
Sind auf der Frommen Sturtz bedacht
Mit ungemenschter Mörder Macht.
Das Teuffelsbindnüß/ so sie schliessen/
Ist: Bluht/ als Ströhme zuvergiessen.
    Verfolgte Kirche/ Wache!
Und trag dem Höchsten deine Sache
Mit Feurigen Gebehten für.
Dein Breutgam wird sich zeigen dir/
Und dieses Heer der düstern Hellen/
Mit tapfern Muhte/ glücklich fällen.

Der vierdte Auffzug

Es eröfnet sich eine Kammer/ woselbst die Streitende Kir-
che/ auf ihren Knien/ vor einem Crucifix in Gebeht und
Trähnen lieget. Unterwährender ihrer Andacht werden von
Fünf Stimmen/ und so viel Instrumenten die vier Ersten
Verse des Geistlichen Kirchen-Liedes: Wo GOTT der HERR
nicht bey uns hält etc. gesungen und gespielet.

Although the theorbe is not mentioned, it may be assumed that it
nonetheless accompanied each piece with the all-important bass
line.

Two musical *Zwischenspiele* of 1684 by Stieler survive separately from the texts to which their performances were appended. "Musicalische Freuden-Feyer," consisting of a "Vorspiel" and five choruses similar to those for *Basilene*, was performed with a text deriving from a prose comedy by Christian Weise, probably the opera libretto *Floretto*, as discussed above. The "Vorspiel" exhibits Stieler's usual metrical variety: two strophic songs (one four-beat trochaic solo, one four-beat dactylic ensemble) and two sections of madrigalic dialogue. The choruses, all strophic, include regular four-beat iambic and trochaic songs and three iambic songs with more complex patterns. The final chorus is iambic until the last strophe, when it changes to shorter dactylic lines. "Winter-Lust," designed to accompany the opera *Filopiste* (as discussed above), has an autonomous "Vorspiel" in which Bruma (Winter) wins a *Streitgespräch* with Flora, Ceres, and Pomona. It contains a few instructions for musicians, especially for intrumental music. This "Vorspiel" is predominantly madrigal dialogue with three inlaid solos in strophic verse, one three-beat iambic, the others four-beat trochaic. The finale, also four-beat trochaic, is sung by the ensemble. As in "Freuden-Feyer" and *Basilene*, the choruses are strophic with a variety of verse forms. The last one, probably a *Tanzlied*, has seven-line strophes in dactylic rhythm with the following pattern of beats per line: 4-4-4-4-2-2-4.

Thus each of the prose dramatic texts written, translated, or produced by Stieler is provided with some kind of frame which is presented musically. In addition to such musical frames, several of Stieler's texts contain inlaid songs or episodes of instrumental music—in common with many other plays of the period. *Die erfreuete Unschuld* of 1666 contains a scene in which the "Hof-kapelle," assembled on stage in preparation for a wedding of the chief characters, accompanies the comic servant Scaramutza, whose voice is identified here as a tenor, in his rendition of a serenade song ("Ständchen"). This folksy, comic song consists of eight four-line strophes, each with a two-line refrain, in *Knittelvers*—the verse form of pre-Opitzian poetry in Germany which either counts the total number of syllables per line, or, as here, has a regular number of accented syllables (usually four) but an irregular number of unaccented syllables between them. As with the *Knittelvers* "Zeitungslied" in *Die Wittekinden*, use of this verse form here both parodies bad or old-fashioned poetry and identifies the lower social class of the *Versschmied* who stitched it together. After Scaramutza finishes serenading his girlfriend, he requests some dance music, and the stage directions indicate that the orchestra complied with a "Tanzlied."

Only one other prose play from the Rudolstadt years indicates the use of music during the acts of the play: in one scene in *Der betrogene Betrug* (III, ix), "ein Chor Musicanten" or "Spielleute"—on hand on stage, as Scaramutza tells us, for the wedding—provide music for Scaramutza to drink and dance to, including his "Leibstückgen," his favorite piece.

The two plays of 1680 both make some use of music outside the musical frame. In *Bellemperie* Scaramutza sings snatches of church hymns in a distracted manner at the beginning of one scene (p. 20), and, naturally enough, the play-within-the-play is provided with a musical framework, albeit much less complete than that of Stieler's "real" plays. The internal play is announced by trumpets and begins with a ballet by the actors. There are no directions to indicate whether or not the musicians were on stage, as actors in the play. But in *Willmut* two internal songs are explicitly to be performed by members of the cast together with musicians placed on the stage. The first, a seduction song designed to lead the protagonist astray, has the direction: "Hier wird musiziert und nachgesetztes Lied . . . gesungen" (p. 65). The second, a moralizing song for his instruction, was apparently sung by members of the cast, but also, perhaps, by the audience, as the directions indicate: "Eine Vertöhnung wird aufgezogen . . . indessen man dieses Lied vom bösen Gewissen absinget" (p. 97). Both inlaid songs were in iambic verse, although the form of the strophes of each is delightfully different and quite complex.

For all of these uses of music during the performance of Stieler's dramatic works, particularly since there are no surviving scores, enormous problems remain. Who composed this music? Was it all composed for these particular texts, or were some of the texts written to fit pre-extant music? Was every dramatic text or portion of one set in verse meant to be performed musically? What did this music sound like, what were its sources and influences, how up-to-date was it for its day? And how much of a musician was Stieler himself?

In the attempt to reconstruct Stieler's musical dramas, or at least to describe what they may have sounded like, it is necessary to look to extant scores for dramatic texts from the period. Unfortunately, this task is severely limited by the fact that it was not only Stieler's scores that were accidently lost or purposely discarded, but indeed nearly all scores of operas and *Singspiele* in Germany of the period. As far as I have been able to ascertain, of all the German operas from their beginnings in 1627 until the end of Stieler's dramatic oeuvre in 1684, only two complete or nearly complete scores to dramatic texts of any literary merit remain: Sigmund Theophil Staden's[37] score to Georg Harsdörffer's chamber opera *Seelewig*, as published in Harsdörffer's *Frauenzimmer Gesprächspiele* of 1644,[38] and Marc Antonio Cesti's score (with acts III and V missing) for Francesco Sbarra's libretto for the festive grand opera in Italian, *Il Pomo d'oro* of 1666-67, preserved in a manuscript in Vienna.[39] Additionally, arias from two of the many operas by Johann Löhner (1645-1705), the only Nürnberg composer involved in writing opera from Staden's death in 1655 until around 1700, have been preserved as popular excerpts.[40] Since there seems to be no extant music for any *Singspiel* of the period that greatly resembles those by Stieler, we have no infallible way of ascertaining how much of any text was set to music or how various kinds of versification were handled in this less presumptuous and presumably less sophisticated form. And of other dramas which used (or might have used) music in the choruses or *Zwischenspiele*, or in the imbedded lyrical poetry, few musical settings remain.[41] Apart from these few sources, then, we are left with hundreds of dramatic texts and libretti published during the period whose only clues to musical presentation are to be found in versification and in occasional stage directions—unfortunately almost all consisting only of the comment that the following words were to be sung. However, the extant music for shorter, non-dramatic texts of the period is quite extensive, so that certain assumptions can be drawn on the basis of comparisons of the verse forms in the dramatic texts—particularly the strophic ones—with similarly constructed texts for sacred and profane vocal music, including the settings for Stieler's own songs of the *Geharnschte Venus*, which may be most pertinent here.

The seventeenth century in Germany has been called the "Generalbasszeitalter," a term which refers to the dominance of the bass line in composition and performance. The bass provides the skeletal structure of the piece, while the treble or melody line is

only decorative harmony which works as augmentation and en-
hancement, but is never allowed to dominate. This characteristic
of Baroque music is clearly seen, as Heinz Becker has pointed
out,[42] in variant copies of Baroque music in which only the treble
parts differ in any significant degree, and in the personnel lists of
Baroque instrumental groups, where bass instruments—such as the
contrabass, cello, and bassoon, whose loud, low tones are
responsible for producing the bass line—augment their dominance
by their relatively high numbers in comparison to the other
instruments—as many as one third to one half as many bass as
treble instrumentalists are listed for orchestras before the middle
of the eighteenth century (Becker, pp. 69 and 71).

Becker ties the structural significance of the bass line to
another definitive characteristic of Baroque vocal music,
improvisation: "Der Baß bedeutete somit nur ein vorfixiertes
Gerüst, das harmonische Arrangement hierzu wurde freizügig
gehandhabt, nicht anders wie auch ein Jazzarrangeur die Freiheit
hat, eine vorgegebene Melodie harmonisch individuell zu inter-
pretieren" (p. 69). Thus each Baroque opera, each Baroque vocal
performance, was a process of full realization of the music,
"spontan, aus dem Augenblick," not just an interpretation of it.
And as with modern jazz, improvisation did not mean a chaotic
rendition; the sketchy system of notation defined the limits of
improvisation, and certain conventions which were part of every
instrumentalist's education at the time determined most of the
choices. Even such specific decisions as voice type for a particular
role, or which instruments played which parts, were ruled by con-
vention, and thus did not require explicit statement: the symbolic
hierarchy of high notes "above" low notes determined the vocal
soloists, for the most part, while certain instruments were traditionally associated with particular contexts (e.g., trumpets with
rulers, battles, and triumphs; see Becker, pp. 68-69).

Beginning with the earliest Italian operas and culminating
already in Monteverdi, the goal of *dramma per musica* was *parlare
musicalmente*, and thus the monodic recitative, a form of musical
presentation in which words and ideas can be clearly and expressively communicated, came into its own. When arias later intrude,
especially during reflective moments in the text, and the music is
allowed more latitude to develop its own integrity *(bel canto)*, the
plot is still forwarded by means of recitative *(recitativo secco)*.

The challenge was, by the middle of the seventeenth century in Germany, not only for the composer to provide appropriate settings for pre-extant texts, but also for the poet to provide texts which lent themselves to musical composition. An examination of the metrical systems employed by several other poets who wrote texts intended to be set to music for which notation still survives should provide a useful point of departure for analysis of Stieler's musical metrics.

Stieler's strophic verse in his dramatic works exhibits great variety and virtuosity, both of which qualities make comparison with *Seelewig* desirable, since Harsdörffer's libretto consists almost entirely of strophic verse and even set lyrical forms (e.g., "Sonnet," in I, i), the exceptions being in non-strophic Alexandrine verse ("Vorrednerin," plus stichomythic dialogue, I, iii). The songs in *Seelewig* show remarkable variety in their rhythmic and strophic patterns, and many could stand by themselves as poems or as pieces of vocal music. Strophic verse is employed here for dialogues, monologues (solos), duets, and ensembles. As music historian Peter Keller has indicated, however, the musical settings reveal a twofold structure which is not entirely parallel to that of the metric systems. Keller, using the term strophic only for those verses which Staden has set to repetitions of a single melody, defines strophic music as "das continuo begleitete Sololied."[43] The other type of setting, non-strophic, he terms "durchkomponiert." *The International Cyclopedia of Music and Musicians*[44] defines this crucial concept: "*Durchkomponiert.* . . A term used for a song which does not have the same music for each verse, as do the so-called strophic songs and simple folksongs, but which brings new musical material to meet the demands of changing textual content." Keller maintains that the non-strophic music here is not recitative, but "ariose"—composed of strung together arias, "Arietten," and "mezz'arie."[45] This "ariose" setting is especially evident for Seelewig's part, according to Keller. Yet Harsdörffer himself identifies the "durchkomponiert" type of setting as recitative. In placing the *Seelewig* text and music in his *Frauenzimmer Gesprächspiele*, Harsdörffer has provided a running commentary not only on the meanings, but also on the techniques of the work. One of the conversationalists, Cassandra, whose task it is to assess and explain the musical setting, describes this twofold type of presentation: "Wil man wenig Noten haben/ so kan es/ als ein

Lied/ von vier Reimzeilen zu den anderen gesungen werden/ oder
durch und durch Erzehlungsweis in die Music gesetzt werden" (p.
45). In the margin Harsdörffer has added the remark "in genere
recitativo" to the latter method. In Stieler's strophic verse in
dramatic texts, the distinction from non-strophic verse is perhaps
much clearer than in Harsdörffer's text, and it is possible that all
those passages I have described as "strophic" above in the descriptions of Stieler's verse forms would have been set to "strophic"
music of the sort Staden composed or, more contemporaneously,
the composers of the *Geharnschte Venus* song cycle.

But since Harsdörffer's *Seelewig* was set to music in its
entirety, the *Judith-Tragödie* of Martin Opitz and a *Singspiel* by
Sigmund von Birken, both of which contain musical settings only
for the choruses, might together provide a better point of comparison with Stieler's prose plays. Opitz's *Judith*, a transla-
tion/adaptation of an Italian opera libretto by Andrea Salvadori
(*Istoria di Iudit*, 1626, composer Marco da Galiano) is written
entirely in verse (madrigalic dialogue—heavily laden with
Alexandrines—and strophic choral pieces), following the example
of its original. Although it was not published until 1635, Opitz
probably completed the work in 1628.[46] Mara Wade feels that it
was intended for a musical performance at court at that time, but
there is no record of such an event, and it was apparently not set
to music in this form. Several years after its publication, *Judith*
was reworked by Andreas Tscherning (the cast expanded from
eight to twenty, two initial acts added, several choruses given
additional text material); the choral pieces were set to music by
Appeles von Löwenstern (under his pseudonym, "Matthaeo Leo-
nastro de Longueville, Neapolitano"). The revised work, complete
with the musical settings (each for three tenor voices and a basso
continuo), was performed in Thorn in 1643[47] and published in
Rostock in 1646.[48] All the choruses penned by Opitz and set to
music by Löwenstern are made up entirely of three-beat iambic
lines (Tscherning's choruses are predominantly iambic pentameter);
some—for the most part those Opitz himself delineated as containing strophic boundaries—are set strophically (that is, with repeating musical units) by Löwenstern; others are instead *durchkomponiert*. Nearly all exhibit a characteristic of Italian operatic music not
present in *Seelewig*: the repetition of partial lines—usually of a
single metric foot—to enhance the emotional content and to offer

the opportunity for musical variety. Brief analysis of numbers 2, 3, 4, and 5 (Opitz's chorus at the end of his Act I and his imbedded choral pieces of Act II) will serve as definitive descriptions of this musical setting. Numbers 2 and 3 are *durchkomponiert* settings, each of which begins with simple, syllabic presentation of the first three lines, then dissolves the metric structure of the next two or three into an intense ariose passage by means of repetition and recombination.[49] Number 2 ends with this emotional elaboration, while number 3 returns to straight syllabic setting for the remainder of this rather long chorus. The choral pieces which appear in the midst of Opitz's Act II, on the other hand, are treated strophically. The first "Chor der Wache" (II, iii) is set as a simple *Lied* with refrain; the second (II, iv), an anti-drinking song, has no refrain, and adds complexity with the repetition of the next-to-the-last phrase (one metric foot) of each strophe. The answering drinking song sung by two soldiers (II, v), also strophic, uses a new (but related) tune which incorporates no repeated metric units of text. It might be fair to surmise that Stieler's musical *Zwischenspiele* may well have had similarly varied settings, both strophic and *durchkomponiert*, but any assumption that they may have been expanded in ariose passages in the Italian style, as in most of Löwenstern's, would have to confront the fact that the settings in the *Geharnschte Venus* and of later songs exhibit little of this sort of elaboration.

Birken's *Psyche* (1652)[50] is also written entirely in verse of varying metric schemes, some of which is strophic, and yet, once again, music is provided (and apparently intended) only for the *Zwischenlieder* for tenor solo. Some regularity is achieved since each of the five *Zwischenlieder* has five strophes, but the strophic form of each chorus is entirely different. Except for the second chorus, which is in iambic meter, all are trochaic. Unusual intermeshing of varying line lengths and rhyme schemes causes the songs to sound much like madrigal verse, and they may in fact have been constructed in emulation of the free-form effect of the madrigal. However, the musical presentation is not at all similar to recitative: strophic music composed by Georg Walch[51] is provided for each chorus, and there is no evidence of the *durchkomponieren* technique at all. Another play by Birken, *Silvia* (1656), does not have musical choruses, but does include the music for an imbedded strophic song in the original manuscript in Nuremberg.[52] Walch's fairly straightforward *Lied* settings might well be comparable with the strophic passages in Stieler's *Zwischenspiele.*

It would also be appropriate to compare Stieler's strophic texts to those of school dramatist Christian Weise for which we do have musical settings, although they postdate most of Stieler's oeuvre. Using the term "Arie," Weise often employs musical prologues and epilogues, as well as songs and musical prayers imbedded in the prose text of the action. He does not, however, make use of vocal music in *Zwischenspiele* or choruses. Complete scores (except for the comic songs) exist for two biblical plays which use a great deal of music: *Jephtha* (1679) and *Abraham* (1680), which were published together.[53] The score was composed by Moritz Edelmann, as Weise notes.[54] *Jephtha* begins with an *Aria* and closes with a *Lied*; each act has at least one song. Music is provided at the end of the text for all except two songs, a love song from Act II and a humorous song in Act IV. It is likely that they used well-known tunes. *Abraham* has an instrumental "Vorspiel" (a sort of overture, as did *Seelewig*) and a very complex prologue aria (consisting of a duet, alternating solos, chorus, duet, solos, and chorus again), but lacks an epilogue aria. There are fewer internal musical texts: a humorous folksy song in Act II without published musical setting, a religious song in III with music, and a prayer song in IV with the direction to use the setting for one of the religious pieces from *Jephtha*. A comedy of 1681 contains an epilogue set to music by Edelmann as well: *Bäurischer Machiavellus*[55] ends with an aria sung by four characters accompanied by two trumpets, four trombones, and tympani. The aria prays for guidance for the city fathers of Zittau, where the play was performed by school boys. Others of Weise's plays were obviously intended to have similar musical contributions, but since scores were not published with the texts nor composers named, we know as little about them as we do about Stieler's. Weise's lyrics, in general, exhibit much less variety and virtuosity than those by Stieler (or Birken), and thus demand considerably less of the composer. Most are either iambic or trochaic, usually four-beat lines; some have refrains. Final choruses, as with Stieler, offer the opportunity for a few dactylic rhythms. That at the end of *Jephtha*, presented by two vocal parts and continuo, probably constitutes an attempt by Weise to write madrigalic verse; the setting is "durchkomponiert," and although not "strophic"—no line of melody is repeated—is perhaps more in "ariose" than in "recitative" form.

Meyer, in her essay on the music of the *Geharnschte Venus*,[56] offers possible identifications for the composers of Stieler's songs (only their initials are provided above their compositions) that differ strikingly from those in the older entry in Eitner's biographical dictionary of musicians.[57] She discusses the characteristics and analyzes the quality of some of the individual compositions. The songs are in what Meyer terms "den neuen monodischen Stil," that is, solo vocalist with a single bass instrument in accompaniment ("continuo"). Each of the seventy songs is strophic: each has units of verse which are set to a melody that is repeated for each strophe. Meyer suggests that these melodies, however, were not as rhythmically regular as we might expect today, and advises: "Viele Lieder gewinnen an Lebhaftigkeit des Ausdrucks, wenn man ihren Vortrag rhythmisch freier gestaltet und dem Rezitativ anähnelt" (pp. 189-90). She thus sees similarities between some of the settings and Italian musical drama (p. 190). She is apparently referring to the sort of musical setting Keller terms "durchkomponiert" and Harsdörffer describes with "durch und durch Erzehlungsweis gesetzet." Four of the songs, although containing units of text which follow a single pattern that is set to a single musical presentation, are clearly madrigalic: each "strophe" is a madrigal which would follow the standard rules for this lyric short form: nine to fourteen lines, a fluid pattern of rhyme pairs (including, in one poem, the "Waise" or orphaned line that is mandatory in Italian madrigals), every line a different length that avoids pairing with any other. Two of these madrigalic songs were penned to fit pre-extant musical settings, each supposedly French ("Französische Blamande," "Franz. Ballet"); the most interesting, both from the point of view of the musical setting by Martin Coler and from that of Stieler's versification, is "Die Schein-keusche."[58] Other songs, on the other hand, are like a rather old-fashioned sort of aria, the bar song: each strophe consists of two metric patterns, of which the first one is repeated immediately, although with new textual material, thus creating the pattern AAB. These bar songs, which make up a large group in the song cycle—eighteen of the seventy songs are of this type—usually have strophes of six or eight lines each, although one has ten lines. The repeating pattern is normally two lines long, but in one case includes three lines; the

pattern that does not repeat may be two or four lines long. Many
of these bar songs were set to music by Martin Coler, who seems
to have enjoyed this form; three use pre-extant French musical
pieces; and four were set to music by Caspar Stieler himself, who
apparently felt comfortable with this form, as well as with the
more traditional *Lied* form. It should be appropriate to compare
the settings of *Die Geharnschte Venus* with the texts for Stieler's
music dramas of at least his first period of activity, 1665-69 in
Rudolstadt and Eisenach-Weimar.

Settings accompanying later Stieler songs appended to the collection *Der Bußfertige Sünder, oder Geistliches Handbüchlein*
(1679), edited by Stieler, can profitably be used in examining the
portions of later dramatic works once set to music.[59] The last eight
tunes ("Zugabe etlicher neuen Lieder nebst Gesangweisen") are
probably attributable to Stieler's pen. These melodies, all designed
for strophic settings of hymn-like songs with multiple strophic
units, are of several types: three are bar songs, much like those in
the earlier *Geharnschte Venus* (each strophe uses the AAB pattern
of musical setting without repeating any verbal material), while
the rest are the kind of strophic presentation he had also already
used in the earlier collection in which there are no musical repetitions within a strophe. One of these, which uses a tune by famous
composer Adam Krieger[60] ("nach der schönen Melodey des
Krügers fünfter Arie"), is very complex rhythmically, with three
repetitions of a long madrigal-like pattern. Another, using shorter
rhythmic units and shorter strophes, utilizes an interesting technique for emphasis of the name Jesus and the other terms in the
text for the godhead, "Erlöser" and "Vater." The two syllables are
set with half or whole notes, the only long notes in the melody
aside from those that end the lines or phrases. In the five strophes
the poet has had to contrive so that these key names always occur
in the same slots in the verse patterns, in spite of the different
text in which each occurrence is to be found. It is perhaps significant that no composer is named for the relatively simple bar
songs or the folksong-like strophic tunes—presumably Stieler himself was responsible—while the musically more difficult form, the
madrigal, is adapted from a published aria by a professional composer. Stieler may well have made similar decisions for the verse
texts in his dramatic works, particularly the later ones: a profes-

sional composer for the madrigal verses and possibly himself as the provider of the strophic songs.

Much of the versification in Stieler's dramatic works is indeed not strophic, nor simply continuous pentameter or Alexandrine lines, but madrigalic. For Stieler, following German redesigning of the madrigal by Opitz, Ziegler, and others, madrigal verse contains lines of varying lengths, but has a dominant rhythm throughout—iambic predominates, although dactylic, as described above, occurs on occasion, and is even quite frequent in *Der göldene Apfel*. Each line normally ends with a rhyme word, although the patterns of rhyme have many options and shift constantly. Rhyming lines frequently have different length, and repeating patterns of line lengths or rhyming pairs are seldom allowed to form.

Madrigal verse originated in Italy as the verse form for dramatic texts—especially pastoral dramas—and became very popular by the third quarter of the sixteenth century. It soon became an accepted lyric genre, as the publication in Germany already in 1596 of a popular collection of Italian madrigals indicates.[61] Its widespread popularity in the late sixteenth century has been linked to the potential it offers for a more organic relationship between the emotional content of a text and its musical setting: "It [the madrigal] set the pace for stylistic developments that culminated in the Baroque period, particularly those involving the expressive relationship between text and music, and must be regarded as the most important genre of the late Renaissance."[62] This new style of musical settings free to augment the emotional content of the texts was an important precondition to the development of the operatic genre.

Opitz was apparently the first to use madrigal verses in German verse drama when he translated the pastoral opera *Dafne* in 1627;[63] like Italian madrigal verse of the time, his verses are sometimes iambic, sometimes trochaic. He continued this rhythmic variety in his *Judith* opera translation of 1628-35, as discussed above, but it was not destined to be universally accepted in Germany. As Wolfgang Keyser states in his *Kleine Deutsche Versschule*,[64] most Germans who set their hands to the verse form after the Opitzian reform of verse-making quickly add some sort of order to the rhythmic freedom of the Italian originals. The German language, with its potentially regular pattern of accented and unaccented syllables, did not seem appropriate for the rhyth-

mic variety so charming in Italian, a language in which syllable
length counts for more than accent. A short treatise on the subject
by Caspar Ziegler in 1653, *Von den Madrigalen*,[65] written at the
request of his relative, the famous composer Heinrich Schütz, in
order to aid in the composition of madrigal verse appropriate for
musical settings, seemingly preserves the Italian method of versification—syllable counting. A line should consist of six or seven
syllables (depending on whether the rhyme was masculine or feminine) or ten or eleven syllables. Yet, since Ziegler followed the
Opitzian reform of German verse in using regular meter consisting
of alternating stressed and unstressed syllables, all of his examples
in fact consist entirely of iambic three-beat and five-beat lines.
Ziegler lauds the freedom of the madrigal verse form and delin-
eates the areas in which this freedom is evident: it need have no
set number of lines, the lines vary in length (although only five-
beat and three-beat lines are acceptable, unlike the Italian
madrigal, which has much more freedom in this area), the lines
need not all end in rhyme words, and the rhyme pattern may show
considerable variation. He ends his treatise with some comments
on the musical settings for madrigal verse which are pertinent here
and will thus be quoted at length:

> Ich muß aber zum Beschluß errinnern/ das kein einziges
> *genus carminus* in der Deutschen Sprache sich besser zu der
> Musick schicke/ als ein Madrigal. Denn darinnen lest sich
> ein *Concert* am allerbesten ausführen/ und weil die Worte so
> fein in ihrer natürlichen *construction* gesetzt werden können/
> so kömbt auch die Harmony umb so viel desto besser und
> anmuthiger. . . . Weil nun ein Madrigal viel freyer ist und
> sich der Reime halber so sehr nicht binden darff/ auch der
> natürlichen Art zu reden näher kömt/ so meyn Ich/ sol es
> einem *Componisten* auch viel leichter und besser auf seinem
> Chartelle (eine Art Pergament)/ als ein Sonnet/ fallen.
> Sonsten aber wird ein Madrigal/ (was die blossen Verse/
> nicht aber die *composition* belanget) dem *stylo recitativo* fast
> gleich gemacht/ und halt Ich besagten *Stylum recitativum*,
> wie ihn die Italianer in der Poesie zu ihren Singe Comedien
> gebrauchen vor einen stets werenden Madrigal/ oder vor et-
> liche viel Madrigaln/ doch solcher gestalt/ daß ie zuweilen
> darzwischen eine *Arietta*, auch wohl eine *Aria* von etlichen
> *Stanzen* lauffe/ welches denn sowohl der Poet als der Com-
> ponist sonderlich in acht nehmen/ und eines mit dem andern
> zu versüssen/ zu rechter Zeit abwechseln muß. (pp. 41-42)

Although he hedges somewhat ("fast gleich"), Ziegler clearly equates madrigal versification with recitative musical settings. He then goes on to express the opinion that composition of madrigals is not as easy as it might sound:

> Nun solte sich einer einbilden/ es were ein Madrigal oder der *Stylus recitativus*, weil er sogar nicht gebunden ist/ gantz leichte und ohne alle mühe zumachen; Alleine Ich wil lieber zwantzig Strophen lange Verse/ die man sonst Alexandrinisch nennet/ als ein einzig Madrigal zu wercke bringen. (p. 43)

The connection that Ziegler draws to the versification of *Singe Comedien* was followed by several later writers of poetical treatises and was not absent in earlier efforts, albeit without using the term "madrigal." In his *Poetischer Trichter* of 1648, for example, Harsdörffer mentions the possibility of musical settings for *Freudenspiele* using terms that are connected elsewhere with recitative: "Die Handlungen werden in den Freudenspielen mit der Music ohn Gesang unterschieden. Wann aber die gantze Verfassung in ungebundener Rede/ so könte man wol darzu gewidmete Lieder singen lassen: sonst aber/ wann es durch und durch Verse und keine Lehren beygebracht/ so ist die Music allein genug/ jedoch/ daß sie nach Beschaffenheit deß Inhalts bald traurig/ bald fröhlich sey."[66]

Albrecht Christian Rotth, in the chapter on comedy in his *Vollständige Deutsche Poesie* of 1688, is more explicit and might, in fact, be describing Stieler's dramatic oeuvre in many particulars. He explicitly advises the use of predominantly iambic verse in relatively short lines, and then discusses madrigal versification: "Insonderheit ist die Madrigalische Arth beliebt/ ja auch nöthig/ wenn singende Comödien aufgeführet werden/ . . . Denn der Thon kan alsdenn besser der Materie nach eingerichtet werden/ als in einer anderen Art Verse."[67] He advises that such madrigal passages be ornamented with occasional strophic interruptions:

> Uber dis dienet auch dieses zur Nachricht/ daß hin und wieder ein oder das andere Versgen von einer Arie mitunter das gespräche/ ehe man sichs versiehet/ in solche singende Comödie mit eingemischet werden kan/ welches entweder ein fein *Morale* oder sonst eine feine kurtze Beschreibung in sich fasset. Und in dieser Arie mögen als denn Jambische oder Trocheische oder Dactilische Verse gebraucht werden/

so gilt es gleich viel. Ja man kan auch/ wenn etwan ein
Versgen von der Arie gesungen worden/ in dem gespräche
fortfahren/ und bald unversehens abermahl ein solches Sing-
versgen in die Arie mit einmischen entweder eben daßelbe
oder das auf dasselbe sein Absehen hat/ oder das eines gantz
andern Inhaltes ist.[68]

In Book I, where Rotth discusses the madrigal proper, that is, the
Italian short poem of up to 15 lines ("ein kurtzes Gedichte (a)/ das
etwas scharffsinniges in sich fasset (b)/ ohne gewisse Mensur der
Reime (c)/ und nachmahls bey dem Leser ein sonderliches Nach-
dencken verursachet,)"[69] he describes the madrigal verse form in
detail, as it is best applied to the German language:

Jedoch ist fleißig zu beobachten/ daß der kleineste Madrigal
. . . aus lautern Jambus bestehet. . . . Die kurtzen Verse
können sechs- sieben- bisweilen acht-sylbig seyn/ die lang-
sten nicht wohl über 11 ausschreiten. . . . Es wehre denn
Sache/ daß man üm eines beßern Nachdrucks und richtiger
Construction willen die Verse frey lauffen liesse. Denn
alsdenn deuchte mir/ sey es auch bey einem Madrigale nicht
so gar unrecht/ wenn man gleich den Abschnitt im Verse
nicht einmahl in acht nimmt/ weil ein Madrigal gleichsam
eine ungebundene Rede darstellet.[70]

Rotth also firmly connects madrigal versification with recitative
musical settings when he points out that the limitations of the
short madrigal poem in no way preclude the use of madrigal
verses for musical dramas:

Wenn man aber gantze *Comoed*ien oder *Tragoed*ien mit dem
heutiges Tages so benahmten *stylo recitativo* schreibt und
darinne eine Madrigalische Verß-Arth braucht (wie sich
denn fast keine besser schickt/ als diese/ wie die *Comoed*ien
sollen gesungen werden/) so mögen die Verse frey lauffen
und bindt man sich nicht an die vorgeschriebenen 14. oder
15. Zeilen.[71]

In the third book, where he discusses such musical dramas, Rotth
criticizes the Italian mode of madrigal versification, followed by
some Germans (he mentions Hofmannswaldau's translation of *Il
Pastor fido*), in which iambic and trochaic verses are both possible.

   Rotth's doubts about this type of mixed versification in
German seem to have assailed most German practitioners of the
madrigal after Opitz. For instance, Harsdörffer, in his *Seelewig*, a

pastoral opera where one would naturally expect to find madrigal verse, prefers to use a few regular Alexandrines and a variety of regular strophic forms which almost verge on the rhythmic freedom of madrigals, as Staden's compositions of them show. If one examines the first song by Künsteling at the opening of the first act, for example, one is struck by the shift in rhythm—from iambic to trochaic—which Staden's composition has forced upon the text in the interior lines of each of the first two strophes. While in Harsdörffer's poetic text the variation is subtle (the removal of the *Auftakt*), in Staden's setting it has become an imitation of the sudden shifts in rhythm of the Italian madrigal verse, not unlike what Opitz's German verses to *Dafne* must have been in Schütz's lost score. Thus Harsdörffer's strophic versification could well be seen as the creation of a German equivalent, a parallel form which fully takes into account the particular demands of the German language, yet offers its composer the opportunity to explore a current Italian style. Hence Harsdörffer's application of the term *in genere recitativo* for the *durchkomponiert* sections, at least.

Yet Harsdörffer's contribution was destined to be substantially without followers, and later poets continued, until Stieler, to struggle somewhat unsuccessfully with the demands of the madrigal. Gryphius, for instance, uses irregular line lengths for dialogue in both of his *Festspiele—Majuma* (1653) and *Piastus* (1660)—yet tends to keep them in groups or patterns according to length, and does not use varying rhythms. He tends in these musical plays,[72] as in his *Verlibtes Gespenste* (also of 1660), to prefer Alexandrine lines for serious parts, four-beat lines for less serious ones. Stieler's formal regularity for the madrigal, however, will come solely in his insistence on a single meter, usually iambic—resulting in a verse form almost identical with the free verse of the eighteenth century. And his successful versification may well have had an effect upon the librettists of the Hamburg opera of the last quarter of the century and beyond.

Since, as Rotth indicates, madrigal verse was normally the metric vehicle for recitative, it is possible that the long portions of Stieler's musical dramas in this form did indeed resemble the Italian recitatives of the early seventeenth century, and even those of German opera and oratorio of the later seventeenth century. But it is more probable that some form of "ariose" recitative, which approaches the melodic beauty of the aria while retaining its rhythmic versatility, would have been more appropriate. Keller's discussion of Staden's setting of *Seelewig* may, in fact, be pertinent for Stieler's madrigalic verse. But an even more appropriate comparison, perhaps (although it cannot be the source since it was composed after several of Stieler's plays and was presumably not even known to him until 1669—if then) would be Cesti's score for *Il Pomo d'oro* (1666-67). This Viennese opera, written and composed by Italians whose roots lay in the innovative circles of musicians in Venice and Florence, is written entirely in madrigal verse, although some of the parts are treated strophically; that is, some repeating patterns are allowed to form, and the composer has taken advantage of that fact to provide strophic settings—arias within the madrigal text. Dialogue is, for the most part, "durchkomponiert," yet not recitative in the sense of narrative, rhythmically free presentation, but rather "ariose." Particularly melodic excerpts can be, and have been, performed in isolation; as noted above, it is even possible that Stieler followed the original rhythms exactly in parts of his translation in order to allow such piecemeal performance. It is easy to imagine this sort of musical setting for Stieler's verses, especially in the choruses and *Zwischenspiele*, but also in *Melissa* in its entirety. The less melodic sort of setting would perhaps have been more suitable, however, for most of *Die Wittekinden*, Stieler's other verse drama.

The texts of musical dramas by Opitz and Gryphius, almost certainly without scores, were probably well known to Stieler. Yet it is another creator of musical drama who would logically be the best candidate to have been the more direct source for Stieler's approach to versification: Anton Ulrich of Braunschweig-Lüneburg, whose musical dramas performed at the court of his father in Wolfenbüttel between 1656 and 1663 were known to the young count Albert Anthon of Schwarzburg-Rudolstadt, who himself may even have witnessed one of them during his stay at the court of his great-uncle in Wolfenbüttel in 1659 as part of his *Bildungsreise*.[73] Several of the texts of Anton Ulrich's plays—*Amelinde* (1657) and *Jacob des Patriarchen Heyrat* (1662)—are to be found in the library in Rudolstadt, formerly the possession of the counts (later princes) of Schwarzburg-Rudolstadt. *Amelinde* is even bound in the same volume with three of Stieler's dramatic contributions to the festivities there.[74] Because the 1664[?] edition of *Amelinde* seems even to have been printed in Rudolstadt, there remains the possibility that this *Singspiel* was performed there at that time.[75] Like Stieler's musical dramas, the libretti of the *Singspiele* and *Singballetten* by Anton Ulrich have survived without their scores. Frederick Lehmeyer and Rand Henson, in two recent Berkeley dissertations, have postulated that while some of the plays had scores composed by the *Kapellmeister* Johann Jacob Löwe,[76] others, including *Amelinde*, were probably set to music by the stepmother of Anton Ulrich, Duchess Sophie Elizabeth, who was not only a dramatist in her own right, but also a student of composer Heinrich Schütz.[77] She had also provided the music, still extant, for the children's *Singspiel* by Schottel, the *Friedens Sieg* of 1642, which one scholar even considers the first German opera.[78]

The *Singspiele* by Anton Ulrich[79] exhibit patterns of versification in many ways similar to the musical portions of Stieler's plays: madrigal-like verses carry the dialogue and narrative sections, for the most part, while emotional or private thoughts are often conveyed in strophic verse, mostly in the tradition of the German *Lied*, and the choruses and ensembles always use strophic format. Most of Anton Ulrich's *Lieder*, however, are trochaic rather than iambic, although some show extremely complex forms and rhythms. *Amelinde*, seemingly one of the most likely texts by Anton Ulrich to have influenced Stieler directly, is a relatively short pastoral allegory, and among Stieler's plays it most closely resembles *Melissa*—a work published and probably written only after Stieler had departed from Rudolstadt. In terms of versification *Amelinde* cannot be the model for Stieler's Rudolstadt plays, for instead of the freedom of the madrigal, even as regularized by Ziegler a few years before *Amelinde* was written, this early *Singspiel* exhibits a marked regularity in its metric scheme for the long passages of dialogue and even many of the non-strophic monologues. Aside from two strophic songs, the first act of *Amelinde* is made up entirely of lines three, six, or five beats in length. The first two scenes, in fact, organize lines of these three types into repeating patterns which could well be demarcated with strophic boundaries. Other scenes are entirely Alexandrine or alternate between pairs of six-beat and five-beat lines. However, several later *Singspiele* of Anton Ulrich show more significant similarities to Stieler's metric systems—*Jacob des Patriarchen Heyrath* (1662), an edition of which was apparently printed in

Rudolstadt at the same time as *Amelinde*, and *Der Hoffman Daniel*
(1663). Both make use of true madrigal verses, perhaps in consideration of Ziegler's reforms. Yet even here the lines still have a
tendency to lengthen out in places to six beats (like those of
Gryphius of this same period), with only occasional imbedded
five-beat lines to evoke the irregularity of the madrigal form, thus
conveying the rather ponderous feeling of tragic Alexandrines—a
tone alien to Stieler's own lighter versification.

Rather than seeing the texts (and perhaps scores) of Anton
Ulrich's *Singspiele* as crucial influences on Stieler, it might be
more appropriate, in spite of the possible publication and performance of *Amelinde* and *Jacob* in Rudolstadt in around 1664, to
see the Wolfenbüttel productions as merely the inspiration for the
activities in Rudolstadt. Count Albert Anthon's accounts of the
performances may have given Stieler the idea to create musical
dramas, to use the Muses and other Greco-Roman deities in his
frames (although it is interesting to note that the celebratory
frame with the nine Muses for Anton Ulrich's *Amelinde* was
omitted in the Rudolstadt edition), and to end some of the plays
with miniature ballets, modelled perhaps on the *Singballete* of the
Wolfenbüttel court. But Stieler's plays, aside from *Melissa* and *Die
Wittekinden*, were written predominantly in prose. And Anton
Ulrich's preference for subject matter—either allegorical-pastoral
or biblical—finds only a few echoes in Stieler's oeuvre. Stieler's
Heldenspiele with comic relief provided by Scaramutza represent a
totally different tradition of courtly theater, one deriving in part
from comedies by Gryphius (*Horribilicribrifax* and *Das Verlibte
Gespenst*), but also more directly from the Italian sources of that
tradition, as Hinck has shown, at least in part.[80]

One question pertaining to the *Singspiele* of Anton Ulrich,
however, has bearing on the problems of reconstructing the musical presentation of Stieler's *Singspiele*, and indeed, all examples of
the genre. Although Anton Ulrich's *Singspiele* are written entirely
in verse, Lehmeyer maintains that only the strophic songs were
presented musically.[81] His assumption, however, is based, as Pierre
Béhar has shown,[82] on the eighteenth-century definition of *Singspiel* which Lehmeyer has applied, without further exploration,
backwards into the mid-seventeenth century for the genre given
this appellation by its creators. While Lehmeyer's claim is certainly
possible, and may in fact be true for the scenes entirely in

Alexandrines in *Amelinde*, I agree with Béhar that it is much more likely that the drama was presented musically in its entirety. With their mixture of three-, five-, and six-beat lines, the passages which are neither Alexandrine nor strophic, although too regular to be termed madrigal versification, would lend themselves to the sort of "durchkomponiert" musical setting that graced Harsdörffer's *Seelewig* and probably Opitz's "more correct" madrigals in the Italian tradition in his *Dafne*. Béhar has convincingly shown this, in fact, to be the case. He points to the fact that "Singspiel," the appellation Anton Ulrich uses for his musical dramas, is the same as the term that defines those texts in the "Singballet" *Ballet der Natur*, which are explicitly designed to be sung, and that the concept "nach italienischer Arth," which Anton Ulrich applies to one of his *Singspiele*, is even in the same wording as the generic subtitle of Harsdörffer's chamber opera *Seelewig*, a piece set entirely to music and performed in Wolfenbüttel just two years before *Amelinde*, as mentioned above. It might be pertinent to point out here that Staden had little trouble setting Harsdörffer's Alexandrine lines, and even Stieler's *Geharnschte Venus* contains an Alexandrine song ("Ein Degen hält den andern in der Scheide"). Béhar also bases his assumption that Anton Ulrich's *Singspiele* were entirely set to music in part on the fact that, as for the singing roles in the *Singballete*, no names of courtiers and young ducal relatives appear, whereas it was the custom to produce *dramatis personae* lists for the theatrical and dance performances there, providing a veritable "Who's Who" of the younger generation at the Wolfenbüttel court. Béhar concludes: "Anton Ulrichs Singspiele lassen sich also in keiner Weise von der traditionellen Form der italienischen Oper unterscheiden. Dieser entsprechend bestanden sie aller wahrscheinlichkeit nach in einer wechselnden Folge von Liedern und Rezitativen" (pp. 783-84). Actually, it would probably be more apt to posit a musical pattern resembling a mixture of strophic and through-composed settings, much as in Staden's score for *Seelewig*, especially for the early texts, like *Amelinde*.

More influential for Stieler's madrigalic versification, in all probability, was Königsberg poet Simon Dach, who penned two operas, *Cleomedes* in 1635 and *Sorbuissa* in 1644, both with music set by Heinrich Albert.[83] Albert claims that his music for *Sorbuissa* was among his best, implying that Dach's text had great musical potential. The madrigalic portions of the text of *Sorbuissa* do not survive, but those of *Cleomedes* do,[84] and it is immediately possible to see what it is about Dach's madrigal verses that distinguishes them from those of Stieler's other predecessors in the attempt to write recitative texts. Stieler is the only German to follow Dach in using iambic rhythms exclusively, and is guided by him as well in choice of line lengths (two to six beats, but with three- and four-beat lines predominating) and in the avoidance of any pervasive patterning of line length or rhyme pairs. Most remarkable at this early date, and apparent again in the verses of Stieler, is the clever use of natural syntactical pauses to create variety and naturalness for the line endings.

Dach's two early operas with their innovations in recitative verse were not generally available to librettists until after 1680, when the madrigalic portions of *Cleomedes* finally appeared in print for the first time; the isolation of Königsberg and the fact that the two texts were connected to very specific occasions of only local concern were undoubtedly to blame. Yet Caspar Stieler, probably alone of all later poets of operatic texts, had the opportunity to know the texts and to work under the tutelage of their author, for he was a student at the University of Königsberg from 1653 to 1656. Not only did he have the opportunity to attend lectures of the famous professor of Poetics and to absorb certain elements of Dach's style and verse-making, but it is also highly probable that he attended, or even participated in, the revival performance of *Sorbuissa* there in 1656.[85]

Stieler's use of madrigalic passages for recitative shows a steady process of refinement during the period from his first known attempts in the *Zwischenspiele* for *Der Vermeinte Printz* in 1665 to the comic masterpiece of 1683, *Floretto*, but within the variety and over the time span of two decades, his talents and insights have put their stamp on all of these texts designed to be set musically as recitative. That no single musical setting survives is a tragedy for the historians of German-language opera.

Musical performances, whether of brief songs, of choruses, or of entire texts, constituted an important part of seventeenth-century German theater, yet the fact that the musical settings have, with only a few exceptions, not been preserved, while texts, many of them lavishly illustrated, survive as monuments to the performances, cannot be ignored. The enormous production of even largely forgotten musicians of the period could speak for the speed and ease of composition according to the practice of the times. Hans Michael Schletterer, in his early study of the German *Singspiel* (1863), expresses this idea, seeing the music as derivative from spiritual music: "Wie leicht waren also die Tonsätze zu den Singspielen herzustellen; eine etwas raschere Bewegung, eine muntere Melodie, mit etwas mehr Schnörkeln als sie sonst in der Kirche angewendet wurden—und die Composition für das Singspiel war fertig."[86] And while a large repertoire of spiritual music was kept at Rudolstadt, and considered important enough to catalogue in 1700,[87] the worldly music, including perhaps the musical settings for Stieler's musical dramas, was neglected, possibly even already discarded as something for which there was no further use. Had it existed only in sketches? Was it only hack work? Did much of it consist of borrowed or even well-known tunes reused for the performance? On the basis of the few surviving musical settings for dramatic texts of the period—*Seelewig*, *Il Pomo d'oro*, and the choruses and songs from a few plays by Martin Opitz, Christian Weise, and Sigmund von Birken—one would have to postulate that, on the contrary, Stieler's musical texts received at least workman-like musical settings composed by someone with some musical training.

Among the possible composers is, of course, Stieler himself. His compositions for a few of his own songs in the *Geharnschte Venus* five years previously, although the work of a dilettante, are evidence of at least rudimentary musical training. Hans Engel, in his essay "Musik in Thüringen,"[88] has provided a picture of musical activity in Erfurt, Stieler's birthplace, which helps to explain how this son of a pharmacist from a long line of pharmacists could have acquired such training. He quotes a passage written by Michael Altenburg of Erfurt in 1620 describing Thuringia as a natural home of music and musicians:

> Man bedenke nur das, wie in allen Örtern die Musica in vollem Schwange gehet. — Ist doch bald kein Dörflein bevoraus in Thüringen, darinnen Musiker, beides vocalis und instrumentalis, nicht herrlich und zierlich den Örtern nach sollte florieren und wohl bestellt sein. (p. 207)

Altenburg goes on to praise "Musikpflege" in the schools of Erfurt. Engel offers other substantiating details for individual towns, including Erfurt, of which he notes (p. 225) that it was an important music publishing city already in the sixteenth century and that the "Ratsgymnasium" had a "chorus musicus" beginning in 1561. Another long established musical institution in Erfurt was the "Korrende," a boys choir for indigent children, who collected or earned money by singing. Professional musicians with official posts in the town, who could have offered musical training beyond the mere reading of music, included the "Stadtpfeifer" and "Stadtmusikanten" with salaries paid by the city, and the organists of the various churches. Johann Ambrosius Bach, the father of Johann Sebastian Bach, was one such member of Erfurt's "Ratskompanie" of musicians. Engel concludes his discussion of music in Thuringia with a comment that has perhaps special meaning for Caspar Stieler, lover of folklore, folk sayings, and dialect: "Das volkstümliche Lied und das Liedersingen sind in Thüringen zu Hause" (p. 266).

Kathi Meyer, in her essay on the music for *Die Geharnschte Venus*, was probably correct in her assessment that Stieler's level of training was merely that of a dilettante, for, in spite of the absence of anyone in the position of *Kapellmeister* upon his arrival in Rudolstadt, and in spite of the fact that he apparently served this function informally in 1665, when the musicians for the wedding festivities are listed with "1 Herr Cammersecretarius" at their head, as noted above, a need for a *Kapellmeister* was evidently perceived very soon thereafter. Apparently either the compositions for *Der Vermeinte Printz* and *Ernelinde* by Stieler or by some other member of the "pick-up" *Kapelle* (e.g., Johann Conrad Hammerschmidt, violinist and "Rentschreiber," perhaps a relation of the important composer Andreas Hammerschmidt, whose songs appear in Erlebach's catalogue of the collection of music books in the Rudolstadt library in 1700—see note 19) were found wanting; or Stieler, if he was the composer, found the task too arduous and time-consuming, given all his other duties. In any case, the new *Kapelldirector*, Wolf Ernst Roth (or Rothe) apparently arrived in Rudolstadt no later than the fall of 1666, and possibly soon after the wedding in 1665.[89] For the Rudolstadt plays after *Der Vermeinte Printz* and *Ernelinde* Roth is indeed the likely composer.

Roth, musician in the *Hofkapelle* in Dresden in 1657 and composer of a collection published there in 1660, according to Eitner,[90] has eighteen spiritual songs under his name listed in Erlebach's catalogue of the Rudolstadt musical manuscript collection.[91] Few of his compositions survive. One of them, published by Kinkeldey (p. xii), is actually a setting for five voices of a Stieler *Trauerode* of 1681 (as Höfer pointed out)[92]—an indication that Stieler, who was at the time no longer in residence at Rudolstadt (nor was Roth, who had retired in 1676), had found him a congenial composer to whom he still wished to entrust his verses. Kinkeldey offers an analysis of Roth's abilities: "Sie (die Ode) zeigt ihn als wirklich interessanten Harmoniker, und wenn auch die melodische Erfindung am Anfang nicht hervorragend erscheint, so ist doch der zuversichtliche Aufschwung der Melodie am Schluß im Anschluß an den Text und die Behandlung der ganzen Stelle als ein durchaus künstlerischer Einfall zu bezeichnen" (p. xii).

Another musician whose name has been suggested in this context—and even falsely connected with the texts, as noted above—is Georg Bleyer. As Höfer has shown, however, Bleyer cannot be considered a possible composer for any of the plays of 1665 or 1666, since he was not yet in Rudolstadt, but he could possibly have provided the score for the last two, which Stieler may have sent from Eisenach where he was then established.[93] Bleyer was a jealous and paranoid young man, as Höfer has shown, whose temper often led to altercations with other members of the court in Rudolstadt, but whose talents (or whose plight) appealed enough to the royal family in Rudolstadt that they continued to give him "second" chances until around 1678. His compositions of spiritual songs in Erlebach's catalogue number some 154. Hired as "Kammerschreiber," obviously an inferior replacement for the departing "Cammersecretarius" Stieler, Bleyer was allocated only a small part of Stieler's responsibilities and income. Never satisfied with this position, he always worked to be accepted as a musician and, above all, to become *Kapelldirektor* in Rudolstadt—a goal he was never able to achieve.

After his move to Eisenach in late 1666, Stieler could have continued to rely on Wolf Ernst Roth for compositions for both his musical dramas (the two Rudolstadt plays of 1667 and *Melissa*) and his poetry, as Roth's setting of the *Trauerode* of 1681, discussed above, would tend to imply. But he would also have come in contact with some local composers—for instance, Johann Christoph Bach, organist of an Eisenach church beginning in 1665, who also is known to have participated in the *Hofkapelle* and thought to have composed music for the court.[94] The music for Stieler's plays of 1680 and those he directed and for which he provided musical interludes in 1684 could well have been provided by Johann Samuel Drese, court organist in Jena until 1683 (Stieler spent the years 1678 to 1680 in Jena)[95] and thereafter *Kapelldirektor* in Weimar (Stieler arrived at his new position in Weimar in 1680).[96] Drese, according to Engel, was indeed responsible for music and performance of "musikdramatischen Aufführungen" with texts written by court poets Georg Neumark and Caspar Stieler.[97]

But even if some other composer or composers wrote the musical settings for the plays, in Rudolstadt and, later, in Eisenach and Weimar, Stieler's knowledge of music was still evident in his abilities as a versifier of eminently singable lyrics. The variety and virtuosity of his prosody, the light and flowing madrigal verses without a trace of the ponderous rhetorical bombast of the Alexandrine, must have provided a pleasant challenge for a composer. For Stieler, beginning already with his *Geharnschte Venus*, verse implies and demands musical settings— compositions which, in the absence of a composer, he was willing to, and capable of, undertaking himself. Even without surviving scores, the texts of his *Singspiele*, *Singende Zwischenspiele*, and imbedded songs make Stieler an important figure in the evolution of the early German *Singspiel* and opera.

8

Ways and Means: The Comedic Tools

Stieler's Poetic Language

Caspar Stieler, a dramatist whose style has aroused the scorn even of those scholars who have devoted a great deal of effort to the study of his dramatic works, and Caspar Stieler, the avid collector of words, enthusiastic purveyor of stylistic excellence, and active member of the *Fruchtbringende Sprachgesellschaft*, would hardly seem to be one and the same man. The time for another challenge to his authorship of the Rudolstadt and Weimar plays ascribed to him by Conrad Höfer has passed; the task at hand is to show that previous criticisms of Stieler's use of language in his plays were, like many pronouncements of "positivist" scholars, judgments based rather on modern taste than on success according to the intentions of the author and within the aesthetic of his own times. The attempt will be made here to offer a more objective description and analysis of the phenomenon of Stieler's language.

Höfer has noted that Stieler's language in his dramas exhibits characteristics of various standardized styles of his times in addition to the language of daily life: the style of pathos of the English Comedians, the mannered or Marinistic style of the Silesian poets, and the language of the courts as disseminated by the chancelleries (*Kanzleisprache*).[98] Although Höfer mentions the social class of the speakers of the "language of everyday life" and *Kanzleisprache* in Stieler's plays, he does not make the rather obvious connection to Opitz's social hierarchy of dramatic style in his *Buch von der Deutschen Poeterey*.[99] Stieler himself advises such appropriateness in his *Die Dichtkunst des Spaten (1685)*:[100]

> . . . . Sonst ist der Kunst zu wieder,
> wenn Skaramutzens Ernst sich einem Statsmann gleicht,
> der Vater seinem Sohn an Raht und Klugheit weicht.
> Der Jüngling als ein Greis, ein Greis wie jener redet,
> ein Kriegsheld in Gefahr verblaßet und verblödet.
> Es sey denn, daß es so erfordre das Gedicht,
> daß auserordendlich wer anders spielt und spricht,
> als Stand und Alter will.

In fact, Stieler's variety of styles, which might be disturbing in narrative fiction, is appropriate to Opitzian drama, in which each character is to speak using his or her proper stylistic level. The speech of everyday life, praised so highly by Höfer and Hinck, while fitting when used by servants and clowns, would be jarringly unsuitable if used by a princess or duchess.[101] But Höfer's list is actually a mixture of stylistic levels and stylistic influences, and most of his criticism is directed at the artificiality and stiffness he perceives in all styles other than that of "everyday life." Höfer, a child of his own times, idealizes naturalistic language (dialect, folk elements, simplicity) as the only natural language. He does not recognize that placing such language on stage is as much a schema or artificial mode for the representation of reality as is use of a pathetic or mannered style. And it is even questionable whether the "ordinary speech" of kings and queens was so different from the language Stieler places in their mouths in his plays; after all, in a century when "All the world's a stage/ And all the men and women merely players," self-stylization of expression to conform with notions of social or political role might be expected. In any case, it would hardly seem inappropriate to a seventeenth-century audience to hear such a stylized representation of discourse at court coming from the lips of characters who play the roles of rulers. After all, language on stage is public discourse, even if it represents private speech acts. Just as such an "unnatural" mode for the representation of human communication as opera could be accepted as illusionistic, or at least mimetic,[102] so, too, is every literary style, every fictional speech act, merely a schematic representation of reality. Höfer's implicit criticism of Stieler's admixture of "incompatible" styles would certainly find less of an echo today. Since Höfer seems to discern the most stylistic unnaturalness and stiffness in *Der Vermeinte Printz*, it is this text which will provide the material for an analysis here.

In the first act of *Der Vermeinte Printz*, among twenty-two scenes, six are in the low-life style which Höfer terms "everyday language," while ten exhibit the stiff formality of *Kanzleisprache* or a formal rhetorical tone. Eight scenes use a more natural but elevated form of discourse, and four show, in some speeches, use of Marinistic elements, or at least Petrarchistic imagery which makes no pretense at "naturalness." It is possible to make generalizations about the reasons underlying these stylistic choices.

The main sort of stilted style used in Stieler's works is characterized by typical constructions from the *Kanzlei*: "dahero," "dero," "seithero," "hinfüro," etc., as well as those slavish terms characteristically used by bureaucrats and courtiers towards royalty: "unterthänigst," "gnädig," "Ehrerbietigkeit." This style is used either in those scenes in which there exists a disparity of social class (normally between a member of the royal family and someone of lesser nobility or from the ranks of the advisers and bureaucrats), or in scenes in which the role of the speaker as king or "prince" is the primary mover of the dialogue. An example or two of each possibility will suffice to demonstrate this observation.

In the first scene, the "prince" converses with two royal advisers about the gender of a nude in a painting. The "prince's" claims, based on a lack of knowledge of her own true gender, are in the exaggerated language of pathos, a fitting stylistic indication of the depths of her emotional reaction, while the advisers, in their muddled attempts at sex education, utilize the formal language of the courtier. Nearly every statement made by these two gentlemen is accompanied by some honorific title for the "prince" they are addressing—"gnädigster Herr," "Eure Hoheit," "Durchlauchtigster Printz"—often used as the third-person subject of the sentence in order to avoid the direct address of peers which would be considered presumptuous toward their social superior. Their stilted style of speaking is an appropriate, and perhaps even realistically depicted, level of discourse designed to demonstrate the disparity in social class of the speakers from that of the person to whom they are speaking. Other scenes in which disparities in social class elicit this form of discourse are scenes ii (the advisers address the king), viii (Rosalve addresses the "prince"), x (Rosalve and Alphonsus address the "prince"), and xv (Alphonsus addresses the "prince"). Such discourse also occurs in briefer passages within scenes when such class distinctions come to the fore.

In all his appearances the king uses this style, obviously not to admit his inferiority, but rather to make it clear that he is speaking not as a father or as an individual with private problems, but solely in his role as king. This use of stilted language by the king is especially clear in scenes ii and iv. Zelide/Floridor uses it herself in scene viii when she pretends, in the role of prince, to woo Rosalve (Rosalve, as usual, responds using the same style in order to acknowledge her social inferiority). In this role-playing mode Zelide/Floridor intermingles elements from Marinistic style (especially Petrarchisms) to establish her identity as "lover," all in the service of perpetuating the deception about her true gender.

This other sort of stilted style, the rhetorical style of declarations of love, is otherwise primarily used in monologues which directly address the audience (Rosalve in vii, the Princess of Naples in vi, and Zelide/Floridor herself in xvii). "O fremde Gewalt und Handlung der Liebe!" exclaims the Countess Rosalve (p. 10), proclaiming her love for Alphonsus. And the Neapolitan Princess, in her disguise as Lirindus, issues an emotional rhetorical question energized by an exaggerated Petrarchistic image in order to announce her love for the assumed prince: "Was hilfft dich [!] nun/ arme Princessin/ daß dein Hertz/ in der nähe/ durch die Flammen der allerhellesten Augen verbrennet wird?" (p. 9). Zelide/Floridor uses a graphic mythological allusion to describe her plight as lover: "Was werde ich Betrübte/ doch endlich vornehmen? Die Liebe ist gleich jenem Adler/ der Hertz und Inngeweide mir lebendig zerzerret und verzehret" (p. 27).

A natural, but elevated stylistic tone, appropriate to the speaker's social class and to the occasion—he or she speaks with a social equal—occurs briefly in a number of scenes, including those in which "Floridor" speaks from her loving woman's heart (rather than from her roles as prince and male heir) to Alphonsus. And in both the scenes in which the two advisers, who had used stilted and obsequious speech to their "prince" and king, speak alone together, this elevated natural style of dialogue predominates; only when they touch on trivial bureaucratic matters, rather than those higher affairs of state, do they slip once again into the language of the chancelleries.

All of the scenes in which the comic characters appear are characterized by the coarse speech deemed natural or appropriate to the lowest social classes; even their masters who appear in these scenes seem to stoop to their level. At any rate, in this first act, a stilted or elevated style appears in only two instances in the midst of these scenes: Scaramutza pretends to be Pantalon's social better in scene xiii and, in this role-playing venture, uses the formal style of a courtier in order to convince Pantalon that he is a desirable bridegroom for his daughter; Alphonsus's letter to Rosalve ending their courtship, read aloud by its recipient in scene xviii, is couched in the formal style advised for all letters, even love letters, at the time.

Aside from the various levels of style apparent in Stieler's dramatic works, there are other characteristics of his style which merit examination. That most of these idiosyncrasies are to be found entirely or predominantly in the low-life scenes tends to support Höfer's claim[103] that it is Stieler's own everyday language that the dramatist puts in the mouth of his comic character, Scaramutza. Chief among these idiosyncratic usages, of course, is the use of dialect forms and local or student slang. Höfer has already identified many of these usages,[104] following in the footsteps of Köster's similar analysis of the language in his book on *Der Geharnschte Venus*;[105] a few typical examples are "löffeln" (*Studentensprache* for "buhlen"), "die rote Suppe" (slang for blood), "Läpsch" (Thuringian dialect for a stupid, lazy person). Höfer and Köster used such idiosyncrasies to place the pseudonymous author of the songs and plays in the Thuringian town of Erfurt in their successful efforts to identify him.

A healthy tone of folksiness lifts the low-life language of Stieler's fools above the merely coarse and eliminates any derisive attitude toward the language or its speakers. This tone is achieved through the liberal use of colorful oaths and curses, dozens of different terms of endearment and derision (*Kosenamen, Scheltnamen*), folk maxims, and other simple formulaic structures typical of such sayings and of riddles. In addition, Stieler seeks the sources for his own fresh metaphors in the low-life jargon of the craftsman and laborer, as well as in his own activities (writing, gambling, the theater).

Some of the curses (*Verwunschungen*) are merely colorful ways of saying "get lost" or "may you suffer for this" (for example, "Daß das Hoffleben were/ wo der Pfeffer wüchse" or "Da schlage Pulver und Bley zu"). But most, naturally enough, are euphemisms for blasphemous turns of phrase ("Potzschlapperpenk," "beim Schlapperbenck"—"curse the sacrament" or "by the sacrament"; "Potztausend"—"curse the devil," from the concept of the Devil as "Tausendkünstler"; "Deß dich . . . "—incomplete version of "daß dich der Teufel hole," found throughout the plays). Perhaps the most intriguing of these is the repeated use of curses having to do with "Velt" (Valentin). Four of the uses are oaths: "Potz Velten" (VP, p. 36), "vor allen Sanct Velten" (*Ernelinde*, p. 114), "Felsherget" (VeltsherrGott) (*Bellemperie*, p. 106), "vor alle velts Krankheit" (*Willmut*, p. 21). The fifth, reflecting on the sickness of which St. Valentin was the patron saint—epilepsy—is a curse modeled on the usually incomplete "daß dich . . . ": "daß euch die Felskrankheit" (*Basilene*, p. 50). Another is used as a euphemism for the Devil: "Wie nun zum Hencker/ hat Sankt Velten dich besessen" (*Floretto*, p. Gv).[106]

Sankt Velten—a short form of Sankt Valentin—is a euphemism for the Devil based on the similarity of the saint's name with the old German name "valant."[107] It was a popular appellation in curses, oaths, and exclamations, especially in Thuringia, where Valentin ranked with Ruprecht, Antonius, and Quirinus as one of the "vier Botschaften"—those patron saints of illnesses who, along with their respective diseases, were favorites in such expressions.[108] Valentin was connected with epilepsy—"Fallsucht"—traditionally, but also in folk etymologies, which saw a similarity to another name for the disease ("St. Veits Tanz") and to a common curse referring to it ("Valthin!"—fallt hin für Fallsucht).[109]

Scaramutza and other comic wooers use an amazing variety of often insulting endearments to the girls they are pursuing. They may refer to sexual promiscuity ("du Unterbettchen," "Bettschelmchen," "Schlaffgesellchen") or use female sexual organs, directly or metaphorically, as metonymy ("Britzschgen" or "Pritsche"; "Sack," "Säckgen," "Schlepsack"; "Klunte," "Klunkermutz"; "Hurenbalg," "Schandbalg"). Other insulting endearments incorporate curses ("Tausenthürchen," "Tausentschätzchen," "Diebesding," "Mordgesichtgen"). Many equate the girlfriends with animals or utilize animal imagery (pets: "Kammerkätzgen"; horses: "Mähre," "Haberstrohschlückerin"; and other farm animals: "Stiertzche"; small wild animals: "du arme Kröte," "ein Zeißgen," "die Fuchschwänzerin," "du stolzes Pfauenzägelchen"). Several use the imagery of garment materials: "mein Lepsch," "mein Hünerfleischgen." Young women are frequently referred to as "das Mensch" or "das Ding." These, like other endearments for young women, are quite often diminutive: "Dingelgen," "Dinglichen." Stieler's pervasive use of diminutives in comic scenes, in fact, is also an idiosyncrasy which makes his style readily identifiable.

The male characters around Scaramutza and his fellow clowns are the recipients of a staggering number of different insulting appellations. Many are scatological ("Plackscheisser," "du Unflath," "Neßler," "Matzpompe," "Misthämmel," "Garsthämmel," "Küh-Fladen"), while others are based on the imagery of unsavory eating ("du Breypeppe," "Lecker") or filthy animals ("Kröte," "Püffel," "Schandhengst," "Schmierflegel," "Schweinbeltz"). Many have to do with tradesmen and craftsmen or laborers who are objects of scorn: "Krämermatz," "Scheerenschleifer," "Schornsteinfeger," "Federschmucker," "Besenbinder," "Bürstenbinder," "Schuster." Some are even the insults of Stieler's own profession: "Blackscheußer," "Tintenklecker." Many equate the object of the insult with an unformed chunk of wood, dirt, stone, or metal: "Scheid," "Knoll," "der hölzene Pater noster," "Schleiffstein," "Stuckeysen," "Klotzsch," "unbehobelt Holtz," "Speiderling," "Schielen Dieb." Some use folk appellations with a long tradition: "mein Herr Urian," "Wurm Velten," "die alte(n) Susannenbrüder," "ein Plumprian," "der funffzehenhut," "das Hempelmänchen." The variety is endless: "Vögel," "Bluhte," "Pengel," "Reckel," "Schermotz," "Schlüffel," "Tropf," "Tuckmeuser," "Matzquinte," "Kasten."

The many references or allusions to card games (e.g., "das Gebetbuch," the slang term for cards; "Nu will ich hie König werden/ und du solst das nächste Schwein bey der Saue Seyn," card-playing jargon) and dice-throwing ("du tausent Eß"—Taus Eß—and "Mahl oder Unmahl") would tend to point to Stieler's own predilection for these activities, at least in his heedless youth. The imagery of public punishment and torture, not, one hopes, similarly a part of Stieler's personal experience, is likewise recurrent in most of the plays ("der Spanische Mantel oder der Französische Kehrbesen," "Staupbesen," "Staupenschlag," "steupen," "unausgesteupt").

One element of folklife that appears throughout Stieler's plays, although more frequently in the comic scenes, is the use of imbedded bits of folk wisdom: *volkstümliche Sprichwörter*. A typical sample would include both common and less widely spread sayings which have been recorded in exactly that form by Grimm or Wander:[110]

Alter hilft vor Tohrheit nicht.
Gut Ding will Weile haben.
Herrn Gunst erbet nicht.
Wer nicht selber kömt/ dem wird der Kopf nicht gewaschen.
Ein Narr macht ihr zehne.
Noht bricht Eisen.
Schweinsköpffe lassen sich nicht
                ohne Hundesköpffe erwerben.
Wormit man ümgeht/ das hänget einem an.

Stieler loves to offer only the first half or the key words of a well-known adage, leaving the audience to remember the rest:

> Es ist nur ein übergänglichen sagt der Fuchß
> 　　(da zog der Jäger ihm das Fell über die Ohren.)
> Das Hemd ist mir näher als der Rock
> 　　(das Fleisch aber näher als das Hemd.)
> Wer weiß/ wo Haase laufft
> 　　(sagte Hans, und legte sein Garn auf dem Dache aus.)
> Fette Suppen/ und hohe Sprünge
> 　　("Es sind gute bissen zu Hofe, aber man
> 　　muss hohe Sprünge danach tun.")

Elsewhere, he alters common sayings or mixes up several. The effect is a humorous sense of incongruity:

> Es sol auch einem Stein geoffenbahret seyn.
> 　　("Es möchte einen Stein erbarmen.")
> Der blinde schlug den Lahmen.
> 　　("Der Blinde trägt den Lahmen.")

Frequently he rephrases adages to fit his context or offers variations on the "standard" version which may be regional rather than esoteric variants:

> Der Baum fällt nicht auff den ersten Streich.
> Glück heget Neid.
> Gnade/ Gnade: darvon ist meines Nachbars Katze gestor-
> 　　ben. ("Vor lauter Gnade stirbt die Katze Hungers.")
> Noht lernet Brot suchen. ("Noth sucht Brot.")

At times these maxims seem to guide wise choices by the characters or to explain motives or events; but usually they become as ridiculous as Polonius's advice to his children in Shakespeare's *Hamlet*:[111] these simple and traditional formulations of wisdom have become laughable clichés. The incongruous variants of well-known adages provide an even more overt source of humor in the plays. Hugo Beck has noted the important place of *Sprichwörter* in the comedies of the sixteenth century,[112] and it is clear that they remain, in the comedies of Stieler, central to the comedic function. Harsdörffer in his *Poetischer Trichter* called *Sentenzen* "des Trauerspiels Grundseulen."[113] We might add that popular *Sprichwörter*, at least for Stieler, could well be termed the pilasters of the comedy, since, like pilasters, their structural importance is more apparent than real.

　　Related to the maxims, many of which use rhyme and/or rhythm, is Stieler's (usually Scaramutza's) tendency in some scenes to speak in this mode. In *Basilene*, for example, where this predilection is most pervasive, Scaramutza rhymes: "Jungfer Melindgen/ mein Kindgen" (p. 17); "Gelt Labellchen mein Bettschelmchen" (p. 33); "Labelchen soll auch werden mein Schlaffgesellchen. Gelt du Rabenäßchen" (p. 76); "Komm her mein Gold-Engelchen (küsset sie/ und sie giebt ihme eine Ohrfeige) das sind lauter LiebsSchlägelchen" (p. 73). He loves pairs of rhyming words ("sie lechtzet und krechtzet," p. 53; "Ich mag ihr Kister oder ihr Magister seyn," p. 5; "da ists alles fix oder nix," p. 49). He offers pseudo-ritualistic gobbledegook for the religious ceremony honoring Diana: "oculus paroculus ein Schnabel ist kein Ziegenfuß" (p. 49). These tendencies are also notable in the speeches of the comic characters in *Die Wittekinden* and *Melissa*, where rhythm and rhyme are, of course, necessary for the versification.

Stieler's Use of Classical Antiquity

"Sie ist vom Proteus nicht gemacht; Fidias hat sie aus einem Stück Felsen gebildet," laments Filidor, speaking of the hardhearted Basilene (*Basilene*, p. 12). "Hier ist die vermummte Lais," exclaims Lirindus/Orgille of Alphonsus/Clarice in *Der Vermeinte Printz* (p. 48). These are but two examples of the numerous uses Caspar Stieler makes of his apparently vast education in the classics. Along with the more obvious references to the Greco-Roman pantheon and minor deities whose names had become metaphorical by the mid-seventeenth century, Stieler employs a host of less frequently encountered figures and stories from mythology and from Roman literature in the writing of his plays. His usages take the form of classical settings for several plays, entire masques based on classical myths, a heavenly frame for the earthly events (prologues, epilogues, *Zwischenspiele*), and casual references used (as in the two examples above) as metaphor or analogy. Zeman demonstrates a similar breadth in Stieler's *Dichtkunst* with his "Anmerkungen,"[114] primarily a list of classical allusions explained for the benefit of us latter-day scholars no longer having the advantage of Stieler's classical education.

Two of the plays—the two pastorals—are set in classical antiquity, and the characters are shown participating in the bucolic world of the Roman idyll as they worship the Greco-Roman deities quite literally. In *Basilene*, the temple and the demands of the goddess Diana form the centerpiece of the play; she provides both the complications and barriers of true love and the solution to the problems. She and her brother Apollo are constantly referred to and called upon in the play with a variety of nomenclature (modeled on such classical forerunners as Virgil's usages in the *Aeneid*) that stamps itself both as knowledgeable about antique practices and as a neo-classical attempt at imitation of classical literary forms (Zyntia and Zynthus for Diana and Apollo, Ammon for Jupiter, etc.). The names chosen in this play for the characters, other than those of the protagonists Filidor and Basilene, are taken from mythology and bucolic poetry, just as they are in *Melissa*, Stieler's other pastoral play. In *Melissa* the antique gods Mercury and Amor actually appear on stage as characters alongside their human counterparts; in *Floretto* Apollo speaks to the protagonist directly.

Stieler was responsible for four masques of various lengths based on classical mythology: the essentially autonomous *Zwischenspiel* to *Der betrogene Betrug* (the story of Danaë and the Golden Rain), the full-length opera libretto *Der göldene Apfel* which he translated from the Italian, and the two short masques Stieler provided to accompany the performances he produced in Weimar in 1684. It is in these masques that his vast knowledge of classical antiquity and Roman literature has the opportunity to exhibit itself most fully. The names of the chief gods and goddesses multiply: Jupiter is also Ammon, Diespiter, Zeus, "der Pol," "der alte Nascher mit der Glitze"; Juno (Iunon) is also "die Zyginnen" and "die Saturinnen"; Venus is Dione, "die Liebinne," "die Pafirene," Zypripor, "die Göttin der Gniden," and Zytehre; Diana is Pythia, Zyntie, "die keusche Föbe"; Apollo is Zyntius and Föbus; the muses are "Zyntiens Chor" and Pierinnen; Mercury is Zillenius and "Flügeldiener"; Pallas Athena is Tritoninne; Mars is Gradivus and Mavvors. Even mythological human beings rate a variety of names: Danaë is also "Tochter des Abanten" and Akrisinnen. Stieler likewise takes advantage of the opportunity to show off his detailed knowledge of the myths of Troy, the geography of the real classical world and of its mythological realms, the history of Athens and other classical states, and Roman literary figures. He can allude to a host of minor divinities and the mortals who were caught in their toils, either as personages at the edge of his story or as metaphors for the elements or qualities they traditionally represent (e.g., "Tehtis Schoß" for sea). In these masques the gods and goddesses, accompanied by a few heroic mortals, are the protagonists, so that it is hardly surprising to find a wealth of classical material here.

In most of his plays classical personages, usually gods and goddesses, also figure centrally in the framework of prologue, epilogue, and *Zwischenspiele*, thus providing a "divine" backdrop for events on the human plane. This usage is most notable in *Der Vermeinte Printz* and in the prologue of *Melissa*, but is also present in *Willmut* (Herkules as prologue, Mercury as epilogue), *Basilene* (Mars as prologue, Irene as epilogue), *Ernelinde* (Lucina and Echo as epilogue), *Die Wittekinden* (choruses of the Fates and the Furies), *Bellemperie* (choruses).

Aside from the *Zwischenspiele* to *Der betrogene Betrug*, the most complete example of a frame set in Greco-Roman mythology is formed by the *Zwischenspiele* of *Der Vermeinte Printz*. The gods are concerned about the human events about to unfold on stage and try to provide solutions. In the prologue Jupiter, in the name of *Staatsraison*, orders Vertumnus, god of shape-shifting, to help the deception in which Orimantes has caused his daughter Zelide to participate by causing a total confusion of gender at court. In the choruses between the acts Amor and Venus begin their counterplot: love will cause the deceptions to founder but will also provide the solution to the problems which brought on deception in the first place; Amor manages to drive out Vertumnus and his tricks. In the concluding chorus Hymen and the other gods unite to bless the unions and resolutions brought about by love. It is clear that in this example the gods are merely personifications of qualitites usually associated with them, not deities in their own right, as in the masques, nor symbols of Christian providence, as in some other usages of the period (notably allegorizations of Ovid's *Metamorphoses* and its contents, as in the "Programma Poeticum" appended to Birken's *Teutsche Rede-Bind- und Dicht-Kunst*).[115] The use of Venus and Juno in the prologue to *Melissa*, on the other hand, seems to resemble more closely the usage in the masques in which the classical deities are characters in the plot, and the fact that Cupido and Merkur appear bodily in the dramatic action tends to support linking this short play to the masque genre. Indeed, the intersecting of the plot on the human level with that of the concerns of the divinities in *Melissa* closely resembles that of the fickle shepherd Paris and his beloved Enno in *Der göldene Apfel*, translated by Stieler the following year.

Nearly all the plays employ at least a few casual classical allusions as part of the language, primarily in the scenes exhibiting what Höfer termed the Marinistic type of elevated style. But most are indeed confined to the *Zwischenspiele* except in *Basilene*, *Melissa*, and the courtly masques. In *Die Wittekinden* the pagan children are depicted worshipping the Greco-Roman deities and, before their conversion to Christianity, foolishly attributing events to them instead of to God. Many allusions in the masques, *Zwischenspiele*, and pastorals are exemplary stories from Greco-Roman mythology used as analogies to some present situation: Apollo and Python; Herse's love for Mercury and Diana's for Endymion; and the eternal punishments of Sisyphus, Tityos, and Ixion, for example.

The sources for Stieler's knowledge of classical antiquity and its myths are to be found primarily in the ancient Roman literary works which made up the Latin language curriculum of the time: Virgil's *Aeneid* and "Eclogues," the "Epistles" and "Satires" of Horace, Ovid's *Metamorphoses*, and the orations of Cicero. These same sources also provide Stieler with a fund of famous passages which he can have Scaramutza torture and parody in his execrable Latin (e.g., "steteruntque comae et vox faucibus haesit," *Basilene*, p. 28; *Aeneid* 2, 774 and 3, 48). Indeed, since many of Scaramutza's shorter Latinisms are school Latin (e.g., "Bonus Vesper"), not classical Latin at all, one wonders whether Stieler might not also have had as one of his duties at Rudolstadt the instruction of young nobles in Latin as well as German. A quotation from an imaginary letter from Cicero to Planco Brundisio Scipioni (VP, p. 69), probably a model passage in a Latin textbook or the result of a schoolboy's assignment, would tend to support this contention. In all the classical materials and names used by Stieler in his plays, aside from a great deal of freedom of orthography, I have discovered only one unintentional mistake: Zelotes for Zelos (*Bellemperie*, p. 183).[116] Scaramutza, of course, makes mincemeat of every allusion (e.g., he takes "Bucephalus," the horse of Alexander the Great, for a hero, *Willmut*, p. 64), and each incident offers fresh evidence of his empty pretensions to the learning of his creator.

Humor

The Rudolstadt plays are all identified as "Lustspiel" or "Mischspiel" by their author, and the comic characters and their comic scenes appear in the midst even of the grisly tragedy *Bellemperie* and of the most ominous events in the others. The humor provided by the comedies and by the comic scenes in the serious plays consists of two major types: situational and verbal.

Situational humor includes all sorts of non-verbal actions and gestures which arouse laughter, as well as ridiculous dilemmas and mistaken identities. The most obvious form of "physical" humor is undoubtedly slapstick: characters come to blows, stumble over obstacles and fall down, are dragged off to jail. Related to slapstick are the actions of characters who have eaten or drunk too much or who need to relieve themselves (the visual side of alimentary-tract humor). Scaramutza and his friends and relations are the usual carriers of slapstick humor, but their scenes involve their masters (especially if they are villains, like Pancalier in *Die erfreuete Unschuld* or Burkhard in *Die Wittekinden*) or mistresses. It is in fact typical of Stieler's plays that women are more likely to strike Scaramutza than his male masters. Stieler usually provides stage directions to indicate blows, stumbles, or falls, although occasionally they are obvious enough in the text that stage directions can be omitted.

But situational humor is not limited in the comedies to the comic scenes or characters. There are two main types of situational humor offered by the plot and main characters (from royalty and the upper nobility) themselves: dramatic irony and mistaken identity. The members of the audience in Stieler's comedies of intrigue (VP, BB, EU) are in on the deceptions which will punish the villains, preserve the honor of the protagonist, or bring true lovers together. This dramatic irony in the comic mode (the audience foresees the happy instead of the catastrophic outcome before the characters do) can evoke amusement at the blind and ultimately futile actions of the antagonists or other characters.

The humor of mistaken identity also often depends on dramatic irony—the audience shares knowledge of the truth with the disguised character. Ferdinand doesn't recognize his wife in the drab chaperone of the girl he is now courting (BB); Eleonora fails to understand the significance of her ring on Mendoza's finger (EU); the loves of Ernelinde (*Ernelinde*) and Floridor-Zelide (VP) for their social inferiors only seem hopeless—the audience knows Ferramond and Alphonsus are actually princes of royal birth who have come in disguise to court.

In *Ernelinde* mistaken identity involves presumed incidents of near incest—the protagonist nearly marries in turn her father, her assumed twin brother, and her actual twin brother, all because the twin children of the queen-mother and her stepson were given to others to raise. There is no question here of dramatic irony—the audience is no more aware than the unfortunate king and his daughter of the facts of the matter. Instead the close brushes with incest themselves seem to be the source of laughter, perhaps a sort of nervous release of anxiety. The predicament which resulted in horror and catastrophe in *Oedipus* has here become ridiculous.

In *Der Vermeinte Printz* mistaken identity is mistaken gender. Prince Floridor is really the Princess Zelide—as the audience is well aware after I, iii—and "his" wooing of the Countess Rosalve is thus reduced to a travesty of courtship. Princess Orgille of Naples has come to court disguised as a man, Lirindus, in order to woo the "prince"; her jealousy of Alphonsus, whom she likewise assumes to be a woman pursuing the assumed prince, brings about the dressing of this unfortunate prince in woman's clothes and in his removal to the women's wing of the palace. The king, hearing his "son" accused of dallying with "Clarice" (Alphonsus), is horrified to think that his daughter may be a lesbian. The issue of mistaken gender opens the play, as discussed above, when in the first scene the naive "prince" mistakes a nude female figure in a painting for a male, much to the concern of "his" advisers.

Scaramutza participates in the humor of mistaken identity by feigning an inability to recognize his masters or mistresses and others. In *Die erfreuete Unschuld* and *Die Wittekinden*, for example, he pretends not to know Pantalon; in *Der Vermeinte Printz* he claims to have been much deceived by his "mistress" Clarice (Alphonsus)—whom he knows perfectly well to be male; and in *Der betrogene Betrug* he teases Victoria by treating her like the lady's companion (a glorified servant) she is pretending to be.

Verbal humor is usually tied to Scaramutza and other specifically comic characters, although the butt of the joke is frequently one of the protagonists or the villain of the piece. Some of the various types of verbal humor correspond to the different sorts of situational humor: verbal slapstick (all the name-calling and insults), verbal mistakes and misunderstandings, the risqué or scatological content of overt speech and double entendre.

Although Scaramutza cannot quite rival Shakespeare's Falstaff for the fluency of his curses and insults, he is both inventive and talented in his frequent attempts. In *Basilene* he calls the satyr who attacks Labelle "du Stinckböckigter alter Schelm" (p. 32) and the witch Empuse "der alten eineugichten einfüssigten blitz-schweffel Hexen" (p. 28) or "Die alte Drachen Hure," "die schelm-ische Gabelfahrerin," and "dem alten Hellen Riegel" (p. 18). The language of his insulting appellations and curses was discussed above.

Verbal mistakes and misunderstandings make up a large pro-portion of Scaramutza's humorous language. He is the master of the malapropism, especially when he attempts to use Latin or French. In some instances he seems to make glaring mistakes on purpose, in order to twit the stupidity of someone else ("Fraudu-lenz" for "Audienz bei einer Frau," *Willmut*, p. 34; "Fraudulenz" means "Betrüglichkeit"); in others, he seems himself to have an incomplete knowledge ("Gallerte"—gelatin—for gallery or balcony in a theater; "Du bist nur ein spectaculum und ein auditorium," *Bellemperie*, p. 160—he means spectator and auditor). But in either case, the results can be hilarious. Often the malapropism means the opposite of what he apparently intends to say, as when he uses "Despect" ("Verachtung") when he means "Respect" (*Die Wittekinden*, p. 87). Sometimes he has misquoted some classical author or religious Latin in order to fit his own intentions ("Ego sum omnia tresq; id est. Hahn im Korbe und Hans in allen gassen," EU, p. 19; "Humores mutant rores," from "Honores mutant mores," *Willmut*, p. 43). At times he uses inappropriate Latin adages: in *Basilene* he means "good things come in threes" when he states "Nulla calamitas sola" (p. 29). The little bit of badly pro-nounced French he has picked up and which he uses in his assumption of the cavalier role in *Bellemperie* (p. 158) not only shows misunderstandings of the language fragments, but also an incongruity—in the midst of phrases culled perhaps from a book of basic French expressions for travellers, there lurks a coarse insult: "bäse moäle kü" ("baisez-moi le cul"). And like any elementary pupil of Latin, he sprinkles his schoolboy phrases into his everyday speech in order to show off: "exempli gratia," "sed heus," "Bonus vesper," "inquam," "ut pote." Several phrases of macaroni Latin are undoubtedly remnants of Stieler's own student days: "Ecce ad nagelum usque" (VP, p. 33) for "bis auf die Nägel (des Trinkgefäßes) trinken"; "gassaten gehen" for girl-watching. The use of Latin or French phrases by Scaramutza is often a sign of a pretentiousness which the other characters and the audience would have taken as ridiculous.

Scaramutza often misunderstands (usually on purpose) the words and instructions of others, as when he nearly gives away the secret of Eleonor's identity several times in *Der betrogene Betrug*, or when he is ordered to stand guard in *Der Vermeinte Printz* (II, i). In *Bellemperie* one whole scene is devoted to his witty twisting of Gillette's words into meanings she had not intended (I, iv). She admiringly protests: "Nun/ ich hätte nicht gedacht/ daß ihr so klug wäret/ Skaramutza/ wie ihr einen [!] die Worte im Maule verdrehet," and he replies—to her and to the audience: "Ja/ du tausent Eß/ kennst mich noch nicht recht" (p. 29), a good answer to Höfer's assumption that he is stupid, as much as to hers. Elsewhere in *Bellemperie* he misunderstands "Türkische Kleider" as "Tückische Kleider" (p. 58). Often his teasing misunderstandings twist the unwitting speaker's words into scatological or sexual meanings (e.g., *Bellemperie*, I, iv); the girls he woos are often equally adept at twisting his sexual innuendos into innocent and innocuous terms (e.g., BB I, iv and II, v).

A chief source of verbal humor in the plays—sexual double entendres and puns—is not nearly so pervasive in works by other authors of the time in Germany, although one can find a few in comedies by Gryphius. While German slang was in the seventeenth century, and remains to some extent today, permeated with figurative language used euphemistically for sexual matters, there seems to be no reference source concerning historical use of sexual puns.[117] English-language *Germanistik* has perhaps the advantage of studies on puns in Shakespeare, among others, and such dictionaries of sexual puns as Partridge's *Shakespeare's Bawdy*.[118] It is amazing how many of the puns listed in that work for Elizabethan English apply equally well to counterparts in seventeenth-century German.

The best extended sexual pun in Stieler's dramas—and one which finds echoes in his other works as well—is that on "Ehre" as a euphemism for virginity or the virginal sexual organ of a girl. This pun extends through two of Scaramutza's scenes in *Basilene*

(II, iii and iv). Labelle thanks Scaramutza for beating and chasing off a satyr who has attempted to assault her sexually: "habt dank mein lieber Scaramutza . . . der alte Bock hette mir doch meine Ehre genommen/ wenn ihr nicht gleich da weret gewesen . . . weil ihr es so treulich mit mir meinet/ und mir mein Ehre erhalten habt/ so will ich auch nun nicht von euch lassen." Scaramutza now begins his verbal assault on her "honor": "Ey mit dem Lumpen Ehren: gib du mir deine/ so will ich dir meine geben/ so verliert keines nichts. Meinstu nicht/ daß meine Ehre so gut ist als deine?" She replies that, once lost, "Ehre" is gone forever. He answers by asking her where she keeps it: "Wo hastu denn deine Ehre/ weise sie doch her/ daß ich sehe/ ob sie schön oder heßlich ist." She chooses to misunderstand him, but by this time the audience will surely take her comments according to Scaramutza's meaning when she claims: "Die Ehre ist das gröste Kleinod bey den Weibs-bildern." In the following scene the pun continues. After terming his master, the priest Theofred, "Eure Ehrwürde," the discussion begins once again. Theofred wishes to know if Scaramutza had robbed Labelle of her "Ehren." Scaramutza replies, "wir haben . . . untereinander von der Ehre geredt/ es ist aber nichts draus wor-den." Theofred and Scaramutza then reuse the word "Ehre" or the phrase "in Unehren" as an extension of the pun another five times in the scene. The term "Ehrengriffgen," meaning a caress, appears several other times in the plays, and, as Höfer has pointed out,[119] Stieler has an entire poem devoted to it in *Die Geharnschte Venus*.

Scaramutza and the other comic characters are not the only purveyors of sexual double entendres, although other characters may not be using them consciously (I cannot doubt, however, that Stieler is). One example from the highest echelons of the social hierarchy in Stieler's plays should suffice. In the first scene of *Der Vermeinte Printz*, in which Zelide/Floridor disputes with the advisers about the gender of the nude Andromeda in a painting, two hilarious puns appear. When the "prince" insists that the body, which, as only she knows, resembles her own, is male, as she then believes herself to be, one bemused adviser tries subtlety: "Es fehlet noch üm ein merckliches/ gnädigster Herr/ daß es kein Mannsbild ist." And in case the audience didn't catch the pun, the "prince's" answering puzzlement—taking "ein merckliches" as some sort of physically visible attribute—will elicit the desired uproarious laughter: "Und woran? an dem Barte? Habe ich doch auch keinen." The pun on the lack of the proof of virility continues when the other adviser, in exasperation, declares: "Die Warheit ist Handgreifflich." It is possible that, as with Shakespeare, it was necessary in this scene, and in many others, to use stage business and the language of gesture to make the double meanings clear.

Sexual innuendo provides one sort of verbal humor, and the lack of euphemisms or the uncouth mentioning of sexual or scatological matters in front of ladies of high rank offers yet another. Scaramutza's and Pantalon's discussion of Brechta's desires for the Black Knight embarrasses her, but prompts laughter in the audience (*Die Wittekinden*, I, xii); Scaramutza's expressed wish to peek at Gillette as she uses a chamber pot brings a sharp reprimand from her and laughter from the audience in *Bellemperie*, I, iv. In one scene (*Basilene*, I, vii) he actually flirts openly with the women in the audience and discusses the events of the marriage bed with them—half the members of the audience thus become the embarrassed butt of his jokes.

Perhaps the most delightful form Stieler's humor takes in his plays is self-referential, either playing on his own name or profession(s), or on those of his alter ego, Scaramutza. Such self-referentiality is by no means limited to the plays. Köster pointed out the acrostichon and anagram in *Die Geharnschte Venus*;[120] one should also be aware of the definition offered for "Stieler" in our author's pseudonymously published *Der Teutschen Sprachschatz Stammbaum und Fortwachs*:

Stieler/ der/ manubriorum et capulorum artifex, it. petiororum creator. Der erste Stieler ist GOtt gewesen/ qui omnium primus petiolos produxerit, Deus ipse suit. Stieler/ stilerus, nomen est gentilitium compilatoris praesentis onomastici, cognominato Serotinus, der Spate.[121]

To the hero of *Basilene* he has given his own pen name of the period, Filidor—a circumstance which the audience would probably have taken as more humorous than pretentious. In his production of *Krieg und Sieg der Keuschheit* in 1684 he likewise gives this same pen name to the main character. In the plays it is not clear whether there are puns on his real name, although "Caspar," as a folk-name for the Devil, appears in *Willmut*, p. 34, and Stieler once uses the idiom "mit Strumpf und Stiel außrotten" in *Basilene*, p. 37. References to brooms, broommakers, and brushmakers—although never overtly connected with the terms "Stiel" or "Stieler"—abound, and make up an image cluster in their own right.

More obvious and certainly intentional are the references in the plays to secretaries. One of the young men loved by a heroine—Ferramond in *Ernelinde*—is made her secretary, a position from which he rises to first place in her heart and a high rank in the land. In *Die erfreuete Unschuld* (I, viii), the hopes for analogous advancement from Stieler's own post (a real possibility—the secretary who followed him at Eisenach rose soon thereafter to the post of minister) are expressed, with a good deal of self-irony, in Scaramutza's social satire of upward mobility. Of the examples of persons whose pretensions place them above their actual station, the series containing the *secretarius* is the most ambitious and thus, in the seventeenth-century social context, the most ridiculous: "Ein Schreiber wil ein Secretarius: ein Secretarius, ein Raht: ein Raht/ ein Cantzler: ein Cantzler der Fürst (seyn)" (p. 19). In other passages, Scaramutza aspires to that "high" post of secretary, referring to it as a position of great honor and high social status (*Die Wittekinden*, I, v; *Willmut*, p. 49). Elsewhere, Pantalon indicates his belief that the title is not far beneath the status of nobleman: "Ich hätte gemeinet/ es solte zum wenigsten ein *Secretarius*, oder ein Schösser mein Eydam werden/ wenn es ja kein Edelman hätte seyn können" (VP, I, xxii, p. 36); he regrets that Scaramutza is not a secretary. In *Die Wittekinden* (I, v) Scaramutza claims to be a sort of secretary ("So hör/ ich bin bald/ wie ein Secretar, Bey unsern Herren General," p. 8), whereas in *Willmut* he denies being any such thing, and does so with the entire catalogue of sarcastic appellations. Asked about some letters which had passed between the prince and Scheinguda, Scaramutza answers: "das müssen die Plackscheisser die *Secretarien* wissen. Und worvor sehet ihr mich denn an? meint ihr wohl/ daß ich so ein Schmierflegel und Dintenklecker sey?" Such claims and denials would be particularly humorous if Stieler himself played the role of Scaramutza. And similarly, Scaramutza's finale in *Willmut* (p. 144) would be all the more hilarious if the secretary Stieler played the part of the character who told the audience to hurry up and leave, since the secretaries, who were all now in the comedy, were needed to write the letters about the events in the play before the replies could be received and the ultimate outcome reported to the audience. This speech, which effectively merges the realities of the play and the audience, would be all the more powerful from the lips of the secretary who wrote the play. One reference in *Die Wittekinden* (p. 17) even makes Stieler's professional territory, the chancellery, a spot for hanky-panky and seduction. Scaramutza, teasing Pantalon with veiled claims that he had seduced Blonje, tells him to seek her and other girls

> . . . dar
> wor Keyser Karl zu Fuß' hingehet/
> Beym Herren *Secretar*.
> Ich mein' in jener Kantzeley/
> Wo man die Pässe pflegt zu siegeln/
> Wüst' ichs/ die Tühr wolt' ich verriegeln/
> Und kein'/ ohn einem derben Schmauß/
> Nicht lassen aus.

The armoured Venus of Stieler's wartime years has become an inkstained Venus, but she is still at home wherever the amorous poet carries out his professional duties. Two further references to Stieler's profession as secretary ridicule the lowly duties to which the professional in that beleaguered position had to stoop— Scaramutza has had "den besten Secretarius am Hofe" write him a speech for the well-wishers at his wedding (VP, III, xii) and has had "den Herrn Kapelldirektor" (Stieler's duties at Rudolstadt seemed to have included this post)[122] compose a love song for his sweetheart (EU, III, iv). Stieler may also be satirizing his own duties in *Die Wittekinden* in the figure of the occasional poet Michele, whose muse serves a journalistic function.[123]

As one might expect, references to the name "Scaramutza" provide a rich source of verbal humor. In *Willmut* (II, x) Scaramutza pretends to misunderstand his name as the insulting appellation "Schermotz" when Scheinguda calls to him, whereupon he takes the opportunity to abuse her verbally in turn: "Du magst wol selber ein Schermotz seyn. Wer ist der Narr/ der so schreyet?" (p. 93). In *Basilene* (I, i) he gratuitously offers the information on how to decline his name, as if it were a feminine Latin noun: "Dominam Scaramutzam (juxta regulam a primae declinationis)" (p. 6). The name is also used as a term for Cupid on the following page: "das kleine Scaramützgen/ den blinden Cupido."

Elsewhere "Scaramutza" is used as a general term for the fool in a comedy (BB, p. 57) or for the funny servant who must accompany every master: "Ihr Gnaden/ wenn ihr in Franckreich zu dem Hertzog reitet/ so bitte ich untertähnig üm die Stadthalterschafft. Ich will schon einen andern Scaramutzen kriegen/ der an meiner Stelle/ eben so ein guter Scaramutza als ich bin/ seyn soll" (EU, II, p. 28).

The generic term for Scaramutza, "Narr," is used ubiquitously in the plays as a source of humor. It is a term of endearment for the girls Scaramutza woos (usually as "Närrchen"); it is an insult which he ironically applies to everyone but himself, the official fool of the play. It finds dozens of uses in slang idioms in which the figurative language is applied, in an ironic twist, to the literal fool, as in *Die Wittekinden*, p. 21, where Scaramutza swears that if he doesn't manage to break through Blonje's virgin defenses this very night, "so solstu mich vor einen Narren schelten." The humorous use of the term "Narr" becomes a major motif in *Willmut*, where Scaramutza's foolishness is exposed at the end as something bordering on evil. In this play the idioms based on "Narr" appear in most of the scenes dominated by Scaramutza (e.g., "einen Narren an einen haben," "jederman weyß/ wer nicht gar ein Narr ist/ daß. . . ," "so ein Narr wäre ich nicht"). But gone is the lighthearted license granted the fool in the earlier plays; bitter irony has replaced it. The cluster of metaphorical uses of "Narr" reaches its climax in a long monologue by Scaramutza (II, vii), his key speech in the play. He begins with a generalization about human behavior, which launches a severe critique of life at court:

Wie gehet es doch so wunderlich zu auf der Welt! Ein Knecht will immer einen Knecht/ und ein Narre den andern haben. Die beyde Narren richten nun aus/ was mir Narren befohlen war/ und bilden sich noch wol was drüber ein: denn sie wissen/ daß ich meines Prinzens Prinz/ Hofemeister/ Praeceptor, Geheimterraht/ Teufel und seine Mutter bin; so mag ich auch hier auf dem Schloss/ ohnangepochet/ in alle Stuben gehen/ denn es hat der ganze Hof und die Pfalzgräfin selber einen Narren an mir gefressen. Es siht mirs auch keiner nicht an/ was vor Narrenkappen und Brillen ich manchem guten Kerl aufsetze/ und ihm was in einem Spiegel zeigen kan/ daß er denket/ er wäre/ wisse und könne noch einmal so viel/ als es in der Wahrheit ist. Es sähe mich mancher nicht über die Achsel an/ wenn er nicht meinte/ es stäcke was grosses hinder mir/ weil ich so in

Gnaden bin. Und/ so bringet es die Mode mit: da ist
manchmal ein Praler bey Hofe/ der hat nichts gelernet/ tritt
vor seinen Herrn und schneidet Lappen/ daß man einem
Elefanten ein Wammes darvon machen könne. Da denkt
denn der Herr: das ist ein treflicher Kerl/ der wird mich in
24. Stunden zum reichen Manne machen/ ziehet ihm einen
sammten Rock an/ und tuht alles/ was er haben will: stracks
tuhts einander Maulaffe dem Herrn nach/ und hält auch was
von ihm/ der dritte/ der vierte/ der fünfte neiget sich und
bücket sich eben so/ und ist wol recht wahr/ was man
spricht: Ein Narr macht ihr zehne.

And in a final twist, he terms his beloved Wunna "die allerärgste
Närrin" because she believes that Scaramutza will be an honored
lord one day at court. He correctly predicts that the fate of
fools—"den Staupbesen," a whipping—will be the only reward for
them both. And in the monologue of the finale he gives the appellation "Narr," and by extension, all the criticisms and punishments
he has associated with it, to the courtiers in the audience: "Das
Ding nimmt ja wol ein beschissen Ende! Aber ich soll erst Nar-
renkleider anziehen/ und bin schon ein Narr/ wenn ich gleich
einen sammten Rock anhätte/ wie der da/ und jener dort" (III, xi).
The tables have been turned, and fools are to be found in the
highest echelons of society. Another sort of ironic usage occurs
when, at the end of the partner piece of 1680, *Bellemperie*, the
fool Scaramutza proclaims himself king as he stands above the pile
of corpses: "Nun will ich hier König werden." A literal fool will
act more morally than the figurative fools once in power: "Gillet-
chen/ wir wollen so schelmisch an einander nicht handeln."
Although no verbal humor based on the term "Narr" appears in
this scene, it can hardly be absent from the minds of the spectators and readers.

"Ein Narr macht ihr zehne"
Scaramutza

Conrad Höfer devoted fourteen pages of his 1904 Stieler monograph to the comic figures in the Rudolstadt plays,[124] expanding on C. Reuling's treatment of the same subject in ten pages in his dissertation of 1890 on comic figures in German literature;[125] yet Walter Hinck still found enough to warrant further discussion in his book on Italian influences on German comedy in 1965.[126] The focus in each of these treatments, reflecting that of the Stieler plays themselves, is the servant Scaramutza.

Scaramutza—Italian Scaramuzza or Scaramuccia, French Scaramouche—is a comic character of the Italian commedia dell'arte created before 1614, perhaps by Silvio Fiorello or his son Giovanni Battista Fiorillo[127] and made famous by Giovanni's brother Tiberio Fiorilli (ca. 1604 to ca. 1694),[128] who made his fortune with this role in the Comédie Italiene in Paris between 1639 and 1684. Fiorilli had apparently already become famous and wealthy in his native Italy before the troupe with which he was associated, led by Giuseppe Bianchi, was invited to France in 1639. Fiorilli remained for most of the rest of his life in Paris, eventually becoming a co-leader of the troupe, which, after 1660, played on alternate nights with Molière's troupe at the Palais Royale Théâtre.[129] In 1664 Fiorilli was awarded an incredible life income of 15,000 livres per year by the king, so great were his abilities and his fame.[130] Molière's respect for his abilities became Fiorilli's chief epitet: "Il fut le mâitre de Molière/ Et la Nature fut le sien." A contemporary and intimate of the French theater of the times, Du Tralage, relates: "Molière held Scaramouche in great esteem for his natural acting. He often went to see him play, and Scaramouche was the model which Molière followed in training the best actors of his troupe."[131] Like most of the other comic figures of the commedia dell'arte, Scaramuccia/Scaramouche was, originally at least, the property of his creator, and was not a ubiquitous stock figure like Hans Wurst or Pickelhering who could be acted by any skilled comic actor. Indeed, Fiorilli was so totally identified with his role that a biography of him, written by a jealous colleague and largely apocryphal, is titled simply *La Vie de*

Scaramouche.[132] It is only in the late 1660s that Scaramuccia begins a triumph as stock figure all over Europe, rivalling Arlecchinio and Pickelhering.

In light of this fact, Stieler's choice of the name, character, and role of Scaramuccia (Germanized to Scaramutza) for his dramatic oeuvre beginning in 1665 can have only one explanation: during his stay in Paris[133] Stieler saw the famous actor perform, perhaps many times, and was so impressed that he adopted Fiorilli's persona as his own.[134] Only in Stieler's two translations of dramatic works (*Ernelinde* and *Der göldene Apfel*) and in the short pastoral *Melissa* (source unknown) is Scaramutza absent, although each of these plays has a similar comic figure or figures. Even in the two theatrical works he produced in 1684, *Die erlösete Treue und Unschuld* and *Krieg und Sieg der Keuschheit*, Stieler's dramatic homunculus, borrowed from the famous Fiorilli, makes an appearance, given words and actions by the director which were obviously inserted in texts written by others. Scaramutza became the hallmark of Stieler's theatrical activities in the small Thuringian and Saxon courts of Germany, as it had been (and continued to be) for Tiberio Fiorilli in Paris. That Stieler's fool bears a variant of the name closer to its Italian origins (Scaramutza/Scaramuzza, Scaramuccia) than to the French (Scaramouche) may point to Stieler's predilection for Italianate comedy over French models (Molière's innovations seem not to have touched him). But one fact not often pointed out about the Comédie Italiene in Paris in the seventeenth century is that it continued to be performed in Italian—the fashionable language at court in Paris, as well as in Vienna![135] Thus it is hardly surprising that Stieler's Scaramutza, in spite of the fact that the young Thespian discovered him in Paris, bears an Italian name.[136]

Other German Scaramutzas did appear in the second half of the seventeenth century, but none, to my knowledge, preceded the comic character in Stieler's Rudolstadt plays. "Scaramuzza der Kurz-weiler" made his appearance as an extemporizing fool in the elaborate marriage celebration of Leopold I (1666-67)[137] and appeared also as a comic figure in the following plays of the seventeenth century: Kröber's *Der Christen Marter-Krohn und Ehren Thron* of 1669, Hallmann's *Adonis und Rosibella* of 1673, Heinrich Marschall's *Des menschlichen Alters Zeitkürzung* of 1676, and a Joseph-play of 1699 in Meiningen.[138] Even Christian Weise uses a character named Scaramutza as a messenger, if not as a comic figure, in his *Lustspiel von der Verkehrten Welt* of 1683, and Christian Gryphius includes "Scaramuzza" among the comic characters from the Italian and Latin traditions acceptable in the *Lustspiel* in his *Schulactus* (dramatized dialogue) on the subject of comedy (1698).[139] Although several scholars have tried to trace the origins of this comic figure in German literature to Stieler,[140] it is equally possible, however, that Kröber, Hallmann, and the other dramatists knew Scaramutza instead from Fiorilli's pan-European fame or from his counterfeit at the Viennese marriage celebrations, especially since mention is made of his appearance in the published accounts of the event.

Scaramuccia ("the little Skirmisher") was created as a member of a comic group of characters of the valet type often referred to as the "Neapolitan trio"; the others were Il Capitano (also called Capitano Matamoros, played by Tiberio's father), and Pulcinella. Scaramuccia was portrayed as cowardly and quarrelsome (a derivation from the ancient Capitano-type), and was known for his claims to vast pseudo-noble genealogies as proof of his respectable birth. In fact, his character type might be termed the "pretentious braggart and charlatan," for the disparity between his audacious claims and the less palatable truth dominates many of his activities and speeches: his delight in listing his "illustrious" ancestors and his titles, his belief that clothes and jewels make the (noble)man, and his braggadocio and cowardice. He is thus a stock character whose function is to satirize a certain ridiculous pattern of behavior of which many of Fiorilli's (and Stieler's) contemporaries were undoubtedly guilty. Furthermore, Scaramuccia was traditionally dressed all in black, thus parodying Spanish court fashions, and he employed satire against civil and military authority, in addition to slapstick and obscenity, as his comic stock-in-trade. Usually included in each performance was an amorous adventure with one or more low-life female characters, usually Colombina, a lady's maid. His role, like that of many other successful stage clowns of the day, was apparently largely pantomime (Fiorilli's true forte) and extemporizing.[141]

Stieler's Scaramutza, although, as Höfer has shown, not a uniform character throughout Stieler's dramatic oeuvre,[142] retains in each appearance most of these basic requisites of the type. To them, as Höfer has also noted,[143] Stieler has added attributes

which place him in the German traditions of the stock comic fig-
ure as well, especially as they derive from the English comedians
(Höfer mentions Thomas Sackville's portrayal of Duke Heinrich
Julius von Braunschweig's Johan Bouset and Jacob Ayrer's Jan
Posset in particular); stock comic episodes tied to Pickelhering,
Hans Wurst, even Til Eulenspiegel, have also been identified.[144]
The late medieval German comic servant, Rubin, who was both
wiser and wittier than his master, may provide a native German
source for the scenes in which Scaramutza is wiser than his betters, while "der dumme Teufel," "Klaus Narr," or the stupid
peasant may be a model for the oaf-like poses he adopts at
times.[145] As in the plays of Heinrich Julius, and unlike those of
the commedia dell'arte, verbal humor reigns supreme in Stieler's
plays over pantomime, alimentary-tract humor, and slapstick
(although none of these theatrical comic techniques is absent).
Scaramutza willfully misunderstands the commands of his social
betters; he takes their figurative words literally; he employs
malapropisms (usually in Latin), either purposely (in his wise
variant in *Der Vermeinte Printz* and *Die erfreuete Unschuld*) or
due to his pretentious stupidity (in *Der betrogene Betrug* and *Bellemperie*); he produces tortured fragments of foreign languages
imperfectly learned; he uses words resonating with sexual double
entendres, or takes those of others in their unintended sexual significance. Höfer has enumerated and cited many of these and
other comic usages.[146] Some of the finest stock scenes are Scaramutza's pantomimic "Praesedenzstreit" with Don Anthon in *Der
betrogene Betrug* (I, viii) and the scene where Scaramutza and the
villain Burckhard take turns stumbling over the ladder Scaramutza
has erected to reach his girlfriend's window for an illicit rendezvous in *Die Wittekinden* (III, i).

In several of Stieler's plays (EU, *Die Wittekinden*, *Bellemperie*), Scaramutza is closely associated with a contemporary off-
shoot of the ancient and commedia dell'arte "capitano" tradition—
that of the self-proclaimed "cavalier." Marianne Kaiser has ably
discussed this theme in her study on Mitternacht, Zeidler, and
Weise. The cavalier theme satirizes the pretensions of a certain
breed of social climber at court and, indeed, criticizes the
tendency of entire courtly societies to ape the glories of knight-
hood which they perceive as a sort of golden age of their own
German past or to emulate the parallel French or Italian medi-

evalizing fashions as a ploy to assert high status. The cavalier may
be a stock comic character modeled on the capitano, or the theme
may be present only in certain characteristics or behaviors of a
single person or set of people in the play. In either form, the
cavalier serves as a parodistic counterpart to the Christian knight
who fights the various manifestations of the Devil in visual and
verbal iconography of the sixteenth and seventeenth centuries
(e.g., Dürer's "Ritter, Tod und Teufel").[147] Stieler even places his
comic "cavalier" in direct juxtaposition with two "Christian
knights" in his dramatic oeuvre: in *Die erfreuete Unschuld* and in
Willmut. In *Die erfreuete Unschuld* Scaramutza appears on horse-
back in one scene (II, xvii), instructing his steed in French as he
practices his cavalier's skills:

> Ala gauche. Ala droite. Passes par la. Pares. Bon! Sa morian,
> encor unefois d'autre maniere. Ala ronde. Pares. Bon! Also
> muß man sich wissen in die Ritterlichen exercitios zu
> qualificieren. Aus dem wege Herr Doctor Forzius, wenn ein
> Kavalier kömmt. (II, p. 29)

That he is no such thing is made clear by the doctor's comments
on his poor horsemanship and low character: "Wer komt hier mit
verhängten Zaume?" and "Er ist ein Bube." In one scene in *Die
erfreuete Unschuld* (II, iv), reused in *Willmut* (III, vii), the self-
proclaimed "cavalier" Scaramutza pretends to misunderstand the
armor worn by the defender of goodness and innocence, thus
twitting the heroic savior just as he heads into battle. The result is
not a lessening of respect for the hero, but insight into the empti-
ness of the pretensions of the "cavalier" and his doubles at court
and in the audience.[148]

Stieler's Scaramutza may entertain the audience with stock
scenes and witticisms, but he is as much individualized in his
utterances as Scaramouche must have been in his gestures. Scaramutza speaks for his author (who may have played the role himself) in passages containing social or aesthetic satire, parody of
individuals (members of the audience or famous political figures),
moral judgments of his social betters, and self-ironization. His
speech patterns also appear to reflect what must have been characteristics of Stieler's own—a rich, varied, and largely metaphorical
Erfurt dialect (with phrases acquired on his travels thrown in for
good measure);[149] a love of folk sayings and proverbs; a delight in
teasing and mystifying the ignorant with his brilliance in foreign

languages; and, especially in *Basilene*, his predilection for folksy doggerel in the form of catchy rhythms and silly rhymes, as discussed above. And in general, he prefers sexual innuendos and double entendres to the coarse obscenity of his prototypes. Furthermore, his little love affairs, unlike those of the Italian source character, presumably lead to married happiness (like Stieler's own?); the vices he shares with Scaramouche and Scaramuccia—the love of strong drink in his cup, good food on his plate, and a pretty girl in his bed—are somehow all modified and made more socially acceptable in Stieler's version.

Stieler's sense of humor has expanded upon the comic repertoire of his source, further serving to make Scaramutza a very individualized fool. It is difficult even today, from the perspective of our own age of black comedy, democracy, and "enlightenment," not to be shocked at Scaramutza's black humor, total irreverence towards authority and religious institutions, and blatant sexuality (especially in *Basilene*). While the latter two sources of humor can certainly be understood according to the theory that comedy allows us to relax, if only vicariously and briefly, from the repressions of our social structures, the presence of black humor, "Galgenhumor," in Stieler's plays is more difficult to explain. Overt in *Die erfreuete Unschuld* and *Basilene*, where Scaramutza claims to look forward to the execution or sacrifice of the heroine because she will be unclothed and because he enjoys watching bloodshed and suffering, this strain of humor is less obvious and less offensive in the serious scenes of the late plays (*Bellemperie* and *Willmut*, where his belittling of the tragic situation merely seems to fulfill the function of comic relief). Yet in either case, Stieler's black humor is an anomaly in his age—and a startling one. Such humor could be seen as a refusal to take life's disasters seriously, the characteristic of a frivolous personality (in Scaramutza, if not in Stieler), or it could reveal a deep-seated cynicism and bitterness in its creator. Yet this humor was undoubtedly designed to arouse laughter as well as horror and disapproval, and thus it is appropriate to ask what Stieler intended this laughter to accomplish: perhaps a violent cathartic release of the tensions built up by the horror and suspense in the plot. In part, the answer may lie in the fact that such horror and suspense— exciting fare, but antithetical to the goals of the heroic-gallant comedy and to its festive context—cannot be allowed to over-

whelm the audience. But Stieler's choice of black humor for his
katastasis, the comic relaxation of tension through laughter,
remains unexplained, for any clowning around could presumably
achieve the same relief.

The social satire of Stieler's comic figure is partly a criticism
of behavior at court among the higher classes and partly a critique
of contemporary morals. In *Die erfreuete Unschuld*, for example,
Scaramutza peers out at the audience and claims to see adulterers
and cuckolds everywhere (II, xiii); in *Der betrogene Betrug* he
criticizes the perfidious actions of Don Ferdinand and contrasts
them to his own fidelity and to that of his social equals (II, v). His
bizarre genealogical claims, traditionally connected with this figure, provide a wonderful mirror for those of Stieler's social betters, and when Scaramutza in *Der Vermeinte Printz* (I, xiii) claims
that his father, grandfather, and all his ancestors were named
Scaramutza, it must have caused a great deal of laughter at the
court of his Schwarzburg patron, most of whose ancestors were
named "Günther." The joke is repeated in his 1680 play, *Bellemperie* (III, viii), probably written for his future patrons in
Weimar—the Saxon dukes whose names have only slightly more
variety. Stieler laughs at the social climbers at court (not excepting
himself) in Scaramutza's depiction in *Die erfreuete Unschuld*:

> Ein ieder will mehr seyn/ als er ist/ und/ was er ist/ wil er
> nicht seyn. Exempli gratia: Fragt einen Stallknecht/ wer er
> sey? So wird er antworten: Ein Bereiter. Den Bereiter:
> respondet: ein Stallmeister. Ein Lackeyen? so wird er sagen/
> ich bin ein Kammerdiener. Ein Schreiber wil ein Secretarius:
> ein Secretarius, ein Raht: ein Raht/ ein Cantzler: ein
> Cantzler der Fürst. . . . (I, viii)

Sometimes, too, Scaramutza is made to carry Stieler's views of
contemporary literature, as when his and Bertha's laughter at the
Knittelvers song of the street poet Michele in *Die Wittekinden* constitutes a slam at all occasional poetry—including, undoubtedly,
Stieler's own:

> Brechta: Was ist diß für ein heßlich Lied/
>   Das mir die Ohren machet gellen?
> Scar.: Ein steiffer Dichter hat diß Lied gesetzet.
>   (I, xii)

Scaramutza's own taste, anything but "steiff," runs to the silly and
the coarse, but also to a folksy and eminently singable sort of

poetry, as in the love song he commissions in *Die erfreuete Unschuld*:

Wer Lust hat auf die daur zu naschen/
Der such' es bey dem lieben waschen.
Im Himmel ist kein schöner Kind/
Alß unsre Wäschermädchen sind.
Hat jemand Lust zu naschen/
Der such es bey dem waschen.

(III, iv)

The song (of which this is the first stanza) with its strophic form and refrains, although from the perspective of a vastly different persona, reminds us of the songs of *Die Geharnschte Venus*, as does that in *Die Wittekinden* beginning "Juch he! wer wolte traurig seyn" (I, xiii).

Not all seventeenth-century German plays had comic figures and comic scenes; the fact that Stieler chose to include Scaramutza in almost all of his plays (including heroic comedies, tragicomedies, a tragedy, and an allegory) demands some sort of explanation. One possibility is to see Stieler's plays as belonging to a particular tradition of dramatic performance in which the comic figure invariably appeared: the rhetorical theater[150] of the Protestant schools, perhaps in emulation of the itinerant stages of the English comedians and/or the Italian commedia dell'arte and of the plays of Heinrich Julius von Braunschweig. One contemporary theorist, Daniel Georg Morhof,[151] does indeed place Stieler in this group of dramatists—but due to his use of prose rather than to the appearance of comic figures and scenes. On the other hand, many theatrical performances designed for festive occasions at various German courts also incorporated a comic figure into the action or at least placed him on the periphery. For example, the opera *Il Pomo d'oro* designed for Emperor Leopold's wedding included the antique Thersites-figure, Momo, while other performances designed for the same event included Scaramutza, as noted above. Thus it could also be maintained that Stieler's own festive plays written for small German courts belong, in their use of a comic figure, to a tradition of festive courtly performances.

Yet the fact that Gryphius and Lohenstein never include a comic figure in tragedies or heroic comedies (and that Gryphius's use of them in *Peter Squentz* and *Horribilicribrifax*, his two satirical comedies, is not as comic relief for heavier scenes, as in either of the two traditions outlined above), ought perhaps to lead to another conclusion: that use of comic figures and comic relief in serious plays in the seventeenth century was totally a matter of personal preference rather than genre-specific. Gryphius and Lohenstein apparently found it unnecessary and even undesirable to lighten the effect of their ponderous tragedies, and their personal philosophies and thematic intentions found no outlet in the words and deeds of a fool. Stieler, on the other hand, chose not only to make use of comic relief in order to express, perhaps, his own inability to remain pessimistic, or to take anything or anyone seriously for long, but also to create a single comic figure, Scaramutza, who would become his mouthpiece, uttering under the guise of foolishness and with fool's freedom those devastating criticisms of his social betters that no self-interested bureaucrat dared express in his own right. Somehow the speeches of the Scaramutza of the early plays in particular come across to us as the words of that younger Stieler, Filidor der Dorfferer, who reveled in sensuality and moral permissiveness, who faced adventures with joie de vivre and tribulations with optimism, and who studied, worked, fought, and wooed with an attitude so carefree as to border on the picaresque. If, in Stieler's late plays, Scaramutza's humor has darkened (in *Bellemperie*) and his sensuality has fallen into disrepute with his creator (in *Willmut*, which ends with a denunciation of Scaramutza as "Wahn" and with a list of his forthcoming punishments), such shifts in the author's own self-image during that time, in view of the troubles in his personal and professional lives, should hardly surprise us. Assuming that Stieler played or intended to play Scaramutza in performances of the 1680 plays, as I surmise he did for the Rudolstadt plays, then the fool's assumption of the reins of government at the end of *Bellemperie*, after the death of the morally corrupt rulers, constitutes a claim staked out for Stieler's own perceived ethical and intellectual superiority over his social betters. And the rejection of Scaramutza as "Wahn" in *Willmut*, if Stieler were to play the role, could indicate self-criticism on the author's part, especially of his own youthful actions and character in the past—an attitude which also appears in his *Teutsche Secretariat-Kunst*: "Ich bekenne/ daß/ so oft ich meine vorige Schreiberey lese/ darob einen ekel empfinde und mich meiner misbrauchten Übereilung schäme,"[152] and in his chosen pseudonym and motto in the *Fruchtbringende Gesellschaft*:

"der Spahte, übertrifft den Frühzeitigen."[153] Stieler's Scaramutza seems, in any case, whether in his manifestations as silly bumpkin or as smug and superior satirist, to be the barely concealing persona of a clever and witty author. In short, Stieler's Scaramutza is as much to be identified with his author as Fiorilli's Scaramouche. And it is this Italian tradition of authorial identification with an entirely esoteric comic figure to which Stieler's Scaramutza belongs, rather than to any German or European tradition of a particular fool or fools.

So Scaramutza intrudes into the serious plots of Stieler's plays as a vehicle for his author to take part in his own work of art, to become a character in his own text. Once in the position, he proceeds, like a *Praecursor* in a sixteenth-century play, to guide the reactions of his audience, to disrupt emotional involvement, especially when it might tend to become uncomfortable, and to offer an ironic distance which encourages rational reception of the staged representations, while at the same time, as a member of the social group to which the members of the audience also belong, linking the reality of the play to the reality of the spectators. In this function, Scaramutza might best be termed "chief manipulator of audience reception."

His intrusions into the reality of the "Perseda" playlet in *Bellemperie* and his illusion-breaking behavior throughout the play itself are exemplary for his function in all the Stieler plays. Scaramutza provides commentary for *Perseda*, usually addressed directly to the interior audience, and slips in and out of his role in the playlet at will—after all, he plays "Scaramutza" in both plays. Not only does he turn to the exterior audience at the common end of the interior and exterior plays with the proclamation that he is the new king, but he also constantly uses theatrical metaphors in the double significance of their figurative and literal (original) meanings, e.g., "Komödie spielen" (p. 128) and "Komödie halten" (p. 159). Scaramutza appears in his costume for the interior play during scenes which belong exclusively to the exterior play, eliciting mocking and ironic questions about his true identity from the characters in the exterior play. Similarly, his illusion-breaking actions and speeches in all of Stieler's plays are designed to evoke metaphysical questions about identity and role-playing, reality and play-acting.

The German Jesuit Jacob Pontanus theorized in his *Institutio Poetica* of 1597,[154] following Lucretius, that the "tragic pleasure" experienced by the audience of a tragedy, alluded to in Aristotle's *Poetics*, results when the members of the audience recognize the fact that the play is only an imitation and that the horrifying events in no way affect their own safety. A comic character can produce such "tragic pleasure" by drawing attention to the fact that the audience is only watching a play (as Scaramutza often does), but he can also deprive the audience of this pleasant experience in serious drama by eliminating the distinctions between staged reality and audience reality, by connecting or bridging the two. Such bridges to the reality of the audience invade the "safe" isolation of the spectator, as, for example, when Scaramutza addresses the audience directly. In some instances he appears to speak to particular spectators, in others he claims to know of many among them who share some vice or shame with the characters on stage. Because Scaramutza's excursions into the reality of his audience, like his behavior to the other characters in the play, involve clever insights into hypocrisy and vice, the members of the audience are exposed to the same risks as the characters: since Scaramutza sees through them, his insights could bring them public ignominy. For this reason Scaramutza's bridge to the audience would be perceived as a sort of pontoon bridge, like that thrown across the Hellespont by Xerxes on his way to Thermopylae—a means of invasion into the spectators' territory and a threat to their safety. The gulf between spectators and play, which allowed them to feel smug in their isolation from unreal events, suddenly itself proves illusory. The tonic of "tragic pleasure" is denied in order to move the members of the audience to evasive or corrective action in their own lives. The result may be a group of people who consciously recognize their own vices and who feel a strong impulse to make some changes. This affective theory of Scaramutza's presence in Stieler's oeuvre does not necessarily contradict or preclude that of William Willeford, for instance, in his attempt to understand the attraction of the archetypal figure of the fool in theatrical performances of every culture.[155] But my emphasis on potential audience reaction does bear out my other claims of Stieler's talents and experience as a consummate Thespian, who is always conscious of the potential results of a performance of the text before an audience.

In all the plays in which Scaramutza appears, except *Die er-freuete Unschuld*, Stieler's mouthpiece has the final word in a sort of finale (in *Die erfreuete Unschuld* Blandine must do so in his stead, for Scaramutza is in jail). For each of the Rudolstadt plays, all romantic comedies, the finale includes an invitation to the ensuing multiple wedding, including his own, and a plea for appropriate gifts. The disgraced Scaramutza has the floor at the end of *Willmut*, but he announces that he is excluded from the joyous festivities of the royal wedding and begs to be taken home by some new patron in the audience, who, he hopes, will be more forgiving. The Scaramutza of the tragedy *Bellemperie* is also the final speaker of the play, and instead of announcing a wedding (although it is clear that he and Gillette are "ein Päarchen"), he invites the audience to his forthcoming coronation and delivers the moral of the story. But in each instance, the speaker of the finale bids the audience a good night in a neighborly fashion reminiscent of the *Fastnachtspiele* of the previous century, or notifies the spectators that they need no longer wait around, for the play is over (in spite of the fact that most plays still have a *Nachspiel* to follow). Much as the early *Fastnachtspiel* is purported to have done by means of the same technique,[156] Scaramutza/Stieler thus reinstates his friendly relationship to his patron and fellow courtiers in the audience at the end of each play—an action which not only reestablishes him in their good graces after critical and satirical utterances directed at them during the play, but which also reintegrates the illusion of his dramatic fiction into the reality of the festive occasion.

IV

EPILOGUE

Stieler's Legacy

10

Prescriptions, Proscriptions, Scripts

Stieler's poetical treatise—actually a verse discourse modeled on Horace's *De Arte Poetica*—marks the end, not the beginning, of his poetic works; after 1685, the date of the unpublished manuscript of *Die Dichtkunst des Spaten*,[1] Stieler apparently wrote and produced no more plays and penned only scattered *Gelegenheitsgedichte*. His rambling and personable instructions in the *Dichtkunst* for writing plays and poems, like his handbooks on the duties of a secretary or on the art of letter-writing, depend on an earlier period in which the author himself was involved in the craft directly. Stieler's *Dichtkunst*, unlike the prose poetical treatises of Harsdörffer or Birken upon which he often seems to depend, is neither expository in style nor overtly theoretical in content or structure. He treats such standard theoretical topics as genre and subgenre, stylistic levels, or plot types, only as they happen to occur to him as he deals with his chief topics, all matters of practical concern to an aspiring poet: *Erfindung, Anordnung, Wörterschmuck*.

Conrad Höfer mentioned the *Dichtkunst* briefly in his book of 1904,[2] in a sort of excursus, but treated it only superficially and incompletely. In 1926 the original discoverer of the manuscript, Bolte, published excerpts of the work (including much of the section on drama) with a slightly more detailed description of the remainder and more apt analysis than that provided by Höfer. In 1975 the manuscript was finally published in its entirety by Herbert Zeman, whose "Nachwort"[3] provides a useful and thorough summary of the topics and analysis of the intentions of the work as a whole. Further analysis of the section on drama, the goal of which will be a confrontation with Stieler's own dramatic works, is necessary here.

Following sixteenth- and seventeenth-century tradition, Stieler sees the origins of drama in the satyr plays of the ancient Greeks, but departs from Opitz and other Renaissance theorists in seeing drama unequivocally in first position among the literary genres. He directly or indirectly excludes several types of popular drama (the "Posse" and the melodramas of the itinerant theater) from his literary canon, but goes on to describe two major subgenres which differ in mood (one arouses laughter and joy, the other sadness and tears, lines 847-56). He briefly discusses tragedy without offering much in the way of a theory (851-76), then turns to his main interest, dividing the non-tragic subgenre into four types: *Komödie* or *Lustspiel* (911ff.), *Mischspiel* (1603), *Heldenspiel* (1609), and *Allegorie* (1706), while returning to the topic of tragedy once more as well (1561ff.). Although he, like Opitz, lists appropriate plots and character-types for each genre, he insists repeatedly that each story will make its own generic demands felt, based primarily on the simple formula of whether the plot conveys—especially at the end—happiness or sadness.

The *Lustspiel* is a drama which depicts everyday life realistically and arouses laughter at the ridiculous in order to help people perceive similar faults in themselves and correct them; the *Lustspiel* should not arouse resistance, revulsion, or sorrow:

> . . . sondern bloß mahl' ab das Tuhn der Welt
> mit frischem Farbenstrich', als ein belebt Gemähld',
> aus dem ein ieder kan sein' eigne Tohrheit richten,
> das, was ihm fehlet, sehn, und lachend das vernichten,
> was Schad' und Spott gebiehrt, und Vorwurf wirken mag.
>
> (955-60)

But Stieler is adamant that the *Lustspiel* is not a farce and that what he has in mind is not low comedy of the type of the *Fastnachtspiel* or *Schwank*: "Lust- ist kein Boßenspiel" (916). The clowns from popular comedy are not to make an appearance here; as surely as Gottsched was to do forty-five years later, Stieler banishes "Pekelhering" and "Hans Supp" from the stage as "ein kahles Affenfest" (914-19). The humor and stylistic level, too, must rise above those in the popular theater (931-36). Furthermore, persons of high social class should not appear (969-84). Stieler briefly defines the *Mischspiel* as a mixture of the elements of tragedy and comedy (1603f.), then passes on to a more involved description of a third non-tragic type, the *Heldenspiel*—a term and concept which he has apparently inherited from Birken,[4] but which he himself, on the basis of his own experience, is much better suited to define. He describes plays in which characters from royalty or the high nobility appear, as in tragedy, but in which the plot revolves around love and ends in a joyful resolution of conflict:

. . . Oft geht was ohne Graus
und sonder Wirrung fort, lauft auch vergnügt hinaus,
daß Spieler Fürsten sind und hohe Standspersonen
. . . .
und diese Schaulust wird ein Heldenspiel genennet,
worinn kein Ehrgeitz, nicht megären Fackel brennet,
und keine Nemesis in Blut' ihr Schwert färbt rot,
noch eine Haubtgefahr der Standeswürde droht.

(1603-12)

The fourth non-tragic type he differentiates from the rest as
totally fictional, for whose plot and characters the author alone is
responsible. But since Stieler sees such fiction as possible only as a
cloak for allegory, he terms this type the "allegorical" play. And
even here events and characters must be plausible—a demand
Stieler makes repeatedly for all dramatic types.

Stieler's treatment of the dramatic subtypes focuses most
extensively and intensively on the *Lustspiel*, but his own dramatic
production includes no single play which fits this description or
this theory, although the Scaramutza scenes in all his plays might
be seen to fulfill the demands of Stieler's affective theory of
laughter in the comedy. While the younger Stieler termed four of
the six Rudolstadt plays "Lustspiele" and indeed, used this term as
well (along with "Trauerspiele" and "Mischspiele") on the collective
title page of 1665, the plays are in actuality more like "Heldenspiele," according to his own definitions. Stieler also used the term
"Lustspiel" to denote the genre of his *Willmut* of 1680, which is
clearly an allegorical drama. Only *Ernelinde* and *Die erfreuete
Unschuld* do indeed seem to fulfill Stieler's later theoretical
requirements for the term which he uses to describe them,
"Mischspiel." He does not address the generic term he provides for
Die Wittekinden—"Singspiel"—in his *Dichtkunst*.

Stieler follows the Nürnberg writers of poetics in offering
criticisms of antique dramatic practice from the modern Christian
perspective and in describing the new genres of dramatic practice
in his own age. He laments the frequent absence of poetic and
divine justice in the plays of the ancients, finding that the
demand for a functional purpose for drama is not met in such
plays. He points out that the *Mischspiel* and the *Heldenspiel* are
types absent among the Greeks and Romans; in speaking of the
characters of high social class in the *Heldenspiele*, for example, he
remarks:

worvon dem Altertum nichts pflegte beyzuwohnen,
das bloß auf Rach und Sturz, Schreck- und Verzweifeln sach
und keine Liebe ließ dem Statsnutz kommen nah!

(1612-14)

And he also notes that in modern drama the choruses of the
ancients have been replaced by musical *Reyen*:

. . . was vor der Chor versüßte
und teilt' in Handlung ab, tuht ietzt der Saiten-Klang.

(1775f.)

However, he does not go so far as Harsdörffer and Birken in con-
demning the use of pagan deities in modern plays, or in advising
the use of biblical archetypes for all possible topics.

Stieler insists, following Horace, that all literature must provide both "Ergetzlichkeit" and "Nutz," and criticizes popular
theater especially (and some plays from antiquity) on the basis that
they provide only the former. But he also follows in the footsteps
of Aristotle's affective theories of drama, providing an elaborate
theory for the good to come of arousing laughter in the audience
(955-60, as quoted above), and constantly alluding to the usefulness of tears, without, however, confronting the Aristotelian
theory of the tragic emotions and their catharsis, as Harsdörffer
does,[5] and without formulating any affective theory for the
Heldenspiel, as Jacob Masen and Birken do.[6]

Why, it might be asked, should Stieler dwell on theoretical
speculation about a genre for which he has never provided an
exemplar, the *Lustspiel*, while ignoring those for which he has?
Has Stieler rejected his much earlier preference for the heroic
comedy by this date? In fact, in late 1684, less than a year before
work on the *Dichtkunst*, Stieler made what was apparently his final
foray into involvement with theater, when he produced, as discussed above, two operas with plots typical for heroic comedies.
Although we cannot be sure that he chose the texts to be performed, Höfer believes him responsible for alterations to the performance scripts quite in his usual mode—a clue that, by 1685,
Stieler can scarcely be suspected of preferring the *Lustspiel* to the
Heldenspiel. Perhaps the answer to the question is to be found in
the very absence of such an affective theory of laughter in other
poetics of the period,[7] leading Stieler to digress at length on this
point while giving short shrift to theoretical concerns well covered
by Birken, Harsdörffer, and others. Besides, although the plots

and characters of his Rudolstadt comedies are certainly of the "heroic" type, most scholars seem to agree that the comic scenes and the laughter they arouse are the true focal points in the plays—for their author and for their audiences. The alimentary-tract clowns "Hans Supp" and "Pekelhering" may be banned from the stage of the *Lustspiel*, but not the sophisticated Scaramutza, perhaps more a stock comic character than a clown. Scaramutza's name crops up only once in the *Dichtkunst* (1103), but his function is addressed there several times under the more anonymous term, "Narr" (e.g., 1809-10). One thinks of the distinction Shakespeare makes between "clown" and "fool" in his plays.

Offering practical advice, rather than a systematization of poetical theory, seems to be the intention of the *Dichtkunst*, yet Stieler's prescriptions and proscriptions for the aspiring dramatist or dramaturgue are nearly hidden under the mass of examples and detailed lists. He does offer tidbits based on his own vast experience, such as the necessity of suspense in an effective plot, how to plan impressive scene changes which do not challenge the technical abilities of the theater, and tips on appropriate costuming and pomp for royal characters without losing sight of the realities of the pocketbook. Yet he does not discuss, as Harsdörffer does, the appropriate sorts of plays or appropriate themes and plots for particular social contexts, occasions, or acting personnel—factors which certainly influenced his own writing and production of plays.

Stieler's treatment in the *Dichtkunst* of the *Mischspiel* consisted in only three lines (squeezed between the passage contrasting tragedy and comedy, and that describing the related *Heldenspiel*), to the effect that joy and sorrow can comfortably be combined in a single play of this type (p. 53, lines 1601-03), but this dramatic subgenre had already received a more extensive rendering in conjunction with the script of his first foray into making a *Mischspiel*. Several of the "Singende Zwischenspiele" Stieler provided for use as choruses to *Ernelinde*, appended to the text of the play in the only edition, dramatize the controversy surrounding the theory and practice of this type of play since its "invention" in 1589 by Giambattista Guarini for his *Il Pastor fido*. Stieler's treatment of the topic following the first act involves a *Streitgespräch* between the personifications of comedy and tragedy, *Die Spitzfindigkeit* and *Der Ernst*. The former speaks for laughter, but also for love and marriage—the appropriate combination of optimistic subject matter for Stieler's heroic-gallant comedies—while the latter scorns them all as frivolity and sin, preferring stern virtue and threatening the punishments of Nemesis for the guilty. While neither convinces the other, the *Zwischenspiel* ends with a chorus of fauns and forest nymphs praising love and marriage—obviously reflective of Stieler's own views. Following the second act, another pair of personifications, *Melankoley* and *Freude*, continue the dialectic of tragicomedy. Melancholy, solemn in her depressed mood, scolds Joy for her noisy celebration of her delight in nature. Finally, however, the two agree to tolerate each other's mood, to live and let live, and to divide up responsibility for appropriate parts of the play. *Freude* claims Ernelinde, for whom a happy ending is in store, while *Melankoley* will take charge of the miserable Isabelle. The chorus at the end of this *Zwischenspiel* is perhaps an allusion to the origin of the tragicomic genre, Guarini's pastoral play, for in it shepherds and shepherdesses praise the pastoral life as one of joy, contrasting it to the melancholic tone which is more often found in the palaces of the rich and powerful.

In fact, Stieler's two *Zwischenspiele* for *Ernelinde* present, in dramatic form, an argument which had raged for a time after the appearance of *Il Pastor fido*, and his views echo those of Guarini himself, who in 1601 found himself forced to affix a defense of his mixed-genre play to the new edition. In this "Compendio della Poesia Tragicomica tratto dai duo Verati per opera dell'autore del Pastor fido," which appears appended to most editions of the play,[8] Guarini answers the charges that his text violates the classical rules for drama in mixing tragedy and comedy by noting that Christianity requires a new world view of optimism, where the virtuous are rewarded and where even evildoers, if properly repentant, can participate in the happy ending.[9] Stieler's dramatized theory of the *Mischspiel*, however, allows more room for the serious, even the "dead serious," in his version. For in *Ernelinde* the guilty are punished for their sins, no matter how repentant: the sinful Isabelle commits suicide in her despair, haunted by visions of Nemesis and hellfire. Yet the play is not allowed to end on this note; the scene of tragic horror is followed by another in which the true lovers are united, and by a final *Zwischenspiel* in which Lucina, goddess of childbirth, lauds married love and prophesies wedded bliss to the newly married princely couple in the audience. And while this tragicomic treatment was provided by Stieler's original (*Ernelinde*, it will be remembered, is a translation), a similar development can be noted in his own tragicomedy, *Die erfreuete Unschuld*, although there Stieler has even further divorced the catastrophe of the guilty character from the happy ending provided for the virtuous lovers by treating them in separate acts.

The Caspar Stieler of the eighties, able to reflect back on his Thespian experiences of several decades, also found an effective and appropriate vehicle for sharing his expertise with contemporaries and with a future readership: in the treatment of a play-within-a-play in his tragedy of 1680, *Bellemperie*, he provides insight into actual dramatic practice of the time. A play with a Turkish setting, *Perseda*, a tragedy of unhappy love (although it is constantly termed "Komödie") is to be performed on the occasion of a royal wedding. The Christian slave woman Perseda, wooed by the Turkish Sultan, finds among the male slaves her lost beloved, Erastus. Assignment of the roles for *Perseda* is informative: three of the four speaking roles in the play are to be performed by the three princely young people at court—the Castilian and Portuguese princes and the Castilian princess Bellemperie. The surprise of the court at the fact that the aged minister Hieronymus is to play the fourth role indicates that the usual actors in courtly performances were the younger members of the high nobility, although elsewhere, in his earlier plays, Stieler hints that courtly bureaucrats—especially secretaries and clerks—were often considered appropriate draftees for roles left unfilled by the young nobles.[10] The assigned roles were parallel to the level of each amateur actor in the actual social hierarchy of the court. Considering the fact that male actors apparently continued to play female characters at the time on the itinerant stage, following English usage, it is worth noting that no surprise whatsoever is expressed when the princess takes upon herself the leading role. Had Stieler felt that any of the procedures followed in the preparations for *Perseda* were improper in the view of his own society, he could surely have made alterations in his source without damaging the fabric of his plot; thus it is probably not inappropriate to conclude that the procedures followed by the courtly characters in *Bellemperie* were those actually used in Weimar or in nearby courts.

Roles are given to the actors to be memorized, but there are no rehearsals—perhaps only to allow the intrigue to be successful. (Bellemperie and Hieronymus have in mind a different ending for the play—murder of their two co-actors and the royal members of the audience and their own suicides.) Costumes and props are found in a well-stocked costume room, which is apparently a permanent repository for such things, indicating frequent usage for performances or at least drawing room games (charades?).

There seems to be a ready-made stage, for there is no talk of setting up a temporary structure, and the stage has a front curtain which is apparently opened at the beginning of the play. We see the amateur actors gathered before the performance, already in their costumes, jokingly comparing their roles in the play and in real life (VIII, iv and v). They also list the usual justifications for such performances before royal audiences: theater is "ein Spiegel des menschlichen Lebens; eine Lehrschule guter Sitten; eine Reinigung der austretenden Begierden/ und eine uralte Gemütsbelustigung der Könige und Fürsten" (pp. 64-65). At the last minute the actors decide to begin the play with a "ballet"—an amateur dance performance in which the younger members of the cast can show off their gracefulness and adeptness at this courtly pastime. A further discussion of the purpose of their theatrical activities ensues: "Wir spielen aber Königen zu Ehren und uns selbst zuvergnügen"—an appropriate activity on a wedding day, especially since it is done at the request of the bride, as her brother points out (p. 146). The kings in the audience expect "Kurtzweil," and are stunned when the dead characters on stage do not rise to receive their applause. Scaramutza, a servant in the main play, is let out of jail to become Scaramutza the fool in the interior play, and his actions playing himself are exactly those of the Scaramutza of each of Stieler's plays: he peeks out from behind the curtain, talks to the spectators, teases his social betters, provides a running commentary in addition to prologue and epilogue, and offers verbal and slapstick humor. He also causes several of the disasters, as when the Turkish Sultan trips over Scaramutza's lance upon entering the stage for the first scene, that must have plagued (or graced) all amateur theater of the time—as so hilariously portrayed in Gryphius's *Herr Peter Squentz*.

Thus in his *Bellemperie*, Stieler has provided a dramatized account of the context and the activities surrounding a typical courtly performance, a miniature record of contemporary practice in the form of concrete representation. This internal play, together with that in *Herr Peter Squentz*, although fictionalized and undoubtedly distorted to fulfill the purposes of their authors in creating a play-within-a-play, can offer perhaps more useful material for a study of actual theatrical practices of the period than the various contemporary poetical treatises. And that is true even for the treatise written by perhaps the most experienced all-round Thespian of the day, Caspar Stieler.

Lines of Influence and Interconnection

One legacy of Caspar Stieler's dramatic oeuvre is his influence upon later dramatists, most notably Christian Weise and Johann Christian Hallmann.[11] While Weise is best known today for his satirical comedies, like *Der bäurische Machiavellus*, and his tragedies, like *Masaniello*, he also wrote a number of heroic or romantic comedies. In fact, his first dramatic text, *Die triumphirende Keuschheit* (1668), as discussed above in the account of the performances in Weimar in 1684, is such a play; after a pause in dramatic production (1688-1702), Weise again took up his pen to write romantic comedies, most notably *Körbelmacher* and *Liebesalliance*. All three comedies named here exhibit a typical romantic plot structure, with complications and intrigues forming its very core. In place of the episodic structure which dominates the rest of Weise's dramatic oeuvre, these comedies, like those of Stieler (and the European tradition to which both authors adhere), utilize classical ("closed form"), even symmetrical dramatic structures. That the lines of influence should be drawn from Stieler to Weise, rather than directly from foreign-language sources, was demonstrated already above, in the section on the productions of 1684. Weise's first play is entirely derivative from Stieler's Rudolstadt plays, particularly *Die erfreuete Unschuld* and perhaps *Ernelinde*. The late comedies, however, incorporate a new element which truly marks the passage into the eighteenth century, as can be seen by scanning the *dramatis personae* lists: instead of princes and princesses, dukes and duchesses, and other protagonists from the high nobility, we see ordinary people from the middle classes. Weise himself is aware of this shift: "Über Fürsten und Herrn haben andere genug geklaget und geschrieben: hier finden die Leute ihren Text/ die entweder nicht viel vornehmer sind/ als ich/ oder die zum wenigsten leiden müssen/ daß ich mich vor ihnen nicht entsetze" ("Vorwort" to *Ertz-Narren*).[12] These late comedies can no longer be termed "heroic-gallant"; they have abandoned the courtly sphere and now provide texts for a theater of the middle classes. They are simply "romantic" comedies. And while, as Haxel has noted, Weise's continuation of the tradition of the romantic comedy in Germany probably did not lead directly to eighteenth-century German comedy (which again turned to foreign sources),[13] Stieler's works might be seen to mark the begin-ning[14] of romantic comedy in the manner of Shakespeare in German literature—a type of comedy which usually uses Romance-language novellas as its source material and which shares with the novella genre a love of unheard-of or amazing events and a predilection for plots filled with intrigues and complications. And while few have made it into the literary canon in Germany (one might name Lessing's *Minna von Barnhelm*, Kleist's odd *Käthchen von Heilbronn*, and Grillparzer's *Weh dem, der Lügt*), the type is perfectly at home on the stage of the Austrian opera (e.g., Mozart's *Die Zauberflöte*, Beethoven's *Fidelio*, and Strauss's and Hofmannsthal's *Der Rosenkavalier*, to name but a few). Gottsched placed Stieler's and Weise's romantic comedies among the plays of literary and theatrical merit listed in his *Nöthiger Vorrath* of 1757-65, and thus made their existence known to generations of later theatrical writers and producers.

Hallmann's debt to Stieler can easily be seen in his pastoral *Die Sinn-reiche Liebe/ Oder Der Glückseelige Adonis und Die Vergnügt Rosibella*,[15] designed in honor of the second marriage of the Holy Roman Emperor Leopold in Vienna in 1673. Höfer has already pointed out the inclusion of Stieler's dramatic homunculus, Scaramutza, in this play (RF, p. 164). But the plot itself also derives from Stieler, for Hallmann's protagonists in the guise of shepherds borrow not only many motifs from *Basilene*, but even the situation and configuration of the romantic pairings. Adonis, like Basilene and Oridor a devotee of the virgin goddess of the hunt, Diana, flees from the desperate wooing of the ardent shepherdess Rosibella, whose situation and behavior parallel those of Filidor and his sister Melinde in *Basilene*. Hallmann has not followed Stieler in using either the sacrifice plot from Guarini, or the accidental wounding in Montchretien's *Bergerie*, but instead turns to Gryphius's *Verlibtes Gespenste* for his solution: Rosibella, like Sulpicius, feigns death in order to awaken love in the hard-hearted object of her affections. Hallmann has probably focused on the Melinde-Oridor configuration, a subplot in *Basilene*, rather than on the Filidor-Basilene pattern with a male wooer, because of the situation associated with the occasion for which he designed his play. The second marriage into which Leopold is now entering ends fears that this monkish emperor might refuse to embark on matrimony again, a fear fueled by the deaths of his heirs from his first marriage. Thus it appears that, for *Adonis und Rosibella*, at least, Hallmann has turned to that archproducer of plays honoring marriages and other dynastic occasions at court, Caspar Stieler, for his models, rather than, for instance, to the mythological pastoral *Dafne* of Opitz or the allegorical pastoral *Seelewig* of Harsdörffer. One might also point out that Hallmann follows Stieler, not Opitz or Harsdörffer, in using prose for pastoral comedy (also in his *Urania*, an allegory in pastoral guise).

Stieler's most important area of influence on later dramatic texts was undoubtedly his contribution to the development of madrigalic versification for recitative in German-language opera. His introduction, already in the Rudolstadt plays of 1665-67, of a free-form iambic verse suitable for natural-sounding dialogue, further perfected in the two opera texts, *Melissa* and *Floretto*, which I now attribute to him, was to create the basis for successful German-language opera at Hamburg and, later, even in Vienna and Beyreuth. His innovations in madrigalic versification can also be seen to have been of importance for the great musical oratorios of Johann Sebastian Bach and Friedrich Händel which were dependent on the developments in Hamburg.

An interesting case of possible later influence on a prose comedy is Ludwig Tieck's *Die verkehrte Welt* of 1796-99. Although Tieck himself claimed to have been inspired by Christian Weise's play of this name, the result is a spoof on theatrical comedy that uses a pastiche of scenes featuring various European fools, among whom Scaramuz reigns supreme—in more ways than one. The common assumption that Tieck found Scaramuz prefigured in Weise's play is patently false, for the Scaramutza there has only two brief speeches in a single scene, and is not at all a comic fool. Furthermore, like Stieler's fool of that name and unlike Fiorelli's commedia dell'arte figure, Tieck's Scaramuz is very much a punster and challenger of theatrical illusion rather than a mime. However, this play is no romantic comedy in the sense of the term used in this study; apparently only Stieler's fool has survived his century.

Thus while Höfer's reluctant admission that Stieler's dramatic works had little or no influence on later dramatists is not really true, it is probably inappropriate to try to draw direct lines of influence from Stieler's comedies to any comedic production after 1705. However, the European tradition of romantic or heroic comedies to which Stieler's comic works belong is one which continued to bear occasional fruit in Germany and frequent fruit in lighthearted Austria for several more centuries. While Stieler was not the first German to produce original comedies in this mode, he was the only one in the seventeenth century to devote nearly all his theatrical efforts to the genre, resulting in a respectable corpus of published scripts of literary quality.

12

A Challenge

With the impending publication of the dramatic works of Caspar Stieler and the appearance of this monographic treatment, the foundation for further appreciation of the works of this talented dramatist will have been laid. This process will allow Stieler to take his rightful place among the other luminaries of the dramatic genre of Baroque Germany, as he already did a decade or so ago among the lyric poets. But the process will also demand an acknowledgment on the part of Germanists of the validity of the heroic or romantic comedy as a dramatic subgenre of literary merit, and an admission of the existence of such works from German pens. This recognition will require a fresh approach to comedy on the part of Germanists, one which will have to supplement the usual analyses of humor with theoretical explorations of the happy ending and of the relationship of this type of "high" or serious comedy with tragedy and with the courtly-gallant novel. For Germany did indeed produce a writer of comedies in the romantic or heroic mode, Caspar Stieler, whose comic spirit offers both the impetus for such an endeavor and a challenge to us all.

NOTES

Part I: Prologue

Chapter 1: The Comic Spirit in Baroque Germany

1. In using the terms "Romantic Comedy" and "Satiric Comedy," I follow the usage and definitions offered by Shakespearean scholar Nevill Coghill, "The Basis of Shakespearian Comedy: A Study in Medieval Affinities," *Essays and Studies*, 3 (1950), 1-28. In their *Art of the Drama* (New York: Appleton-Century-Crofts, 1935; rpt. 1963), Fred B. Millett and Gerald Eades Bentley similarly divide Elizabethan comedy into two types, which they term "realistic" and "romantic," pp. 95-98. Others term the phenomenon "romance," "heroic comedy," or "tragicomedy." Stieler himself used the term "Heldenspiel" in his theoretical treatise, *Dichtkunst des Spahten (1685)*, ed. Herbert Zeman, Wiener Neudrucke, no. 5 (ms. Weimar; Vienna: Österreichischer Bundesverlag, 1975), p. 53, line 1609, following the usage of Sigmund von Birken, *Teutsche Rede-Bind-und Dicht-Kunst* (Nürnberg: Riegel, 1679; rpt. 1973), pp. 323-40. Stieler's six Rudolstadt comedies are not the sole representatives of the romantic comedy in Baroque Germany, especially if one includes pastoral plays under this heading; even Andreas Gryphius is responsible for several.

2. Even Willi Flemming, who pioneered the objective mode of treatment for Baroque works, falls into at least implicit regionalism in terming satirical comedy "German comedy" and in denying any value to the German followers of the Romanic traditions in his "Einführung," *Die deutsche Barockkomödie*, DLE, vol. 4 (Leipzig: Reclam, 1931), pp. 27-42. In this survey of comedy he ignores Caspar Stieler (although he includes a work of his in another volume in the series) and concentrates on the writers of satirical comedy, Heinrich Julius von Braunschweig, Andreas Gryphius, Christian Weise, and Christian Reuter. He also ignores the popular cousin of the romantic comedy, the pastoral play, among his dramatic types in the DLE series. Even within Gryphius's works, he disregards the romantic-comedy half of the double comedy *Verlibtes Gespenste/Die gelibte Dornrose* and chooses to print and discuss only the *Zwischenspiel* set among German peasants.

3. Joseph Campbell, *The Hero with a Thousand Faces* (New York: Meridian, 1956), in the chapter titled "Tragedy and Comedy."

4. Northrop Frye, "The Argument of Comedy (1948)," in *Theories of Comedy*, ed. Paul Lauter (Garden City, N.Y.: Anchor, 1964), pp. 450ff.

5. Susanne K. Langer, *Feeling and Form: A Theory of Art* (New York: Scribner's, 1953). See Morton Gurewitch, *Comedy: The Irrational Vision* (Ithaca: Cornell University Press, 1975), for an excellent summary of the subject of comic theory.

6. And others, even some who are not dealing with romantic comedy, such as Elder Olson, in his *The Theory of Comedy* (Bloomington: Indiana University Press, 1968), p. 40: "While it would be a rare comedy that evoked no laughter—the comic function is less one of producing laughter than one of producing a lightheartedness and gaiety with which laughter is associated. . . . It involves achieving a state of mind in which we can view human frailties with smiling indulgence."

7. Dieter Kafitz, *Lohensteins 'Arminius': Disputatorisches Verfahren und Lehrgehalt in einem Roman zwischen Barock und Aufklärung*, Germanistische Abhandlungen, no. 32 (Stuttgart: Metzler, 1970), p. 37; Christian Thomasius, *Freymüthige Lustige und Ernsthaffte iedoch Vernunfft- und Gesetz-mäßige Gedanken Oder Monats-Gespräche* (Halle, 1690), p. 661. Giles R. Hoyt has recently criticized this and other systems of classification as arbitrary, and even as detrimental to the appreciation of the Baroque novel, in his "Der höfisch-historische satirische galante landstörtzerische Staats- Helden- Liebes- Barock-Roman or the Babel of Genre in the Seventeenth Century German Novel," *Colloquia Germanica*, 13 (1980), 321-43.

8. Herbert Singer, *Der galante Roman* (Stuttgart: Metzler, 1966), p. 16.

9. Hans Wagener, *The German Baroque Novel*, Twayne World Authors Series, no. 229 (New York: Twayne, 1973), pp. 105-106.

10. Singer, *Der galante Roman*, p. 16; Gerhard Spellerberg, *Verhängnis und Geschichte: Untersuchungen zu den Trauerspielen und dem 'Arminius'-Roman Daniel Caspers von Lohenstein* (Bad Homburg, Berlin, Zürich: Gehlen, 1970), pp. 18-19; Hans Gerd Rötzer, *Der Roman des Barock, 1600-1700: Kommentar zu einer Epoche* (München: Winkler, 1972), pp. 63-64; Volker Meid, *Der deutsche Barockroman* (Stuttgart: Metzler, 1974), p. 48.

11. Spellerberg, *Verhängnis und Geschichte*, pp. 19ff.

12. For Jacob Masen's *Palaestra eloquentiae ligatae*, see excerpt in Willi Flemming's *Ordensdrama* (DLE, *Barockdrama*, vol. 2), and discussion in his *Barockkomödie* (DLE, *Barockdrama*, vol. 4); Sigmund von Birken, *Teutsche Rede-Bind- und Dicht-Kunst*, p. 335.

13. Bernard of Clairvaux, *Sermones in Cantica canticorum*. See Bernard de Clairvaux, *Opera* (Rome: Editiones Cistercienses, 1957ff.), vols. 1 and 2.

14. As described (and deplored) by Denis de Rougemont in his book *Love in the Western World* of 1940, translated by Montgomery Belgion with that title (revised edition, New York: Fawcett, 1966).

Chapter 2: Caspar Stieler: State of the Scholarship

15. *Des Spaten oder Caspar Stielers . . . Teutscher Secretariat-Kunst*, ed. and rev. Joachim Friedrich Feller (Frankfurt am Main: J. B. Andrea and H. Hort, 1726), introduction.

16. Johann Heinrich Falkenstein, *Analecta Nordgaviensia*, IV (Schwabach, 1738); Just Christoph Motschmann, *Erfordia Literata, oder Gelehrtes Erffurth* (Erfurt, 1729), vol. I, pp. 100-123 and 312-14.

17. Johann Christoph Gottsched, *Nöthiger Vorrath zur Geschichte der deutschen dramatischen Dichtkunst* (Leipzig: Teubner, 1757-1765), vol. I. Under the year 1665 Gottsched (mis)cites a volume with the collective title (*Filidors Trauerkunst*[!] *und Mischspiele*, Jena, 1665) containing only *Der Vermeinte Printz* and *Ernelinde* (which he misspells as *Ermelinde*, p. 218). He speculates that *Der betrogene Betrug*, listed under the year 1667 among operas (p. 223), is by the same author, but does not similarly attribute *Die erfreuete Unschuld* (1666; p. 220) to the unknown Filidor.

18. Johannes Moller, *Cimbria literata* (Havniae: Kisel, 1744); this first edition was published some time after the genesis of the work, edited by Moller's sons.

19. Christian Gottlieb Jöcher, *Gelehrten-Lexicon, darinne die Gelehrten aller Stände . . . Nach ihrer Geburt, Leben, merckwürdigen Geschichten, Absterben und Schrifften aus den glaubwürdigsten Scribenten . . . schrieben worden*, Vierter Teil (Leipzig: Gleditsch, 1751), p. 418 (under Schwieger).

20. A. F. C. Vilmar, *Geschichte der deutschen National-Literatur*; edition used here is the fourteenth (Marburg: Elwert, 1871), p. 344.

21. Theodor Raehse, ed., Jacob Schwieger, *Geharnschte Venus*, Neudrucke deutscher Litteraturwerke des XVI. und XVII. Jahrhunderts (Halle: Max Niemeyer, 1888).

22. Albert Köster, *Der Dichter der Geharnschten Venus: Eine litterarhistorische Untersuchung* (Marburg: Elwert, 1897).

23. Conrad Höfer, *Die Rudolstädter Festspiele aus den Jahren 1665-1667 und Ihr Dichter: Eine literarhistorische Studie*, Probefahrten: Erstlingsarbeiten aus dem Deutschen Seminar in Leipzig (Leipzig: Voigtländer, 1904).

24. Willi Flemming, "Einführung: Festspiele," in *Oratorium/Festspiel*, DLE, *Barockdrama*, vol. 6 (Leipzig: Reclam, 1933), pp. 134ff.

25. Conrad Höfer, "Georg Bleyer, Ein Thüringischer Tonsetzer und Dichter der Barockzeit," *Zeitschrift des Vereins für Thüringische Geschichte und Altertumskunde*, Beiheft 24 (1941), 1-92.

26. Walter Hinck, *Das deutsche Lustspiel des 17. und 18. Jahrhunderts und die italienische Komödie* (Stuttgart: Metzler, 1965), pp. 130-36.

27. Herbert Zeman, *Kaspar Stieler: Versuch einer Monographie*, diss. Vienna, 1965.

28. Paul Hankamer, *Deutsche Gegenreformation und deutsches Barock: Die deutsche Literatur im Zeitraum des 17. Jahrhunderts* (Stuttgart: Metzler, 1935), p. 339; Richard Newald, *Die deutsche Literatur vom Späthumanismus zur Empfindsamkeit, 1570-1750* (Munich: Beck, 1951), vol. 5 of *Geschichte der deutschen Literatur von den Anfängen bis zur Gegenwart*, p. 199.

29. When Lohenstein or other prominent poets of the period express similar modesty, however, scholars now usually point out that such a disclaimer was a topos requisite for Christian authors since the Middle Ages. Could the perceived faults with Stieler's language really exist in even hurried works by this prolific author who not only wrote beautiful poetry, but also manuals on style and a dictionary of the German language? Instead, I propose to provide an explanation for the various styles in the plays, particularly the style of courtly address.

30. Horst Hartmann, *Die Entwicklung des deutschen Lustspiels von Gryphius bis Weise (1648-1688)*, diss. Potsdam, 1960. Hartmann stresses the importance of the Rudolstadt comedies, but adds little to knowledge or appreciation of them. He does note the peculiarity most of them demonstrate: the central role of an assertive woman (pp. 135-36).

31. Roy Pascal, *German Literature of the Sixteenth and Seventeenth Centuries: Renaissance—Reformation—Baroque*, vol. II of *Introductions to German Literature* (New York: Barnes and Noble, 1968), p. 234.

32. Bernhard Sowinski, "Die Literatur in der Neuzeit," in *Geschichte Thüringens*, vol. 4: *Kirche und Kultur in der Neuzeit* (Köln: Böhlau, 1972), p. 363. Sowinski follows Goedeke's erroneous spellings for *Ernelinde* and *Bellemperie* and omits *Basilene*, but seems to know the plots of the plays he does mention.

33. Rudolf Schoenwerth, *Die niederländischen und deutschen Bearbeitungen von Thomas Kyds 'Spanish Tragedy'*, Litterarhistorische Forschungen, no. 26 (Berlin: Felber, 1903; rpt. 1977), pp. cvii ff.

34. Conrad Höfer, "Weimarische Theaterveranstaltungen zur Zeit des Herzogs Wilhelm Ernst," Sonderdruck aus dem Jahresbericht des Großherzoglichen Sophienstiftes zur Weimar, Ostern 1914 (Weimar: Hofbuchdruckerei, 1914).

35. Judith P. Aikin, *German Baroque Drama*, Twayne World Authors Series, no. 634 (New York: Twayne, 1982), pp. 90-92 and 120-21.

36. Judith P. Aikin, "The Audience within the Play: Clues to Intended Audience Reaction in German Baroque Tragedies and Comedies," *Daphnis*, 13 (1984), 194-96.

37. Hellmut Christian Wolff, *Die Barockoper in Hamburg (1678-1738)* (Wolfenbüttel: Möseler, 1957), pp. 61-64 and passim.

Chapter 3: Filidor and "der Spahte": A Short Biography

38. Zeman's biography of Stieler in his monographic dissertation, pp. 13-110, supercedes the earlier attempt of Albert Rudolphi, *Kaspar Stieler der Spate, ein Lebensbild aus dem 17. Jahrhundert*, Program Erfurt, 1872, in that it balances the often erroneous accounts of the early eighteenth century against Stieler's own revelations and against documentation. This account relies on Zeman's evidence.

39. Zeman has recorded the Latin dismissal document and provided a translation, p. 21.

40. In his *Teutsche Secretariat-Kunst*, vol. I (Leipzig, 1705), p. 53, Stieler seems to give a reason for never claiming his early literary works: "Ich bekenne/ daß/ so oft ich meine vorige Schreiberey lese/ darob einen ekel empfinde und mich meiner misbrauchten Übereilung schäme." And on p. 62 he indicates a further reason: having to provide dramatic entertainment for the court is outside the proper duties and beneath the dignity of a self-respecting secretary.

Part II: The Plays

Chapter 4: The Rudolstadt Plays

1. The novella, written and first published in 1640, was available to me in a collection of Pallavicino's works owned by the Newberry Library in Chicago, where it is catalogued as *Opere*, 1660. The title page of the novella itself reads: *Il Principe Hermafrodito di Ferrante Pallavicino*, Venetia MDCLVI, Appreso il Turrini.

2. For a detailed examination of this polemical use of courtly comedy, see my article, "Practical Uses of Comedy at a Seventeenth-century Court: The Political Polemic in Stieler's *Der Vermeinte Printz*," *Theatre Journal*, 1983, 519-32.

3. *Lex Salica: 100 Titel-Text*, ed. Karl August Eckhardt, Germanenrechte, N.F., Abt. Westgermanisches Recht (Weimar: Böhlau, 1953), especially article 93, paragraph 6.

4. In *Henry V*, I, i, which relies on the chronicle of Holinshed; see also *Holinshed's Chronicles as used in Shakespeare's Plays*, ed. Allardyce Nicoll and Josephine Nicoll (London: Dent, 1927), p. 72 (Holinshed III, 545-46).

5. On the history of Barby, see Gerd Heinrich, *Die Grafen von Arnstein*, Mitteldeutsche Forschungen, no. 21 (Köln: Böhlau, 1961), pp. 306-33; Johann Heinrich Zedler, *Grosses Vollständiges Universal-Lexikon*, 1732ff. (rpt. Graz: Akademisch, 1961), vol. III, col. 428; *Brockhaus Encyclopädie* (1966), vol. II, p. 300. The core of Barby was land held in fief from the abbey of Quedlinburg, which in turn had received it in fief from the Saxon kings before 1000. Saxony reclaimed this territory in 1659. Other portions of Barby derived from lands received in fief in nearly equally distant times from Magdeburg and Anhalt (which in turn held them from Saxony); these portions likewise were reclaimed by their liege lords in 1659. See W. Fix, *Die Territorialgeschichte des Preußischen Staates* (Berlin: Schropp, 1869), p. 159.

6. Höfer, *Die Rudolstädter Festspiele*, p. 151.

7. According to Heinrich Ferdinand Schöppel, *Die Regenten des Fürstentums Schwarzburg-Rudolstadt* (Regensburg, 1915), p. 25.

8. For more extended speculation on the political stance of this play, see Aikin, "Practical Uses of Comedy," op. cit., especially 530-31.

9. As Höfer has shown, *Die Rudolstädter Festspiele*, pp. 144-48.

10. Other works by Stieler used as sources by the dictionary makers are *Die Geharnschte Venus* (1, 5, 7), *Bellemperie* (1), *Der Vermeinte Printz*, *Die Wittekinden*, *Stammbaum* (his dictionary), *Sekretariat-Kunst*, and *Zeitungs Lust und Nutz*. *Ernelinde* and the other Rudolstadt plays are ascribed merely to "Filidor" in the text, but erroneously to Jakob Schwieger in the index volume's list of sources published in 1971.

11. See Part III (In the Green Room), note 35, below, on this type of poem/song.

12. Walter Benjamin, *Ursprung des deutschen Trauerspiels*, 1928, rpt. "Wissenschaftliche Sonderausgabe," ed. Rolf Tiedemann (Frankfurt: Suhrkamp, 1969), p. 45. This quotation in Benjamin's work led to my interest in the plays of Caspar Stieler.

13. See *Die Dramen des Andreas Gryphius: Eine Sammlung von Einzelinterpretationen*, ed. Gerhard Kaiser (Stuttgart: Metzler, 1968), pp. 297-98.

14. Walter Wenzel, *Wittekind in der deutschen Literatur* (Bochum: Pöppinghaus, 1931), pp. 26-35.

15. See Judith P. Aikin, *The Mission of Rome in the Dramas of Daniel Casper von Lohenstein: Historical Tragedy as Prophecy and Polemic*, Stuttgarter Arbeiten zur Germanistik, no. 21 (Stuttgart: Heinz, 1976), pp. 104, 105, and 108.

16. Höfer, *Rudolstädter Festspiele*, p. 87. The French version of the novella, adapted from Bandello's II, 44, is to be found in Pierre Boisteau and Francois de Belleforest, *Histoires Tragiques: Extraictes des oeuvres Italiens de Bandel, et mis en langue Françoise . . . par Pierre Boaisteau, surnomme Launay . . . (et) par Françoise de Belleforest* (Paris: Jean de Bordeaux, 1580), vol. 1, pp. 111-57.

17. A recent work on the *miles christianus* motif provides a description of this figure, a mixture of traits ascribed to Michael and to Christ: "Der Typus dieses Kämpfers ist, neben Christus, der Erzengel Michael. Dieser führt seit Luzifers Sturz die himmlischen Heerscharen an und ist 'das Vorbild aller männlichen Tugenden, als Krieger und Ritter ohne Furcht und Tadel, als Satansfeind und Drachenkämpfer'." Andreas Wang, *Der 'miles christianus' im 16. und 17. Jahrhundert und seine mittelalterliche Tradition*, Mikrokosmos, Beiträge zur Literaturwissenschaft und Bedeutungsforschung, no. 1 (Bern: Herbert Lang, 1975), p. 87.

18. On this movement, see Walter Nigg, *Das ewige Reich: Geschichte einer Sehnsucht und einer Enttäuschung* (Erlenbach-Zürich: Reutsch, 1944), pp. 270-72; D. H. Kromminga, *The Millennium in the Church: Studies in the History of Christian Chiliasm* (Grand Rapids, Mich.: Eerdman, 1945), p. 17; Eric R. Chamberlain, *Antichrist and the Millennium* (New York: Dutton, 1975); Philip G. Rogers, *The Fifth Monarchy Men* (London: Oxford, 1966); Martin Lackner, *Geistfrömmigkeit und Enderwartung: Studien zum preußischen und schlesischen Spiritualismus, dargestellt an Christoph Barthut und Quirin Kuhlmann* (Stuttgart: Evangelisches Verlagswerk, 1959); Erhard Kunz, *Protestantische Eschatologie von der Reformation bis zur Aufklärung*, (Freiburg: Herder, 1980); and my article on this play, "Romantic Comedy as Religious Allegory: The Millennial Kingdom in Caspar Stieler's *Die erfreuete Unschuld*," *The German Quarterly*, 57 (1984), 59-74.

19. Henry Archer, *The Personall Reign of Christ upon Earth*. See Chamberlain, *Antichrist and the Millenium*, p. 89.

20. On Fritsch, see Faber du Faur, *German Baroque Literature: A Catalogue of the Collection in the Yale University Library* (New Haven: Yale University, 1958), entry for numbers 479-81.

21. Dietrich Korn, *Das Thema des Jüngsten Tages in der deutschen Literatur des 17. Jahrhunderts* (Tübingen: Niemeyer, 1957), pp. 30-31.

22. "Des Spaten," *Der teutsche Advocat* (Nürnberg: Hofmann, 1678), p. 477; see Zeman, *Monographie*, p. 63, and Otto Kinkeldey, "Einleitung: Philipp Heinrich Erlebach, nebst einigen Notizen zur Geschichte der Rudolstädter Hofmusik," in Philipp Heinrich Erlebach, *Harmonische Freude Musikalischer Freunde*, ed. Kinkeldey, Denkmäler Deutscher Tonkunst, vol. 46/47 (rpt. Wiesbaden: Breitkopf und Härtl, 1959), p. xvi, for the possible influence of Fritsch on Stieler and on the royal family in Rudolstadt.

23. *Der Bußfertige Sünder Oder Geistliches Handbüchlein*, "von dem Spaten" (Jena: Hoffmann, 1679).

24. Jakob Masen, *Palaestra eloquentiae ligatae* (1657); see Willi Flemming's introduction to comedy, *Die deutsche Barockkomödie*, vol. IV of *Barockdrama*, DLE, Reihe Barock (Leipzig: Reclam, 1931), p. 22. Sigmund von Birken, *Teutsche Rede-bind- und Dicht-Kunst* (Nürnberg: Christof Riegel, 1679; rpt. Hildesheim: Olms, 1973).

25. On early *Fastnachtspiel* from this perspective, see Eckehard Catholy, *Fastnachtspiel* (Stuttgart: Metzler, 1966), especially pp. 20-24.

26. *Evangelischer Liederschatz für Kirche und Haus: Eine Sammlung geistlicher Lieder aus allen christlichen Jahrhunderten*, ed. M. Albert Knapp (Stuttgart: Cotta, 1837), vol. 1, no. 1064, pp. 462-63.

27. It can also be found in the *Evangelischer Liederschatz*: vol. 1, no. 1029, p. 448.

28. Published in Nicodemus Frischlin, *Operum Poeticorum . . . pars Scenica* (Wittenberg: Berger, 1636); microfilm, Jantz, *German Baroque Literature*, no. 88; Research Publications, Inc., reel 18. Latin choruses follow each act of *Phasma* except the last, which instead ends with two variants on this Luther hymn. The first, sung by "Christus cum suis," uses the first two verses of Luther's text, substituting the more specific "Und steur deß Bapsts und Türcken Mord" for "Und steuer unsrer Feinde Mord" in the second line of the first verse and adding several more original verses. The second, sung by "Satanas cum suis," is a parody of this hymn which prays for the victory of the Roman Catholic Church and other heresies. The first two lines read: "Erhalt die Römisch Kirch O Gott/ Und wehr des Luthers Hohn und Spot."

29. To be found, for example, in *Kirchen-Gesangbuch für Evangelisch-Lutherische Gemeinden ungeänderter Augsburgischer Confession* (St. Louis, Mo.: Concordia, 1892).

30. Their popularity and significance is indicated by the numerous editions and translations, including three or four for each that might have been available to Stieler when he wrote *Basilene*—not that Stieler, with his language ability in Italian, would have needed to avoid the originals.

31. Published only in Antoine de Montchretien, *Les tragedies de Ant. de Montchrestien sieur de Vasteuille plus une bergerie et un poeme de Susane* (Rouen: Jean Petit, 1601).

32. Höfer, *Rudolstädter Festspiele*, pp. 96-98; Zeman, however, offers evidence that Stieler may have used both Guarini's original and a French adaptation of Montchretien in the form of a novella, pp. 224ff.

33. It should be pointed out, however, that the two pastoral plays of Johann Christian Hallmann—*Urania* of the same year as *Basilene* and *Adonis und Rosibella* of 1673—are likewise in prose with verse choruses, although they include *Zwischenspiele* not unlike those for his verse tragedies.

34. In a scene based on that in *Bergerie* in which the seeress Philistille tries to convince the chaste huntress Dorine that she should reject the hunt and become a shepherdess (II, ii).

35. See my article "Guarini's *Il Pastor fido* in Germany: Allegorical and Figural Aspects," *Studi Germanici*, XVI (1978), 125-48; bibliographical references to parallel studies by Italianists are to be found in this article.

36. Sancti Aurelii Augustini Episcopi, *De Civitate Dei*, ed. Emanuel Hoffmann, Corpus Scriptorum Ecclesiasticorum Latinorum, vol. 40 (Prague: Tempsky, 1899), pp. 190-92.

37. Paul Scarron, *Le Romant Comique* (Paris: Toussainct Guinet, 1651); recently republished with notes and commentary by Robert Garapon, Lettres Francaises (Paris: Imprimerie Nationale, 1980).

38. Stieler makes several errors when he gives the title as "Trompeur, trompeur a demy." He cites an edition published in Amsterdam in 1622 which Höfer was unable to find in 1904 (*Rudolstädter Festspiele*, p. 81), and for which I have also found no references.

39. Höfer, *Rudolstädter Festspiele*, pp. 81-85.

Chapter 5: Later Dramatic Texts and Activities

40. *Teutsche Secretariat-Kunst*, vol. 1 (Leipzig, 1705), p. 62.
41. Stieler himself, in his motto, according to Zeman, p. 71, explained the name as "Übertrifft den Frühzeitigen," so I can only speculate about a hidden meaning on the order of the anagrammatic names in *Die Geharnschte Venus*. The Greek "thesp-," from Thespus, first dramatist, also means prophetic (both Opitz and Stieler use the topos of the poet as seer in their poetical treatises) or humble (another traditional topos to describe the poet).
42. Signatur Dd 4739'i.
43. Herr Starke, "stellvertretender Direktor," wrote his surmises to me in a letter of February 13, 1981.
44. See Höfer, *Rudolstädter Festspiele*, pp. 27-28, on Scaramutza's use of diminutive names for his girlfriends.
45. Höfer, *Rudolstädter Festspiele*, e.g., p. 43.
46. Zeman's *Monographie* devotes much space to Stieler's apparently great love for his wife, especially pp. 82-88.
47. As Zeman has shown, pp. 68-72, Stieler was admitted to the "Fruchtbringende Gesellschaft" upon his own application in 1668. However, Zeman's reading of "Wintermonat" in two of the documents as January is patently false (although Grimm's *Deutsches Wörterbuch* allows January as a possible equivalent, that dictionary states: "Die Mehrzahl aller Zeugnisse des 15.-19. Jhs. meint . . . den November"), for Neumark's letter of December 1668 makes sense only if "Wintermonat" refers to the previous month.
48. Stieler's *Hoch-Fürstlicher Ehren-Altar* (Gotha, 1678) contains elegies to the seven princes of that family who died between 1667 and 1676.
49. See Höfer, *Rudolstädter Festspiele*, p. 152. The wedding never took place due to the bride's sudden death.
50. Meliboeus is a character in Nicodemus Frischlin's *Phasma* (1580), as well as in classical Latin literature; Amyntas clearly derives from Torquato Tasso's pastoral *Aminta*. But it is obvious that only the names, not the nature of the characterization in each source, is borrowed.
51. Georg Philipp Harsdörffer, *Frauenzimmer Gesprächspiele*, ed. Irmgard Böttcher, Deutsche Neudrucke, Reihe Barock, no. 16 (Tübingen: Niemeyer, 1968), part XII, p. 102.
52. Signature Q580. It is first discussed by Conrad Höfer, *Rudolstädter Festspiele*, pp. 149-50.
53. Höfer, ibid., p. 149, had claimed that the handwriting was Stieler's, but in his *Monographie*, p. 72, Zeman showed that it was written by some person unknown, with corrections in Stieler's hand.
54. Stieler's post in Eisenach was as "gemeinschaftlicher Cammer- und Lehenssekretarius." On this period in his life, see Zeman, *Monographie*, pp. 63-66.
55. On this opera, see also the introduction by Guido Adler to his edition of the work: Marc Antonio Cesti, *Il Pomo d'oro: Bühnenfestspiel*, Denkmäler der Tonkunst in Österreich, vols. 6 and 9 (Vienna: Artaria, 1896), pp. v-xxvi; Egon Wellesz, "Ein Bühnenfestspiel aus dem Siebzehnten Jahrhundert," *Die Musik*, 52 (1914), 191-217, also published in an English translation by Patricia Kean in Egon Wellesz, *Essays on Opera* (London: Dobson, 1950), pp. 54-81; H. Seifert, "Die Festlichkeiten zur ersten Hochzeit Kaiser Leopolds I," *Österreichische Musikzeitschrift*, 29 (1974), 6-16; and Carl B. Schmidt, "Antonio Cesti's Il Pomo d'oro: A Reexamination of a Famous Habsburg Court Spectacle,"

Journal of the American Musicological Society, 29 (1976), 381-412. None of these studies knows of Stieler's translation. Wellesz also treats this work in the context of Viennese opera of the seventeenth century in his valuable survey, *Der Beginn des musikalischen Barock und die Anfänge der Oper in Wien*, Theater und Kultur, no. 6 (Vienna: Literarische Anstalt, 1922). On Francesco Sbarra as a comic poet, see Marcus Landau, *Die italienische Literatur am öster-reichischen Hofe* (Vienna: C. Gerolds Sohn, 1879), p. 19. On Marc Antonio Cesti, see Hermann Kretzschmar, "Die Venetianische Oper und die Werke Cavallis und Cestis," *Vierteljahresschrift für Musikwissenschaft*, 8 (1892), 1ff.

56. The most famous of these before Leopold were Maximilian I to Maria of Burgundy, and their son Philipp to Joanna ("the Mad"), heiress of Spain, but in general the *Heiratspolitik* of the Habsburg dynasty was justly admired.

57. On these events, see especially Seifert, "Die Festlichkeiten zur ersten Hochzeit Kaiser Leopolds I," op. cit., and Wellesz, *Der Beginn des musikalischen Barock*, pp. 62-67.

58. According to documentation assembled by Alexander Witeschnik, *Wiener Opernkunst von den Anfängen bis zu Karajan* (Vienna: Kremayr and Scheriau, 1959), p. 21, and others.

59. Adler, introduction to the edition, and others.

60. Gottlieb Eucharius Rinck, in the second edition of his biography of Leopold, *Leopolds des Grossen Römischen Kaysers Wunderwürdiges Leben und Thaten* of 1713 (according to Adler, ibid., p. vii), claims that the opera was performed three times a week for a year in 1667-68. Seifert has pointed out that even the performance of 1667 or early 1668 assumed by Adler and others probably never came about, in part because of the unfinished theater, but also because of the death of the imperial couple's first child early in 1668.

61. *Il Pomo d'oro Festa teatrale Rappresentata in Vienna per l'augustissime Nozze delle sacre cesaree e reali maestá di Leopoldo e Margherita componimento di Francesco Sbarra* (Vienna: Matteo Cosmerovio, Stampatore della Corte, 1667 and 1668).

62. Like that of Rinck about the number and frequency of performances noted above, note 60.

63. Theresa Schüssel, *Kultur des Barock in Österreich* (Graz: Stiasny, 1960), p. 124.

64. Sigmund von Birken, *Teutsche Rede-Bind- und Dicht-Kunst*, p. 325.

65. *Der guldene Apfel/ Schauspiel*, facs. ed. Margret Dietrich (Vienna, 1965), according to Schmidt, "Antonio Cesti's Il Pomo d'oro."

66. Nationalbibliothek, Signature ms. 16844.

67. See note 55, above. The missing acts III and V have been largely reconstructed on the basis of a manuscript found recently in Modena. See Antonio Cesti, *Il Pomo d'oro, Music for Acts III and V from Modena, Biblio-teca Estense, ms. mus. E. 120*, ed. Carl B. Schmidt (Madison, Wisc.: A-R Editions, 1982). Schmidt also discusses this portion of the score in his article, "Antonio Cesti's Il Pomo d'oro," op. cit.

68. The aria "E dove t'aggiri" on *Italian Opera*, RCA Victor LM 6030, vol. 5, side one; a selection on *Of Castles and Cathedrals: Music of the Emperors at the Hofburg Castle, Vienna* (Musical Heritage Society CC7).

69. The *Reyen*, basically unchanged from the first edition (1661), appears at the end of Act II; Daniel Casper von Lohenstein, *Afrikanische Trauerspiele*, ed. Klaus Günther Just, Bibliothek des literarischen Vereins in Stuttgart, no. 294 (Stuttgart: Hiersemann, 1957), pp. 77-80.

70. Galeazzo Gualdo Priorato, *Ragguaglio di quanto e seguito nel Terzo Matrimonio di Sua Maestá Cesarea. Anno 1676. 1677. Lettera del Conte Galeazzo*

Gualdo Priorato, all' . . . *Cardinale Barberino* (Vienna, 1677), p. 16v. A copy exists in the Biblioteca Vaticana, Signature Stamp. Barb. Z.I.82.

71. Anonymous, *Der Schütz- und Schatten-reich ausgebreitete Kaisers-Adler/ Oder: Das Glor-grünende Römische Reichs-Zepter/ unsers Allergroß-mächtigsten Augusti LEOPOLDI des Ersten* (Augsburg, 1690), pp. 29-30.

72. Latin: Bella gerant alij: tu, Felix Austria, nube./ Nam, quae Mars allijs, dat tibi Regna Venus.

73. See note 15, above.

74. See especially Jörg Jochen Berns, "Trionfo-Theater am Hof von Braunschweig-Wolfenbüttel," *Daphnis*, 10 (1981), 663-710, particularly 664-73.

75. See Schmidt, "Antonio Cesti's Il Pomo d'oro," pp. 394-95 on these pieces, extant only in the Modena manuscript (see note 67, above).

76. The translation seems to be based on the edition of 1667, not 1668, for the honorific pages reflect the format of the earlier edition. The versions are otherwise apparently identical, but, as Adler has noted, there are minor variants in the text for the manuscript score (edition, p. 205).

77. Höfer, *Rudolstädter Festspiele*, p. 150.

78. Wellesz, *Der Beginn des musikalischen Barock*, p. 72.

79. Zeman, *Monographie*, p. 95.

80. That *Bellemperie* was performed in Meiningen is recorded by Schöppack, *Geschichte der lat. Schule zu Meiningen bis 1705*, Programmheft Meiningen 1843; see Höfer, *Rudolstädter Festspiele*, p. 157. Both dramas were produced by the Rector of Görlitz in 1684 and 1685, according to *Die Mitteilungen der Schlesischen Gesellschaft für Volkskunde*, 16, 251 (see Bolte, *Eine Ungedruckte Poetik*, p. 97).

81. Thomas Kyd, *The Spanish Tragedy*, ed. Thomas W. Ross (Berkeley/Los Angeles: University of California, 1968). Written in the late 1580s, this play was the most popular English drama of the period, overshadowing the works of Shakespeare. There was also a version, now lost, on the continental itinerant stage.

82. *Don Jeronimo, Marschalk van Spanjens Treur-Spel. Vertoont Op d'Amsterdamsche Schouwburgh, Den 12. October, 1638* (Amsterdam: Ioost Hartgersz, 1638).

83. Rudolf Schoenwerth, *Die niederländischen und deutschen Bearbeitungen von Thomas Kyds 'Spanish Tragedy'*, op. cit., pp. cvii ff.

84. As most scholars have noted, it is hardly an improvement, for the vivid metaphors and convoluted phrasing are perhaps as alienating in the prose dialogues of *Bellemperie* to a twentieth-century ear as the appearance of the excessively polite circumlocutions of seventeenth-century bureaucratic jargon in the earlier prose plays. Yet within the stylistic limits Stieler has accepted for the elevated speeches of his noble characters, as much as in the recently preferred low-life speeches of Scaramutza and his fellows, this expert on words constantly reveals his talent and his expertise.

85. In Andreas Gryphius, *Gesamtausgabe der deutschsprachigen Werke*, vol. VII, ed. Hugh Powell and Marian Szyrocki (Tübingen: Niemeyer, 1969). Written ca. 1647-50, first performed 1657 or 1658, published in 1663. Pickelhering facetiously argues that the Pyramus and Thisbe play is a comedy since the actors revive after playing dead: "Das Spiel wird lustig außgehen/ denn die Todten werden wieder lebendig/ setzen sich zusammen/ und trincken einen guten Rausch" (p. 11). And indeed, the actors of the internal play do resurrect at the end of the playlet before the eyes of the audience on stage.

86. The dance of death, with roots in popular superstition, was a frequent subject for late medieval and sixteenth-century poets and visual artists. In the

Ringelreihen of the danse macabre, the dead or a personification of death, often with a fiddle (a *Spielmann*), danced with the living who were soon to die or with the recently dead. The motif was often associated with the Black Death. See Wolfgang Stammler, *Der Totentanz: Entstehung und Deutung* (München: Hanser, 1948), and Hellmut Rosenfeld, *Der mittelalterliche Totentanz: Entstehung—Entwicklung—Bedeutung*, second rev. ed. (Köln/Graz: Böhlau, 1968). Stieler, who was a musician as well as a poet, becomes a sort of latter-day *Spielmann* who lures audience members to join the dance signifying mortality.

Although a dance of death at the end of a drama is novel, dances in which actor and audience joined were popular in the sixteenth century *Fastnachtspiel*, as Eckehard Catholy has shown (*Fastnachtspiel*, Sammlung Metzler, Stuttgart: Metzler, 1966, pp. 24-25, and *Das Fastnachtspiel des Spätmittelalters: Gestalt und Funktion*, Hermaea, Germanistische Forschungen, N.S., no. 8, Tübingen: Niemeyer, 1961, pp. 117-18). These dances, as Catholy demonstrates, serve to destroy any illusion which separates play and audience realities and to integrate the comedy of the play into the jollity of the occasion. Stieler's *Totentanz* functions to destroy that separation instead in order to confront the audience members with their own mortality by even stronger means than those usually employed in tragedy. Cheerful ballets often followed court performances of plays in the seventeenth century, but did not involve audience members, as far as I know.

87. For a treatment of the ending of *Bellemperie* from this perspective in the context of a discussion of a number of plays of the German Baroque, see my article "The Audience within the Play: Clues to Intended Audience Reaction in German Baroque Tragedies and Comedies," *Daphnis*, 13 (1984), 187-201.

88. Other poetical treatises of the period ignore the type as a particular genre, although Birken's example for his *Heldenspiel* is certainly an overt *Allegorie*: see Sigmund von Birken, *Teutsche Rede-Bind- und Dicht-Kunst* (Nürnberg, 1679; rpt. Hildesheim, 1973), pp. 323-30. Harsdörffer defines, but does not name, the type, which he places between his "Freudenspiel" and "Hirtenspiel;" see Georg Philipp Harsdörffer, *Poetischer Trichter* (Nürnberg, 1650; rpt. Darmstadt, 1969), pp. 97-98. Only Stieler's *Dichtkunst* provides a self-explanatory terminology and definition of this type of comedy.

89. On other uses of the "Hercules at the Crossroads" parable, see Erwin Panofsky, *Hercules am Scheidewege und andere antike Bildstoffe in der neueren Kunst*, Studien der Bibliothek Warburg, no. 28 (Berlin/Leipzig: Teubner, 1930); and Judith Aikin, *The Mission of Rome in the Dramas of Daniel Casper von Lohenstein*, op. cit., pp. 111-13.

90. See Aikin, *Mission of Rome*, pp. 230-31.

91. Ibid., pp. 111-13.

92. Höfer, "Weimarische Theaterveranstaltungen," pp. 3-10.

93. Ibid., p. 5.

94. Zeman, *Monographie*, pp. 99-100.

95. Herbert A. Frenzel, *Thüringische Schlosstheater: Beiträge zur Typologie des Spielortes vom 16. bis zum 19. Jahrhundert*, Schriften für Theatergeschichte, no. 63 (Berlin: Gesellschaft für Theatergeschichte, 1965), pp. 178-79 and notes.

96. E.g., Erdmann Werner Böhme, *Die frühdeutsche Oper in Thüringen: Ein Jahrhundert mitteldeutscher Musik- und Theatergeschichte des Barock* (Stadtroda: Richter, 1931), pp. 194-95; Wolfgang Lidke, *Das Musikleben in Weimar von 1683 bis 1735*, Schriften zur Stadtgeschichte und Heimatkunde, no. 3 (Weimar: Stadtmuseum, 1953), pp. 18-19; and H. Engel, *Musik in Thüringen*, Mitteldeutsche Forschungen, no. 39 (Köln: Böhlau, 1966), p. 119. The performances are also listed by Renate Brockpähler, *Handbuch zur Geschichte der Barockoper in Deutschland* (Emsdetten: Lechte, 1964).

97. *Musicalische Freuden-Feyer/* Bey des Durchlauchtigsten Fürsten und Herrns/ Hn. Wilhelm Ernstens/ Herzogs zu Sachsen/ Jülich/ Cleve und Berg/ Landgrafens in Thüringen/ Marckgrafens zu Meißen/ Gefürsteten Grafens zu Henneberg/ Grafens zu der Marck und Ravensberg/ Herrns zu Ravenstein/ Am 19. Octobris des 1684. Heyl-Jahrs Höchst-glücklich eingetretenen Fürstlichen Geburtstage/ Vor und neben dem theatralischen Schauspiele/ (genand) Krieg und Sieg der Keuschheit/ Zu Weimar auf dem Fürstlichen Gartenhause aus unterthänigster Schuldigkeit glückwüntschend vorgestellet. Weimar/ Gedruckt bey Johann Andreas Müllern/ Fürst. Sächs. Hof-Buchdruckern. The only extant copies of this and the *Zwischenspiel* of the other Weimar performance of 1684, "Glückwüntschende Winter-Lust," are to be found in the Zentralbibliothek der deutschen Klassik in Weimar and in the Forschungsbibliothek in Gotha.

98. Frenzel, *Thüringische Schlosstheater*, pp. 178-80.

99. Höfer, "Weimarische Theaterveranstaltungen," p. 7.

100. Available to Stieler in editions of 1668, 1671, 1673, 1678, and 1680. The edition of 1678 is reprinted in Neudrucke deutscher Litteraturwerke des XVI. und XVII. Jahrhunderts, nos. 242-45, ed. Max Freiherr von Waldberg (Halle: Niemeyer, 1914), pp. 175-243.

101. E.g., "Sanct Velten," "löffelt," "botz tausend," "wo Barthel Most holt," "Ertz-Vater," all in the first scene. The creative name-calling in the comic scenes in this play, and the frequent use of diminutives of animal names and other insulting or complimentary names for girls as *Kosenamen*, both point to direct influence from Stieler.

102. This comic opera is discussed in some detail and often used as a source of examples by Hellmut Christian Wolff, *Die Barockoper in Hamburg (1678-1738)* (Wolfenbüttel: Möseler, 1957), vol. 1, pp. 61-64 and passim. While Wolff does not tie *Floretto* to the composer Strungk, all other mentions in music literature do so, and the attribution is apparently secure. On Strungk, see Fritz Berend, *Nicolaus Adam Strungk, 1640-1700: Sein Leben und seine Werke, mit Beiträgen zur Geschichte der Musik und des Theaters in Celle, Hannover, Leipzig* (Hannover: Homann, 1915).

103. Albert Köster, *Der Dichter der Geharnschten Venus: Eine litterarhistorische Untersuchung* (Marburg: Elwert, 1897), pp. 7-14; Conrad Höfer, *Die Rudolstädter Festspiele*, especially pp. 47-69.

104. *Glückwüntschende Winter-Lust/* welche zu unterthänigsten Ehren Der Durchläuchtigsten Fürstin und Frauen FRAUEN CHARLOTTEN MARIEN/ gebohrner und vermählten Hertzogin zu Sachsen/ Jülich/ Cleve und Berg/ Landgräffin in Thüringen/ Marckgräffin zu Meißen/ Gefürsteten Gräffin zu Henneberg/ Gräfin zu der Marck und Ravensberg/ Frauen zu Ravenstein und dero Den 10. Christmonats des 1684. Jahrs höchsterfreulich erschienenen Fürstlichen Geburtstages/ nach geendigter Heil. Weinacht-Feyer/ am 28. iztgedachten Monats und Jahrs Bey den angestellten Freuden-Spiele/ (genand/) Die erlösete Treue und Unschuld/ Auf dem Fürstl. Gartenhause zu Weimar gehorsamst aufgeführt worden. Weimar/ Gedruckt bey Johann Andreas Müllern/ Fürstl. Sächs. Hof-Buchdruckern.

105. Höfer, "Weimarische Theaterveranstaltungen," p. 8. He found the text in the library in Gotha.

106. Höfer knew only of the performance of 1674, and mistakenly placed it in Weißenfels. Frenzel, *Thüringische Schlosstheater*, p. 271, n. 711, and Brockpähler, *Handbuch zur Geschichte der Barockoper*, know both dates and place both performances in Halle.

107. According to Höfer, "Theatralische Veranstaltungen," p. 8.

108. Frenzel, *Thüringische Schlosstheater*, p. 179 and p. 271, n. 713.

Part III: In The Green Room

Chapter 6: "Fette Suppen und hohe Sprünge": Questions of Patronage and Occasion

1. *Die Dichtkunst des Spaten, 1685*, ed. Herbert Zeman, Wiener Neudrucke, no. 5 (Vienna: Österreichischer Bundesverlag, 1975), lines 1883ff.

2. Sigmund von Birken, *Teutsche Rede-Bind- und Dicht-Kunst* (Nürnberg, 1679; rpt. Hildesheim: Georg Olms, 1973), p. 201.

3. On patronage in the Middle Ages see Joachim Bumke, *Maezene im Mittelalter: Die Gönner und Auftraggeber der höfischen Literatur in Deutschland 1150-1300* (Munich: Beck, 1979).

4. See Zeman, *Monographie*, pp. 52-54.

5. Zeman would date their completion after Stieler obtained the new post in January 1680. Due to their lack of possible connection to any courtly occasions or performances in 1680, I see them instead as the results of an attempt to find a new patron.

6. See *Adelsherrschaft und Literatur*, ed. Horst Wenzel, Beiträge zur älteren deutschen Literaturgeschichte, no. 6 (Frankfurt: Lang, 1980); Jan-Dirk Müller, *Gedechtnus: Literatur und Hofgesellschaft um Maximilian I* (Munich: Fink, 1982).

7. See Zeman, *Monographie*, pp. 55-63.

8. Ibid., *Monographie*, pp. 68-72. However, Zeman has misunderstood the date on one letter. See Part II (The Plays), note 47, above.

Chapter 7: Caspar Stieler and the German "Singspiel"

9. *Die Geharnschte Venus oder Liebeslieder im Kriege gedichtet herausgegeben von Filidor dem Dorfferer* (Hamburg: Guht, 1660).

10. In Caspar Stieler, *Die Geharnschte Venus*, ed. Conrad Höfer, Festgabe der Gesellschaft der Münchner Bücherfreunde (Munich: C. Wolf, 1925).

11. Jacob Schwieger[!], *Geharnschte Venus*, ed. Theobald Raehse, Neudrucke deutscher Literaturwerke des sechzehnten und siebzehnten Jahrhunderts, nos. 74 and 75 (Halle: Niemeyer, 1888), p. xiv.

12. Op. cit., pp. 183-93; reprinted with few alterations in the historical-critical facsimile edition of the collection: Kaspar Stieler, *Die Geharnschte Venus oder Liebes-Lieder im Kriege Gedichtet*, ed. Herbert Zeman (München: Kösel, 1968), pp. 19-28; a "Nachtrag" in that edition by Bernhard Billeter adds nothing to her comments on Stieler, although it provides a useful bibliography (pp. 28-29).

13. A book of 108 songs published by Stieler in 1679 and reprinted in 1689 contains 24 pages of melodies, but it is not clear who composed them, either in the information offered by the title page, or in the entry under Caspar Stieler in Robert Eitner's *Biographisch-Bibliographisches Quellen-Lexikon der Musiker und Musikgelehrten christlicher Zeitrechnung bis Mitte des neunzehnten Jahrhunderts* (1903; rpt. Graz: Akademisch, 1959), vol. 9. This songbook is *Der Bußfertige Sünder, oder Geistliches Handbüchlein. Nebst dazu gehörigen Psalmen und christlichen Liedern* (Jena: Nisius, 1679). Other song books published by Stieler that may also have had musical settings in some copies include: *Neuentsprungene Wasserquelle* (Weimar: Schmidt, 1670; Nürnberg: Hofmann, 1675 and 1676; new editions in 1690, 1707, and 1718); and *Jesus-Schall und Wiederhall* (Nürnberg: Hofmann, 1684). I have not encountered any copy which does.

14. E.g., H. Engel, "Musik in Thüringen," in *Geschichte Thüringens*, vol. IV: *Kirche und Kultur in der Neuzeit*, Mitteldeutsche Forschungen, no. 48 (Köln: Böhlau, 1972), pp. 207ff.; H. Engel, *Musik in Thüringen*, Mitteldeutsche Forschungen, no. 39 (Köln: Böhlau, 1966), pp. 171-72; Erdmann Werner Böhme, *Die frühdeutsche Oper in Thüringen: Ein Jahrhundert mitteldeutscher Musik- und Theatergeschichte des Barock* (Stadtroda: Richter, 1931), pp. 129-30, 159-60, and 194-95.

15. Engel, *Musik in Thüringen*, p. 172. Many dictionaries of opera or lists of early operas refer to one or more of Stieler's plays, without seeming to know any more about them than the title. An example of such piecemeal knowledge, and probably the origin of several such mentions, is Hans Michael Schletterer, *Das deutsche Singspiel von seinen ersten Anfängen bis auf die neueste Zeit* (1863; rpt. Hildesheim: Georg Olms, 1975). On p. 189 he lists Jacob Schwieger as author of the musical drama *Die Wittekinden* and on p. 128 lists *Der Betrogene Betrug* as an anonymous *Singspiel*.

16. Peter Gülke, *Musik und Musiker in Rudolstadt*, Sonderausgabe der Rudolstädter Heimathefte (Rudolstadt: Mitzlaff, 1963), pp. 6-8.

17. Böhme, *Die Frühdeutsche Oper in Thüringen*, pp. 194-95; Wolfgang Lidke, *Das Musikleben in Weimar von 1683 bis 1735*, Schriften zur Stadtgeschichte und Heimatkunde, no. 3, diss. Leipzig 1953, pp. 18-19.

18. Conrad Höfer, "Weimarische Theaterveranstaltungen zur Zeit des Herzogs Wilhelm Ernst," Sonderdruck aus dem Jahresbericht des Großherzoglichen Sophienstiftes zu Weimar (Weimar: Hofbuchdruckerei, 1914).

19. Otto Kinkeldey, "Einleitung: Philipp Heinrich Erlebach, nebst einigen Notizen zur Geschichte der Rudolstädter Hofmusik," in *Philipp Heinrich Erlebach: Harmonische Freude Musikalischer Freunde*, Denkmäler Deutscher Tonkunst, vol. 46/47 (1914; rpt. Wiesbaden: Breitkopf und Härtel, 1959), pp. v-xvi. Erlebach was *Kapellmeister* in Rudolstadt beginning around 1680. This volume also contains Erlebach's catalogue (1700) of the musical manuscript collection in the archive of the "Gräfliche Hofkapelle" which will be referred to elsewhere in this study.

20. Willi Flemming, "Einführung" in *Oratorium, Festspiel* (vol. 6 of *Barockdrama* in the Baroque series of Deutsche Literatur in Entwicklungsreihen), (Leipzig: Reclam, 1933), pp. 117-40. Urte Härtwig, "Stieler," in *Die Musik in Geschichte und Gegenwart*, vol. 12, cols. 1298-1300, is among those who follow Kinkeldey and Flemming in seeing Bleyer as the composer of all of Stieler's Rudolstadt plays. She does not speculate as to a possible composer for the plays of 1680, although she lists them as dramas with music.

21. Conrad Höfer, "Georg Bleyer, Ein thüringischer Tonsetzer und Dichter der Barockzeit," *Zeitschrift des Vereins für thüringische Geschichte und Altertumskunde*, Beiheft 24 (Jena: Fischer, 1941).

22. Höfer, "Georg Bleyer," pp. 12-17.

23. Ibid., p. 27. Höfer points out that Bleyer's contract of October 22, 1666, implies the existence of someone, unnamed, currently holding the post. Documents from 1668 make it clear that there is indeed a *Kapell-direktor* at Rudolstadt, although, again, there is no mention of a name, according to Kinkeldey, p. v.

24. Gülke, *Musik und Musiker in Rudolstadt*, op. cit., p. 7, believed that secretary to have been Bleyer, apparently unaware of Höfer's study refuting that possibility. Bleyer was never called "Cammer-Secretarius," but only "Cammerschreiber," a considerably inferior title.

25. *New Grove Dictionary of Music and Musicians*, vol. 15 (London: Macmillan, 1980), p. 643.

26. Ibid., p. 643.

27. Ibid., vol. 1, p. 573.

28. Ibid., vol. 10, p. 834.

29. Conrad Höfer, *Rudolstädter Festspiele*, pp. 41-42.

30. Kinkeldey, *Erlebach*, p. xiii.

31. On this type and its tradition, see Mara R. Wade, *The Early German Pastoral Singspiel*, diss. University of Michigan, 1984.

32. Höfer, *Die Rudolstädter Festspiele*, p. 150.

33. The original libretto and score by Sbarra and Cesti, *Il Pomo d'oro: Bühnenfestspiel*, is published in Denkmähler der Tonkunst in Österreich, vols. 6 and 9, ed. Guido Adler (Vienna: Artaria, 1896).

34. Hellmut Christian Wolff, *Die Barockoper in Hamburg (1678-1738)* (Wolfenbüttel: Möseler, 1957), p. 61. Discussion of this opera continues on pp. 62-64, and Wolff uses a number of quotations from this libretto to make points later in the study.

35. The echo song has a tradition in sixteenth-century Italian madrigal verse and its musical settings, and became very frequent in the seventeenth century not only in Italy but in Germany as well. It had become a commonplace in pastoral drama in Germany, at least, by 1660. The echo is defined by musicians as "imitation in music of a natural echo effect," and more specifically, in the echo song in vocal music, "only the last few notes of each phrase were echoes" (*Grove Dictionary of Music and Musicians*, vol. 5, p. 822). A famous early example of the echo song in musical drama occurs in Cavalieri's *Rappresentatione di Anima, et di Corpo* of 1600. Literary historians define the phenomenon as a type of poetic text and unearth a literary tradition going back to antiquity. Gero von Wilpert's *Sachwörterbuch der Literatur* (Stuttgart: Kröner, 1969), p. 194, offers the following account:

> *Echolied*, Gedicht, dessen Reimwörter durch Echo verdoppelt werden und dessen Verszeilen meist aus Fragen bestehen, auf die das Echo oft verblüffend antwortet, so daß der Wirkung nach die Frage in sich selbst Antwort findet, vielfach in satir. Absicht. Nach Vorläufern in der Antike (*Anthologia Graeca*, Guaradas) und theoret. Untermauerung in den Renaissance- und Barockpoetiken beliebt in dt., franz., engl. und ital. Lit. vom sechzehnten bis zur Mitte des achtzehnten Jh.

Martin Opitz mentions, but does not define echo poems in his *Buch von der Deutschen Poeterey* (1624; rpt. Tübingen, 1966), ch. 5, pp. 21-22. An early discussion appears in Johann Peter Titz, *Von der Kunst Hochdeutsche Verse und Lieder zu machen* (Danzig: Hünefeld, 1642), ch. 16, paragr. 6, excerpted in *Poetik des Barock*, ed. Marian Szyrocki (Rowohlt, 1968), p. 100. Georg Harsdörffer deals with the echo songs ("Gegenhall") as they appear in *Hirtenspiele* in his *Poetischer Trichter* (1650; rpt. Darmstadt: Wissenschaftliche Buchgesellschaft, 1969), XII, p. 101, and cites Pierre Ronsard as his source. Most extensive among German poetical treatises is the section in Sigmund von Birken's *Teutsche Rede-bind- und Dicht-Kunst* (1679; rpt. Hildesheim: Georg Olms, 1973), pp. 136-41. Birken calls such poems "Fraggebände," but notes that the "Lateiner und Griechen" had called them "echoes" and later himself uses Harsdörffer's term "Gegenhall" to describe the phenomenon of the echoing rhyme-word. He offers several examples of well-made echo songs. Other later poetical treatises which discuss the echo poem include: Balthasar Kindermann, *Der deutsche Poet* (Wittenberg: Fincelius, 1664; rpt. Hildesheim: Olms, 1973), pp. 278-79; Albrecht Christian Rotth, "Echo oder Nach-Hall," in *Vollständige Deutsche Poesie* I (Leipzig: Lanck, 1688), Er.

36. Kinkeldey, *Erlebach*, p. xiv.

37. Peter Keller attributes the score to Sigmund Theophil von Staden in his *Die Oper Seelewig von Sigmund Theophil Staden und Georg Philipp Harsdörfer*, Publikationen der schweizerischen Musikforschenden Gesellschaft, series II, no. 29 (Bern: Haupt, 1977). Harsdörffer's own attribution of the score to "dem hochberühmten und kunsterfahrnen Herrn Johann Gottlieb Staden" is generally accepted to have been a mistake, and does not refer to Sigmund's father, Johann Staden, who was already dead in 1644.

38. Georg Philipp Harsdörffer, *Frauenzimmer Gesprächspiele*, Vierter Theil (Nürnberg: Endter, 1644; rpt. Tübingen: Niemeyer, 1968), pp. 51-150 (libretto with commentary) and pp. 489-622 (score with text beneath).

39. Published in Denkmäler der Tonkunst in Österreich in 1896; see note 33 above.

40. Arias from the opera *Triumphirende Treue* were published in *Keusche Liebes- und Tugend Gedancken* (Nürnberg: Gerhard, 1680); forty-four arias from his later opera *Theseus* were published in 1688. See Herald Samuel, "Löhner," in *Die Musik in Geschichte und Gegenwart*, vol. XII, cols. 1097-1100. No entire opera libretto or score exists, however.

41. To be discussed here are those for a few plays by Martin Opitz, Christian Weise, and Sigmund von Birken. Fritz Moser, *Die Anfänge des Hof- und Gesellschaftstheaters in Deutschland* (Würzburg-Aumühle: Triltsch, 1940) describes others by such authors as Simon Dach and David Schirmer as products of a long tradition of courtly theatrical and semi-theatrical events which were set in part to music; although he describes most of these musical settings as lost, he claims that in 1940 several arias by Heinrich Albert to a *Singspiel* by Simon Dach of 1635 (*Cleomedes*) still survived (p. 96).

42. Heinz Becker, "Geprägter Inhalt—Tote Form? Barockoper heute— Marginalien zu ihrer Reinkarnation," in *Elemente der Literatur: Beiträge zur Stoff-, Motiv- und Themenforschung, Elisabeth Frenzel zum 65. Geburtstag*, ed. Adam J. Bisanz, Raymond Trousson, and Herbert A. Frenzel, vol. 1 (Stuttgart: Kröner, 1980), pp. 63-80.

43. Keller, *Die Oper Seelewig*, p. 72.

44. *The International Cyclopedia of Music and Musicians* (New York: Dodd, Mead and Co., 1975), p. 605.

45. Keller, *Die Oper Seelewig*, p. 72.

46. It is published in Martin Opitz, *Geistliche Poemata (1638)*, ed. Erich Trunz, Deutsche Neudrucke, Reihe Barock, no. 1 (Tübingen: Niemeyer, 1966), but the dedicatory letter is dated 1635. In this letter, Opitz claims that he had finished *Judith* "vor etzlichen Jahren." Mara Wade has recently dated the completion of the work at the end of 1628 in a paper titled "Martin Opitz's *Judith* (1635) in the Baroque Age," given at the International Conference on the German Renaissance, Reformation, and Baroque Periods, University of Kansas, Lawrence, Kansas, April 4, 1986.

47. Although Marian Szyrocki, *Martin Opitz*, Neue Beiträge zur Literaturwissenschaft, no. 4 (Berlin: Rütten und Loening, 1956), p. 107, gave 1646 as the date of this performance, Wade has shown that the actual date was 1643.

48. Martin Opitzen *Judith* auffs neu außgefertiget; worzu das vördere Theil der Historie sampt den Melodeyen auff iedwedes Chor beygefüget von Andreas Tscherningen, Rostock, Gedruckt durch Johann Richeln/ Raths Buchdr. in vorlegung Joachim Wildens/ Buchhändlers/ im Jahr 1646.

49. The pattern of the textual lines of number 2 is thus:

A	3 beats
B	3
C	3
D1 D1 D2 D3	4
E1 E1 E2 E3	4
E1 E2 E3	3
F1 F2 F3	3
F1 F1 F2 F3	4

That of number 3 is:

A	3
B	3
C	3
D	3
E1 D	4
D	3
E1 E1 E1 E2	4
E1 E2	2
E1 E2	2
E1 E1 E2 E3	4
F to Y	3 beats each

50. Published at the end of his *Teutsche Rede-Bind- und Dicht-Kunst* (Nürnberg: Riegel, 1679; rpt. Hildesheim: Olms, 1973), pp. 389-516.

51. See Wade, *Singspiel*, pp. 230-45.

52. Blake Lee Spahr, *The Archives of the Pegnesischer Blumenorden: A Survey and Reference Guide*, University of California Publications in Modern Philology, vol. 57 (Berkeley: University of California Press, 1960), p. 78.

53. In Christian Weise, *Sämtliche Werke*, ed. John D. Lindberg, vol. IV (Berlin: de Gruyter, 1973).

54. Ibid., pp. 174 and 207.

55. In Christian Weise, *Sämtliche Werke*, vol. XI. Weise identifies M.[oritz] E.[delmann] as the composer on p. 153.

56. Dr. Kathi Meyer, "Die Musik der Geharnschten Venus," in *Die Geharnschte Venus*, ed. Höfer, pp. 183-93; see note 12, above.

57. Robert Eitner, *Biographisch-Bibliographisches Quellen-Lexikon*, vol. 9, under "Jacob Schwieger."

58. This song, consisting of madrigalic strophes, each of which has ten lines of various lengths that avoid all patterning except rhyme, even uses the orphan lines ("Waisen") so popular in Italian madrigal poetry, but extremely rare in German lyric poetry of the seventeenth century. This poem, in fact, like many songs in the first opera, Rinuccini's *Dafne*, begins each strophe with an unrhymed line, and has another at line seven; thus only eight of the ten lines of each strophe rhyme, forming the pattern WAABCCWBDD.

59. See note 13, above. Eitner indirectly, at least, ascribes the music to Stieler.

60. According to *The New Grove Dictionary of Music and Musicians*, vol. 10, p. 265, Adam Krieger (1634-66), who was active in 1650-57 in Leipzig, where he published his first collection of "arias," *Arien* (1657), was called in 1657 to Dresden. There he was active at court, including collaboration with David Schirmer, who is responsible for the publication of his second collection, *Neue Arien* (1667, republished in 1676), after Krieger's death. The *New Grove*

Dictionary says of Krieger that he brought "German song to a new peak of development, firmly establishing Italian expressiveness in a tradition hitherto dominated by strophic songs." The later collection, especially, exhibits this Italian style; several dialogue songs are not even strophic. Others, however, employ the bar form also prevalent already in Stieler's *Geharnschte Venus*, as well as in his later songbook.

61. Hans Leo Haßler, *Neue Teutsche Gesang nach Art der welschen Madrigalien und Canzonetten*. Others followed quickly. See Dorothea Glodney-Wiercinski, introduction to Caspar Ziegler, *Von den Madrigalen*, Ars Poetica, Texte, no. 12 (Frankfurt: Athenäum, 1971), pp. 5-6.

62. *Grove Dictionary of Music and Musicians*, vol. 11, p. 461.

63. In Martin Opitz, *Weltliche Poemata* (1644; rpt. Tübingen: Niemeyer, 1967), pp. 103-28. Opitz does not name or discuss the versification in the preface to this work.

64. Wolfgang Keyser, *Kleine Deutsche Versschule*, Dalp-Taschenbücher, no. 306 (Bern: Francke, 1965), p. 55.

65. Ziegler, *Von den Madrigalen*, op. cit. (See note 61, above).

66. Harsdörffer, *Poetischer Trichter*, "Die zwölffte Stund. Von den Freuden- und Hirtenspielen," p. 97. The description clearly refers to basso continuo accompaniment and musical settings of the sort which offer the freedom of the recitative to convey the content of the words expressively. Harsdörffer's use of the terms "durch und durch Erzehlungsweis" and "in genere recitativo" in his *Gesprächspiele* in context with the score of *Seelewig* should be remembered here as well.

67. Albrecht Christian Rotth, *Vollständige Deutsche Poesie* (1688), from an excerpt in *Poetik des Barock*, ed. Marian Szyrocki, Texte Deutscher Literatur 1500-1800, no. 23 (Reinbeck: Rowohlt, 1968), p. 209.

68. Ibid., pp. 209-10.

69. Albrecht Christian Rotth, *Vollständige Deutsche Poesie in drey Theilen* (Leipzig: Lanck, 1688), Teil I, D2v.

70. Ibid., D2v-D3r.

71. Ibid., D3v.

72. Dietrich Walter Jöns, in his "Majuma, Piastus" study in *Die Dramen des Andreas Gryphius: Eine Sammlung von Einzelinterpretationen*, ed. Gerhard Kaiser (Stuttgart: Metzler, 1968), discusses their probable musical presentation, pp. 295-97. Jöns feels that more of *Piastus* must have been sung and contrasts the two texts by terming *Majuma* a *Singspiel* and *Piastus* an opera, p. 296.

73. Höfer, *Die Rudolstädter Festspiele*, pp. 6-7.

74. Signatur Ma x Nr, 41, vol. II. The Curt von Faber du Faur collection at Yale also owns the pieces of what once was a single volume in which not only *Amelinde*, but also *Jacob des Patriarchen Heirat* (1662), both apparently printed in Rudolstadt, were bound with several of the Rudolstadt plays. See Curt von Faber du Faur, *German Baroque Literature: A Catalogue of the Collection in the Yale University Library* (New Haven: Yale, 1958), nos. 352 and 353. The library in Rudolstadt also owns a copy of the same edition of the Joseph-play, currently bound with other works of Wolfenbüttel origin. Dünnhaupt does not acknowledge a separate Rudolstadt printing of *Jacob*; however, Spahr describes it in detail. Spahr is not convinced by Faber du Faur's arguments that it was necessarily published by Freyschmidt in Rudolstadt. See note 79 below.

75. Just as *Seelewig* received not just one, but two new editions in Wolfenbüttel in connection with its performance there in 1654. See Joseph Leighton, "Die Wolfenbütteler Aufführung von Harsdörffers und Stadens 'Seelewig' im Jahre 1654," *Wolfenbütteler Beiträge zur Barockforschung*, 3 (1978), 115-28.

76. Only *Orpheus*, written on the occasion of Sophie Elizabeth's birthday, identifies the composer (Löwe). See Frederick Robert Lehmeyer, *The "Singspiele" of Anton Ulrich von Braunschweig*, diss. University of California at Berkeley, 1971, p. 117; and Rand Henson, *Duke Anton Ulrich of Braunschweig-Lüneburg-Wolfenbüttel (1633-1714) and the Politics of Baroque Musical Theater*, diss. University of California at Berkeley, 1980, pp. 82-85.

77. Her plays have recently been made available in a new edition: Sophie Elisabeth, Herzogin zu Braunschweig und Lüneburg, *Dichtungen*, vol. 1 (*Spiele*), ed. Hans-Gert Roloff, Europäische Hochschulschriften, Deutsche Literatur und Germanistik, no. 329 (Frankfurt: Peter Lang, 1980). A section dealing with earlier theater history in the 1941 survey *250 Jahre Braunschweigisches Staatstheater 1690-1940* by Heinrich Sievers, Albert Trapp, and Alexander Schein (Braunschweig: Appelhaus, 1941) provides an early account of her activities as composer, patron of music, and purveyor of musical theater (pp. 26-42), although her activity as probable composer for Anton Ulrich's dramatic texts is not yet recognized. Her activity as a dramatist has been discussed in several recent articles: Hans-Gert Roloff, "Absolutismus und Hoftheater: Das *Freudenspiel* der Herzogin Sophie Elisabeth zu Braunschweig und Lüneburg," *Daphnis*, 10 (1981), 735-53; Hans-Gert Roloff, "Die höfischen Maskeraden der Sophie Elisabeth, Herzogin zu Braunschweig-Lüneburg," in *Europäische Hofkultur im sechzehnten und siebzehnten Jahrhundert*, vol. 3 (Hamburg: Hauswedell, 1981), pp. 489-96; and Joseph Leighton, "Die literarische Tätigkeit der Herzogin Sophie Elisabeth von Braunschweig-Lüneburg," in ibid., pp. 483-88. Her activity as a composer is discussed in *The Grove Dictionary of Music and Musicians*, vol. 17, p. 530; this article includes a bibliography of further secondary literature about her. She was a student, as well as a patron, of Heinrich Schütz.

78. *250 Jahre Braunschweigisches Staatstheater*, p. 30.

79. The plays have recently appeared in a complete critical edition: Anton Ulrich Herzog zu Braunschweig und Lüneburg, *Bühnendichtungen*, ed. Blake Lee Spahr et al., Bibliothek des literarischen Vereins in Stuttgart, nos. 303-4 (1982) and 309-10 (1984-1985) (Stuttgart: Hiersemann). Previously, only *Der Hoffmann Daniel* was widely available, in *Barockdrama*, vol. 5: *Die Oper*, ed. Willi Flemming, DLE (Leipzig: Reclam, 1933), pp. 125-79.

80. Walter Hinck, *Das deutsche Lustspiel des 17. und 18. Jahrhunderts und die italienische Komödie: Commedia dell'arte und theatre italien*, Germanistische Abhandlungen, no. 8 (Stuttgart: J. B. Metzler, 1965), pp. 130-36.

81. Lehmeyer, *The "Singspiele"*, pp. 3-9.

82. Pierre Béhar, "Anton Ulrichs Ballette und Singspiele: Zum Problem ihrer Form und ihrer Bedeutung in der Geschichte der deutschen Barockdramatik," *Daphnis*, 10 (1981), 775-92, especially 781-83. See also Wade, *Singspiel*, p. 328, who agrees with Béhar.

83. Unfortunately, all the music designed as settings for madrigal verse has been lost; only two strophic choruses from *Cleomedes* survive, published in Heinrich Albert, *Erster Theil der ARIEN oder MELODEYEN* (1638); rpt. titled *Arien* ed. Hermann Kretzschmar, Denkmäler deutscher Tonkunst, No. 12 (1958).

84. Both texts appeared in Simon Dach, *Poetische Wercke* (1696; rpt. 1970) and in an edition of Dach's complete works: Simon Dach, *Gedichte*, ed. Walther Ziesemer, Schriften der Königsberger Gelehrten Gesellschaft, No. 5 (1937), II, 281-318. Dach's dramas are little studied. Aside from scattered references, only an inaccessible typescript dissertation treats them: Herbert Bretzke, "Simon Dach's dramatische Spiele: Ein Beitrag zur Literaturgeschichte des 17. Jahrhunderts," diss. Königsberg, 1922.

85. According to Walther Ziesemer, in Dach, *Gedichte*, II, 390. It had also been performed in 1644 and 1645. Although the arias were republished in context with each performance, only a brief prose synopsis remains of what must once have been madrigalic dialogue, as in *Cleomedes*.

86. Schletterer, *Das deutsche Singspiel*, pp. 73-74.

87. See Kinkeldey, *Erlebach*, op. cit., pp. xxii ff.

88. Engel, "Musik in Thüringen," op. cit.

89. See note 23, above.

90. Eitner, *Biographisch-Bibliographisches Quellen-Lexikon*, vol. 8, p. 332.

91. Kinkeldey, *Erlebach*, op. cit., pp. xxii ff.

92. Höfer, "Georg Bleyer," p. 27.

93. Ibid., pp. 12-17.

94. Engel, "Musik in Thüringen," p. 210.

95. Zeman, *Monographie*, p. 86.

96. Ibid., p. 95.

97. Engel, "Musik in Thüringen," p. 229.

Chapter 8: Ways and Means: The Comedic Tools

98. Conrad Höfer, *Rudolstädter Festspiele*, p. 125.

99. Martin Opitz, *Buch von der Deutschen Poeterey* (Brieg, 1624; rpt. Tübingen: Niemeyer, 1966), p. 20.

100. Kaspar Stieler, *Die Dichtkunst des Spaten (1685)*, ed. Herbert Zeman (Vienna: Österreichischer Bundesverlag, 1975), lines 1102-9.

101. Höfer does pay his respects to appropriateness in passing when he points out that Christian Weise was unwise enough to make this mistake, p. 130.

102. On this topic, see Otto Hasselbeck, *Illusion und Fiktion: Lessings Beitrag zur poetologischen Diskussion über das Verhältnis von Kunst und Wirklichkeit*, Theorie und Geschichte der Literatur und der schönen Künste, no. 49 (Munich: Fink, 1979), especially pp. 7-23.

103. Höfer, *Rudolstädter Festspiele*, p. 47: "daß in ihnen [den komischen Szenen] der Dichter so recht reden konnte, wie er es im zwanglosen Verkehr gewöhnt war."

104. Höfer, ibid., pp. 47ff.

105. Albert Köster, *Der Dichter der Geharnschten Venus: Eine Litterarhistorische Untersuchung* (Marburg: Elwert, 1897).

106. See Höfer, *Rudolstädter Festspiele*, p. 34.

107. K. F. W. Wander, *Deutsches Sprichwörterlexikon* (Aalen: Scientia, 1963), vol. 5, cols. 1522-23.

108. Hanns Bächtold-Stäubli, *Handwörterbuch des deutschen Aberglaubens* (Berlin: de Gruyter, 1927-42), vol. VII, p. 854.

109. Wander, *Deutsches Sprichwörterlexikon*, cols. 1522-23.

110. Jakob and Wilhelm Grimm, *Deutsches Wörterbuch*, 16 vols. (Leipzig: Hirzel, 1854-1960); Wander, *Deutsches Sprichwörterlexikon*, 5 vols.

111. *Hamlet*, I, iii.

112. Hugo Beck, "Die Bedeutung des Genrebegriffs für das deutsche Drama des 16. Jahrhunderts," *DVjs*, 8 (1930), 86.

113. Georg Philipp Harsdörffer, *Poetischer Trichter*, p. 81 ("Die eilffte Stund"): "Die Lehr- und Danksprüche sind gleichsam des Trauerspiels Grundseulen; solche aber müssen nicht von Dienern und geringen Leuten/ sondern von den fürnemsten und ältsten Personen angeführet. . . werden."

114. *Dichtkunst des Spahten*, ed. Zeman, pp. 188-272.

115. On the "Programma Poeticum," see Theodor Verweyen, "Daphnes Metamorphosen: Zur Problematik der Tradition mittelalterlicher Denkformen im 17. Jahrhundert am Beispiel des *Programma Poeticum* Sigmund von Birkens," in *Rezeption und Produktion zwischen 1570 und 1730: Festschrift für Günther Weydt zum 65. Geburtstag*, ed. W. Rasch, H. Geulen, and K. Haberkamm (Bern/München: Francke, 1972), pp. 319-79.

116. Zelotes is a name in the Judeo-Christian tradition used both for the God of Israel as a zealous god in the Old Testament, and in the New Testament for the Apostle Simon of Cara as "the Zealot"; Stieler means Zelus (Zelos), son of the River Styx, personification of zeal.

117. Indeed, I have encountered resistence among Germans to my perception of such puns in Walther von der Vogelweide. To find proof that such language was intended to be seen as puns is not easy: with Grimm's *Wörterbuch* it is often a hit-or-miss proposition, and when the great dictionary does indicate that a particular phrase or word is sometimes used in a sexual sense, it usually prudishly fails to explain what that sense is: one finds merely the remark "obzen." Wander's *Deutsches Sprichwörterlexikon*, when it does happen to explicate such a sexual pun, is usually more explicit. Several of the dialect dictionaries do not neglect this area, although, again, consistency is a problem to the researcher.

118. Eric Partridge, *Shakespeare's Bawdy: A Literary and Psychological Essay and a Comprehensive Glossary* (New York: Dutton, 1948).

119. Höfer, *Rudolstädter Festspiele*, pp. 26-27. The poem is "Ehren-Griffe," fourth song in the seventh "Zehen" of GV.

120. Köster, *Der Dichter der Geharnschten Venus*, pp. 111-12; the anagrams are "Karpas" (Kaspar) and "Peilkarastres" (Kaspar Stieler). One might even speculate that one spelling he chooses for his later pen name in the "Fruchtbringende Gesellschaft," "der Spahte," is a clue to yet another anagram: Thaesp, for Thespus, founder of the dramatic genre in ancient Greece.

121. *Der Teutschen Sprache Stammbaum und Fortwachs oder teutscher Sprachschatz* (Nürnberg: Hofmann, 1691; rpt. München: Kösel, 1968), col. 2163.

122. Zeman, *Monographie*, p. 57.

123. Stieler was also expected to report the latest news at the dinner table of his patron, according to a document cited by Zeman, p. 56. Stieler later indicated his special interest in journalism with a book on the subject: *Zeitungs-Lust und Nutz* (Hamburg: Schiller, 1695).

Chapter 9: "Ein Narr macht ihr zehne": Scaramutza

124. Conrad Höfer, *Rudolstädter Festspiele*, pp. 112-23.

125. C. Reuling, *Die komische Figur in den wichtigsten deutschen Dramen bis zum Ende des XVII. Jahrhunderts*, diss. Zürich (Stuttgart: Göschen, 1890), pp. 132-42.

126. Walter Hinck, *Das deutsche Lustspiel des 17. und 18. Jahrhunderts und die italienische Komödie* (Stuttgart: Metzler, 1965), pp. 130-36.

127. Pierre L. Duchartre, *The Italian Comedy*, trans. R. T. Weaver (London: Harper, 1929), pp. 93 and 236ff.; Karl Friedrich Flögel, *Geschichte des Grotesk-Komischen* (Leipzig: Barsdorf, 1914), p. 35, believes that Tiberio Fiorilli created him himself.

128. Duchartre, *The Italian Comedy*, pp. 96-97.

129. Thelma Niklaus, *Harlequin* (New York: Braziller, 1956), p. 75.

130. Duchartre, *The Italian Comedy*, p. 98.

131. Ibid., p. 97.

132. Angelo Constantini, *La Vie de Scaramouche*, ed. Louis Moland (Paris: Barbin, 1878). Constantini was the comic figure Mezzetino in Fiorilli's troupe. Of this "biography" Winifred Smith, *The Commedia dell'arte* (1912; rpt. New York: Blom, 1964), p. 158, states: "The apocryphal *Vie de Scaramouche* has been proved a tissue of falsehoods." Actually, many of the "falsehoods" are a part of the fictional persona of Scaramuccia, not falsifications or fabrications attributable to Constantini.

133. According to Herbert Zeman, *Monographie*, pp. 46-49, Stieler spent extensive time in Paris in 1658-60, possibly divided between two visits (one certainly in 1658; another possibly in 1659 or 1660 before his travels to Italy).

134. See Höfer, *Rudolstädter Festspiele*, p. 203.

135. Niklaus, *Harlequin*, p. 79.

136. One scholar, Flögel, *Geschichte des Grotesk-Komischen*, p. 35, claims that Fiorilli was absent from Paris from 1658 to 1670, but other accounts contradict this statement. Even if he had been in Italy during this time, Stieler could, of course, have seen him perform there instead, since Italy was the next stop on his tour.

137. See Egon Wellesz, *Der Beginn des musikalischen Barock und die Anfänge der Oper in Wien*, Theater und Kultur, no. 6 (Vienna: Literarische Anstalt, 1922), p. 63.

138. This list was compiled by Conrad Höfer, *Rudolstädter Festspiele*, pp. 164-65, and is repeated by Walter Hinck, *Das deutsche Lustspiel*, p. 135.

139. Hinck discusses Weise's usage, ibid., p. 136. On Christian Gryphius and his use of Scaramuzza, see Dietrich Eggers, *Die Bewertung deutscher Sprache und Literatur in den deutschen Schulactus von Christian Gryphius*, Deutsche Studien, no. 5 (Meisenheim am Glan: Hain, 1967), p. 120, and James Hardin, "Christian Gryphius's Lost Schulactus *Von den Lust-Spilen/ Oder Comoedien*," *Daphnis*, 17 (1988), 119ff.

140. Höfer, *Rudolstädter Festspiele*, pp. 162ff.; Curt von Faber du Faur, *German Baroque Literature: A Catalogue of the Collection of the Yale University Library* (New Haven: Yale, 1958), pp. 176-77.

141. On the original Scaramuccia/Scaramouche, see especially Duchartre, *The Italian Comedy*, pp. 236ff., and Niklaus, *Harlequin*, pp. 39-41.

142. Höfer, *Rudolstädter Festspiele*, pp. 112ff. I'm not convinced, however, that he is stupid in *Basilene* or BB. He may have hoodwinked Höfer as successfully as he did his masters with a pose of stupidity.

143. Ibid., pp. 117-118.

144. Ibid., pp. 118-121.

145. Reuling, *Die komische Figur*, describes these two types, pp. 1-13, although he does not attempt to connect them to Stieler's ("Schwieger's") Scaramutza.

146. Höfer, *Rudolstädter Festspiele*, pp. 117-21.

147. Marianne Kaiser, *Mitternacht, Zeidler, Weise: das protestantische Schultheater nach 1648 im Kampf gegen höfische Kultur und absolutistisches Regiment*, Palaestra, no. 25a (Göttingen: Vandenhoek and Ruprecht, 1972).

148. On this topic see Andreas Wang, *Der 'miles christianus' im 16. und 17. Jahrhundert und seine mittelalterliche Tradition*, Mikrokosmos, no. 1 (Bern: Herbert Lang, 1975).

149. Albert Köster, *Der Dichter des geharnschten Venus (Marburg: Elwert, 1897), and Höfer, Rudolstädter Festspiele*, describe the characteristics of this dialect in connection with Stieler.

150. See my survey, *German Baroque Drama*, Twayne World Authors Series, no. 634 (New York: Twayne, 1982), pp. 141-53, for a discussion of this sub-genre and its authors.

151. Daniel Georg Morhof, *Unterricht von Der Teutschen Sprache und Poesie* (Kiel: Reumann, 1682), p. 739.

152. *Teutsche Secretariatkunst*, vol. 1, p. 53.

153. As shown in a document quoted by Zeman, *Monographie*, p. 71, n. 1.

154. Jacob Pontanus, *Institutio Poetica* (Ingolstadt: Sartorius, 1597); see David E. R. George, *Deutsche Tragödientheorien vom Mittelalter bis zu Lessing: Texte und Kommentare* (Munich: Beck, 1972), p. 83.

155. William Willeford, *The Fool and His Scepter: A Study in Clowns and Jesters and Their Audience* (Evanston, Il.: Northwestern University, 1969).

156. Eckehard Catholy, *Fastnachtspiel*, Sammlung Metzler (Stuttgart: Metzler, 1966).

Part IV: Epilogue

Chapter 10: Prescriptions, Proscriptions, Scripts

1. *Die Dichtkunst des Spaten (1685)*, ed. Herbert Zeman, Wiener Neudrucke, no. 5 (Vienna: Österreichischer Bundesverlag, 1975).

2. Höfer, *Rudolstädter Festspiele* pp. 141-42.

3. *Dichtkunst*, pp. 279-95.

4. Birken, *Rede-Bind- und Dicht-Kunst*, pp. 323-24.

5. Harsdörffer, *Poetischer Trichter*, II, pp. 83-84.

6. Birken, *Rede-Bind- und Dicht-Kunst*, p. 335.

7. Several mention laughter as a result (e.g., Augustus Buchner, *Anleitung zur deutschen Poeterey*, ed. Marian Szyrocki, Deutsche Neudrucke, Reihe Barock, no. 5, Tübingen: Niemeyer, 1966, p. 10), but do not see the laughter as central to the usefulness of comedy.

8. Giambattista Guarini, *Il Pastor fido e Il Compendio della Poesia Tragicomica*, ed. Gioachino Brognoligo, Scrittori d'Italia, no. 61 (Bari: Laterza, 1914), pp. 222ff. Guarini's *Compendio* was intended to answer the particularly vocal criticisms of Giovanni Pietro Malacreta, whose *Consideratoni[!] sopra il Pastor fido tragicomedia pastorale del molto Illustre Signore Cavalier Battista Guarini* had appeared in Vincenza in 1600.

9. Guarini, *Il Pastor fido*, p. 246.

10. *Willmut*, p. 144.

Chapter 11: Lines of Influence and Interconnection

11. Höfer, *Rudolstädter Festspiele*, pp. 162-67, traces some possible evidence of influence on minor plays, but considers it tenuous and downplays its possible importance.

12. Heinrich Haxel, *Studien zu den Lustspielen Christian Weises*, p. 41; Haxel discusses these late comedies, pp. 40-44.

13. Haxel, *Studien*, p. 41.

14. He is preceded only by two comedies of Gryphius, *Seugamme* translated from the Italian in the 1640s, and *Verliebtes Gespenste* of 1660, if we limit our count to texts of literary merit.

15. In his *Trauer- Freuden- und Schäffer-Spiele* (Breslau: Fellgiebel, 1684).

BIBLIOGRAPHIES
Bibliography of Printed Plays Cited in the Text

Der Vermeinte Printz. Lustspiel. Rudolstadt: Freyschmidt, 1665.
Ernelinde, Oder Die Viermahl Braut. Mischspiel. Rudolstadt: Freyschmidt, 1665.
Die erfreuete Unschuld. Misch-Spiel. Rudolstadt: Freyschmidt, 1666.
Die Wittekinden. Singe- und Freuden-Spiel. Jena: Neuenhahn, 1666.
Der betrogene Betrug. Lustspiel. Rudolstadt: Freyschmidt, 1667.
Basilene. Lustspiel. Rudolstadt: Freyschmidt, 1667.

All of the above plays are to be found bound, two to five per example, in a collective volume of which a number of copies survive, each with a different configuration of plays; most copies contain only VP, *Ernelinde*, and one other. The title page of this collective volume identifies it as:

Filidors Trauer- Lust- und Misch-Spiele. Erster Theil. Jena: Neuenhahn, 1665.

No "Zweiter Theil" was published, and no "Trauer-Spiele" are to be found in any copy.

Another collective volume that contains any two of the above plays (again, not the same selection in all copies, of which three are known to me) was published in 1674:

Eröffnetes Theatrum oder Neuaufgerichteter Schau-Platz, Schöner anmuhtiger Comoedien und Tragoedien, mit allerhand neuen Erfindungen und Representationen. Durch Mons. du Baas, Königl. Comoedianten zu Paris in Französischer Sprache herausgegeben, anitzo aber ins Teutsche gebracht. Theil I. Jena: [Neuenhahn], 1674.

This is not a new edition, but only new—and untruthful—packaging for leftover pages from 1665-67.

Melissa. Schäfferey. Rudolstadt[?]: Freyschmidt[?], 1668.
Bellemperie. Trauerspiel des Spaten. Jena: Johann Nisio, 1680.
Willmut. Lustspiel des Spaten. [Jena: Johann Nisio], 1680.
Floretto. Weimar[?]: Johann Andreas Müller[?], [1683].

Complete citations for *Der göldene Apfel* and the *Zwischenspiele* of 1684, all in the library in Weimar, are to be found in the notes for those sections.

Chronological Bibliography of Scholarship on Stieler's Dramatic Oeuvre

(Brief mentions appear only in the notes)

Pabst, K. T. "Jacob Schwieger als Dramatiker." Meininger Programm vom Jahr 1847.

Passow, W. "Das deutsche Drama im 17. Jahrhundert." Ibid.

Rudolphi, Albert. "Kaspar Stieler, der Spate, ein Lebensbild aus dem 17. Jahrhundert." Programm des Kgl. Gymnasiums zu Erfurt, 1872.

Paludan, Julius. "Ältere deutsche Dramen in Kopenhagener Bibliotheken." *Zeitschrift für deutsche Philologie*, 23 (1891), 226ff.

Schoenwerth, Rudolf. *Die niederländischen und deutschen Bearbeitungen von Thomas Kyds 'Spanish Tragedy'*. Berlin: Felber, 1903. Rpt. Nendeln: Klaus, 1977.

Höfer, Conrad. *Die Rudolstädter Festspiele aus den Jahren 1665-1667 und Ihr Dichter: Eine literarhistorische Studie*, Probefahrten: Erstlingsarbeiten aus dem Deutschen Seminar in Leipzig. Leipzig: Voigtländer, 1904.

Höfer, Conrad. "Weimarische Theaterveranstaltungen zur Zeit des Herzogs Wilhelm Ernst." Sonderdruck aus dem Jahresbericht des Groherzoglichen Sophienstiftes zu Weimar. Weimar: Hofbuchdruckerei, 1914.

Bolte, Johannes. "Eine ungedruckte Poetik Kaspar Stielers." *Sitzungsberichte der preußischen Akademie der Wissenschaften*, 15 (1926), 97-122, especially 97-98.

Wenzel, Walter. *Wittekind in der deutschen Literatur*. Diss. Münster. Pöppinghaus: Bochum-Langendreer, 1931.

Flemming, Willi. "Einführung." *Oratorium. Festspiel.* Vol. 6 of *Barockdrama*, DLE. Leipzig: Reclam, 1933, pp. 134-40.

Höfer, Conrad. "Georg Bleyer, ein Thüringischer Tonsetzer und Dichter der Barockzeit." *Zeitschrift des Vereins für Thüringische Geschichte und Altertumskunde*, Beiheft 24. Jena, 1941.

Hempe, L. D. "Caspar Stieler's 'Bellemperie,' ein Wort zu einem Rarissimum der deutschen Barockdichtung." *Börsenblatt Leipzig* 114 (1947), 106-107.

Taeger, Hans. "Der Thüringer Barockdichter und -gelehrte Kaspar Stieler mit besonderer Betonung seiner Eisenacher Zeit (1667-77)." *Der Wartburg Türmer*. June 1954, 87-90.

Hartmann, Horst. *Die Entwicklung des deutschen Lustspiels von Gryphius bis Weise (1648-1688)*. Diss. Potsdam, 1960.

Hinck, Walter. *Das deutsche Lustspiel des 17. und 18. Jahrhunderts und die italienische Komödie*. Stuttgart: Metzler, 1965, pp. 130-36.

Zeman, Herbert. *Kaspar Stieler: Versuch einer Monographie*. Diss. Vienna, 1965.

Aikin, Judith P. *German Baroque Drama*. Twayne World Authors Series. New York: Twayne, 1982.

Aikin, Judith P. "Practical Uses of Comedy at a Seventeenth-Century Court: The Political Polemic in Caspar Stieler's *Der Vermeinte Printz*," *Theatre Journal*, 1983, 519-32.

Aikin, Judith P. "The Audience within the Play: Clues to Intended Audience Reaction in German Baroque Tragedies and Comedies," *Daphnis*, 13 (1984), 187-201.

Aikin, Judith P. "Romantic Comedy as Religious Allegory: The Millennial Kingdom in Caspar Stieler's *Die erfreuete Unschuld*," *The German Quarterly*, 57 (1984), 59-74.

Aikin, Judith P. "Satire, Satyr Plays, and German Baroque Comedy," *Daphnis*, 14 (1985), 759-78.

Index